ARTIFICIAL INTELLIGENCE
MACHINE LEARNING
AND
DEEP LEARNING

ARTIFICIAL INTELLIGENCE
MACHINE LEARNING
AND
DEEP LEARNING

Oswald Campesato

MERCURY LEARNING AND INFORMATION
Dulles, Virginia
Boston, Massachusetts
New Delhi

Publisher: David Pallai
MERCURY LEARNING AND INFORMATION
22841 Quicksilver Drive
Dulles, VA 20166
info@merclearning.com
www.merclearning.com
1-800-232-0223

O. Campesato. *Artificial Intelligence, Machine Learning and Deep Learning.*
ISBN: 978-1-68392-467-8

Library of Congress Control Number: 2019957226

202122321   Printed on acid-free paper in the United States of America.

*I'd like to dedicate this book to my parents –
may this bring joy and happiness into their lives.*

CONTENTS

Chapter 3: Classifiers in Machine Learning

PREFACE: THE ML AND DL LANDSCAPE

What Is the Goal?

The goal of this book is to introduce advanced beginners to basic machine learning and deep learning concepts and algorithms. It is intended to be a fast-paced introduction to various "core" features of machine learning and deep learning, with code samples that are included in a university course. The material in the chapters illustrates how to solve some tasks using Keras, after which you can do further reading to deepen your knowledge.

This book will also save you the time required to search for code samples, which is a potentially time-consuming process. In any case, if you're not sure whether or not you can absorb the material presented here, then glance through the code samples to get a feel for the level of complexity.

At the risk of stating the obvious, please keep in mind the following point: *you will not become an expert in machine learning or deep learning by reading this book.*

What Will I Learn from This Book?

The first chapter contains a very short introduction to AI, followed by a chapter devoted to Pandas for managing the contents of datasets. The third chapter introduces you to machine learning concepts (supervised and unsupervised learning), types of tasks (regression, classification, and clustering), and linear regression (the second half of the chapter). The fourth chapter is devoted to classification algorithms, such as kNN, Naïve Bayes, decision trees, random forests, and SVM (Support Vector Machines).

The fifth chapter introduces deep learning and delves into CNNs (Convolutional Neural Networks). The sixth chapter covers deep learning architectures such as RNNs (recurrent neural networks) and LSTMs (Long Short Term Memory).

The sixth chapter introduces you to aspects of NLP (Natural Language Processing, with some basic concepts and algorithms, followed by RL (Reinforcement Learning) and the Bellman equation. The first appendix covers Keras, whereas the second appendix covers TensorFlow 2.0.

Another point: although Jupyter is popular, all the code samples in this book are Python scripts. However, you can quickly learn the useful features of Jupyter through various online tutorials. In addition, it's worth looking at Google *Colaboratory* that is entirely online and is based on Jupyter notebooks, along with free GPU usage.

How Much Keras Knowledge Is Needed for this Book?

Some exposure to Keras is helpful, and you can read the appendix if Keras is new to you. If you also want to learn about Keras and logistic regression, there is an example in Chapter 3. This example requires some theoretical knowledge involving activation functions, optimizers, and cost functions, all of which are discussed in Chapter 4.

Please keep in mind that Keras is well-integrated into TensorFlow 2 (in the tf.keras namespace), and it provides a layer of abstraction over "pure" TensorFlow that will enable you to develop prototypes more quickly.

Do I Need to Learn the Theory Portions of this Book?

Once again, the answer depends on the extent to which you plan to become involved in machine learning. In addition to creating a model, you will use various algorithms to see which ones provide the level of accuracy (or some other metric) that you need for your project. If you fall short, the theoretical aspects of machine learning can help you perform a "forensic" analysis of your model and your data, and ideally assist in determining how to improve your model.

How Were the Code Samples Created?

The code samples in this book were created and tested using Python 3 and Keras that's built into TensorFlow 2 on a MacBook Pro with OS X 10.12.6 (MacOS Sierra). Regarding their content: the code samples are derived primarily from the author for his *Deep Learning and Keras* graduate course. In some cases there are code samples that incorporate short sections of code from discussions in online forums. The key point to remember is that the code samples follow the "Four Cs": they must be Clear, Concise, Complete, and Correct to the extent that it's possible to do so, given the size of this book.

What Are the Technical Prerequisites for This Book?

You need some familiarity with Python, and also know how to launch Python code from the command line (in a Unix-like environment for Mac users). In addition, a mixture of basic linear algebra (vectors and matrices), probability/statistics, (mean, median, standard deviation) and basic concepts in calculus (such as derivatives) will help you master the material. Some knowledge of NumPy and Matplotlib is also helpful, and the assumption is that you are familiar with basic functionality (such as NumPy arrays).

One other prerequisite is important for understanding the code samples in the second half of this book: some familiarity with neural networks, which includes the concept of hidden layers and activation functions (even if you don't fully understand them). Knowledge of cross entropy is also helpful for some of the code samples.

What Are the Non-technical Prerequisites for This Book?

Although the answer to this question is more difficult to quantify, it's very important to have a strong desire to learn about machine learning, along with the motivation and discipline to read and understand the code samples.

Even simple machine language APIs can be a challenge to understand them at first encounter, so be prepared to read the code samples several times.

How Do I Set up a Command Shell?

If you are a Mac user, there are three ways to do so. The first method is to use `Finder` to navigate to `Applications > Utilities` and then double click on the `Utilities` application. Next, if you already have a command shell available, you can launch a new command shell by typing the following command:

```
open/Applications/Utilities/Terminal.app
```

A second method for Mac users is to open a new command shell on a MacBook from a command shell that is already visible simply by clicking `command+n` in that command shell, and your Mac will launch another command shell.

If you are a PC user, you can install Cygwin (open source *https://cygwin.com/*) that simulates bash commands, or use another toolkit such as MKS (a commercial product). Please read the online documentation that describes the download and installation process. Note that custom aliases are not automatically set if they are defined in a file other than the main start-up file (such as .bash_login).

Companion Files

All of the code samples and figures in this book may be obtained for download by writing to the publisher at info@merclearning.com.

What Are the "Next Steps" after Finishing this Book?

The answer to this question varies widely, mainly because the answer depends heavily on your objectives. The best answer is to try a new tool or technique from the book out on a problem or task you care about, professionally or personally. Precisely what that might be depends on who you are, as the needs of a data scientist, manager, student or developer are all different. In addition, keep what you learned in mind as you tackle new challenges.

O. Campesato
San Francisco, CA

INTRODUCTION TO AI

This chapter provides a gentle introduction to AI, primarily as a broad overview of this diverse topic. Unlike the other chapters in this book, this introductory chapter is chapter is "light" in terms of technical content. However, it's easy to read and also worth skimming through its contents. Machine learning and deep learning are briefly introduced toward the end of this chapter, both of which are discussed in more detail in subsequent chapters.

Keep in mind that many AI-focused books tend to discuss AI from the perspective of computer science and a discussion of traditional algorithms and data structures. By contrast, this book treats AI as an "umbrella" for machine learning and deep learning, and therefore it's discussed in a cursory manner as a precursor to the other chapters.

The first part of this chapter starts with a discussion regarding the term *artificial intelligence*, various potential ways to determine the presence of intelligence, as well as the difference between Strong AI and Weak AI. You will also learn about the Turing Test, which is a well-known test for intelligence.

The second part of this chapter discusses some AI uses-cases and the early approaches to neural computing, evolutionary computation, NLP, and bioinformatics.

The third part of this chapter introduces you to major subfields of AI, which include natural language processing (with NLU and NLG), machine learning, deep learning, reinforcement learning, and deep reinforcement learning.

Although code-specific samples are not discussed in this chapter, the companion files for this chapter do contain a Java-based code sample for solving the Red Donkey problem, and also a Python-based code sample (that requires Python 2.x) for solving Rubik's Cube.

What Is Artificial Intelligence?

The literal meaning of the word *artificial* is synthetic, which often has a negative connotation of being an inferior substitute. However, artificial objects (e.g., flowers) can closely approximate their counterparts, and sometimes they can be advantageous when they do not have any maintenance requirements (sunshine, water, and so forth).

By contrast, a definition for *intelligence* is more elusive than a definition of the word *artificial*. R. Sternberg, in a text on human consciousness, provides the following useful definition: "Intelligence is the cognitive ability of an individual to learn from experience, to reason well, to remember important information, and to cope with the demands of daily living."

You probably remember standardized tests with questions that ask for the next number in a given sequence, such as 1, 3, 6, 10, 15, 21. The first thing to observe is that the gap between successive numbers increases by one: from 1 to 3, the increase is two, whereas from 3 to 6, it is three, and so on. Based on this pattern, the plausible response is 28. Such questions are designed to measure our proficiency at identifying salient features in patterns.

Incidentally, there can be multiple answers to a "next-in-sequence" numeric problem. For example, the sequence 2, 4, 8 might suggest 16 as the next number in this sequence, which is correct if the generating formula is 2^n. However, if the generating formula is $2^n + (n-1) * (n-2) * (n-3)$, then the next number in the sequence is 22 (not 16). There are many formulas that can match 2, 4, and 8 as the initial sequence of numbers, and yet the next number can be different from 16 or 22.

Let's return to R. Sternberg's definition for intelligence, and consider the following questions:

- How do you decide if someone (something?) is intelligent?

- Are animals intelligent?

- If animals are intelligent, how do you measure their intelligence?

We tend to assess people's intelligence through interaction with them: we ask questions and observe their answers. Although this method is indirect, we often rely on this method to gauge other people's intelligence.

In the case of animal intelligence, we also observe their behavior to make an assessment. Clever Hans was a famous horse that lived in Berlin, Germany, circa 1900, and allegedly had a proficiency in arithmetic, such as adding numbers and calculating square roots.

In reality, Hans was able to identify human emotions and, in conjunction with his astute hearing, he could sense the reaction of audience members as Hans came closer to a correct answer. Interestingly, Hans performed poorly without the presence of an audience. You might be reluctant to attribute Clever Hans's actions to intelligence; however, review Sternberg's definition before reaching a conclusion.

As another example, some creatures exhibit intelligence only in groups. Although ants are simple insects, and their isolated behavior would hardly warrant inclusion in a text on AI, ant colonies exhibit extraordinary solutions to complex problems. In fact, ants can figure out the optimal route from a nest to a food source, how to carry heavy objects, and how to form bridges. Thus, a *collective* intelligence arises from effective communication among individual insects.

The ratios of brain mass and brain-to-body mass are indicators of intelligence, and dolphins compare favorably with humans in both metrics. Breathing in dolphins is under voluntary control, which could account for excess brain mass, as well as the fact that alternate halves of a dolphin's brain take turns sleeping. Dolphins score well on animal self-awareness tests such as the mirror test, in which they recognize that the image in the mirror is actually their own image. They can also perform complex tricks, as visitors to Sea World can testify. This illustrates the ability of dolphins to remember and perform complex sequences of physical motions.

The use of tools is another litmus test for intelligence and is often used to separate *homo erectus* from earlier ancestors of human beings. Dolphins also share this trait with humans: dolphins use deep-sea sponges to protect their spouts while foraging for food. Thus, intelligence is not an attribute possessed by humans alone. Many living forms possess some degree of intelligence.

Now consider the following question: can inanimate objects, such as computers, possess intelligence? The declared goal of artificial Intelligence is to create computer software and/or hardware systems that exhibit thinking comparable to that of humans, in other words, to display characteristics usually associated with human intelligence.

What about the capacity to think, and can machines think? Keep in mind the distinction between thinking and intelligence. Thinking is the facility to reason, analyze, evaluate, and formulate ideas and concepts. Therefore, not every being capable of thinking is intelligent. Intelligence is perhaps akin to efficient and effective thinking.

Many people approach this issue with biases, saying that computers are made of silicon and power supplies and therefore are not capable of thinking. At the other extreme, computers perform much faster than humans and therefore must be more intelligent than humans. The truth is most likely somewhere between these two extremes. As we have discussed, different animal species possess intelligence to varying degrees. However, we are more interested in a test to ascertain the existence of machine intelligence than in developing standardized IQ tests for animals. Perhaps Raphael put it best: artificial intelligence is the science of making machines do things that would require intelligence if done by man.

Strong AI versus Weak AI

Currently there are two main camp regarding AI. The *weak AI* approach is associated with the Massachusetts Institute of Technology, and it views any system that exhibits intelligent behavior as an example of AI. This camp focuses on whether a program performs correctly, regardless of whether the artifact performs its task in the same way humans do. The results of AI projects in electrical engineering, robotics, and related fields are primarily concerned with satisfactory performance.

The other approach to AI is called *biological plausibility*, and it's associated with Carnegie-Mellon University. According to this approach, when an artifact exhibits intelligent behavior, its performance should be based upon the same methodologies used by humans. For instance, consider a system capable of hearing: proponents of strong AI might aim to achieve success by simulating the human hearing system, whereas weak AI proponents would be concerned merely with the system's performance. This simulation would include the equivalents to cochlea, hearing canal, eardrum, and other parts of the ear, each performing its required tasks in the system.

Hence, proponents of weak AI measure the success of the systems that they build based on their performance alone. They maintain that the *raison d'etre* of AI research is to solve difficult problems regardless of how they are actually solved.

On the other hand, proponents of strong AI are concerned with the structure of the systems they build. They maintain that by sheer dint of possessing heuristics, algorithms, and knowledge of AI programs, computers can possess a sense of consciousness and intelligence. As you know, Hollywood has produced various movies (e.g., *I, Robot* and *Blade Runner*) that belong to the strong AI camp.

The Turing Test

The previous section posed three questions, and the first two questions have already been addressed: how do you determine intelligence, and are animals intelligent? The answer to the second question is not necessarily yes or no. Some people are smarter than others and some animals are smarter than others. The question of machine intelligence is equally problematic.

Alan Turing sought to answer the question of intelligence in operational terms. He wanted to separate functionality (what something does) from implementation (how something is built). He devised something that's called the *Turing Test*, which is discussed in the next section.

Definition of the Turing Test

Alan Turing proposed two imitation games, in which one person or entity behaves as if he were another. In the first game, a person (called an interrogator) is in a room with a curtain that runs across the center of the room. On the other side of the curtain is a person, and the interrogator must determine whether it is a man or a woman. The interrogator (whose gender is irrelevant) accomplishes this task by asking a series of questions.

This game assumes that the man will perhaps lie in his responses, but the woman is always truthful. In order that the interrogator cannot determine gender from voice, communication is via computer rather than through spoken words. If it is a man on the other side of the curtain, and he is successful in deceiving the interrogator, then he wins the imitation game.

In Turing's original format for this test, both a man and a woman were seated behind a curtain and the interrogator had to identify both correctly.

Turing might have based this test on a game that was popular during this period, which may even have been the impetus behind his machine intelligence test.

Additional interesting updates regarding the Turing test are discussed in these two links:

https://futurism.com/the-byte/scientists-invented-new-turing-test

https://theconversation.com/our-turing-test-for-androids-will-judge-how-lifelike-humanoid-robots-can-be-120696

In case you didn't already know, Erich Fromm was a well-known sociologist and psychoanalyst in the twentieth century who believed that men and women are equal but not necessarily the same. For instance, the genders might differ in their knowledge of colors, flowers, or the amount of time spent shopping. What does distinguishing a man from a woman have to do with the question of intelligence? Turing understood that there might be different types of thinking, and it is important to both understand these differences and to be tolerant of them.

An Interrogator Test

This second game is more appropriate to the study of AI. Once again, an interrogator is in a room with a curtain. This time, a computer or a person is behind the curtain, and the machine plays the role of the male and could also find it convenient on occasion to lie.

The person, on the other hand, is consistently truthful. The interrogator asks questions and then evaluates the responses to determine whether she is communicating with a person or a machine. If the computer is successful in deceiving the interrogator, it passes the Turing Test and is thereby considered intelligent.

Heuristics

Heuristics can be very useful, and AI applications often rely on the application of heuristics. A *heuristic* is essentially a "rule of thumb" for solving a problem. In other words, a heuristic is a set of guidelines that often works to solve a problem. Contrast a heuristic with an algorithm, which is a prescribed set of rules to solve a problem and whose output is entirely predictable.

A heuristic is a technique for finding an approximate solution that can be used when other methods are too time-consuming or too complex (or both). With a heuristic, a favorable outcome is likely but not guaranteed, and heuristic methods were especially popular in the early days of AI.

Various heuristics appear in daily life. For example, many people prefer using heuristics instead of asking for driving directions. For instance, when exiting a highway at night, sometimes it's difficult to find the route back to the main thoroughfare. One heuristic that could prove helpful is to proceed in the direction with more streetlights whenever they come to a fork in the road. You might have a favorite ploy for recovering a dropped contact lens or for finding a parking space in a crowded shopping mall. Both are examples of heuristics.

AI problems tend to be large and computationally complex, and frequently they cannot be solved via straightforward algorithms. AI problems and their domains tend to embody a large amount of human expertise, especially if tackled by strong AI methods. Some types of problems are better solved using AI, whereas others are more suitable for traditional computer science approaches involving simple decision-making or exact computations to produce solutions. Let us consider a few examples:

- Medical diagnosis
- Shopping using a cash register with barcode scanning
- ATMs
- Two-person games such as chess and checkers

Medical diagnosis is a field of science that has benefited for many years from AI-based contributions, particularly through the development of expert systems. Expert systems are typically built in domains where there is considerable human expertise and where there exist many rules that are often of the form: if-condition-then-action. As a trivial example: if you have a headache, then take two aspirins and call me in the morning.

In particular, expert systems became very popular (and very useful) because they can store far more rules than humans can hold in their head. Expert systems are among the most successful AI techniques for producing results that are comprehensive and effective. In fact, expert systems can help humans make more accurate decisions (and even "challenge" incorrect choices).

Genetic Algorithms

One promising paradigm is Darwin's theory of evolution, which involves natural selection that occurs in nature at a rate of thousands or millions of years. By contrast, evolution inside a computer proceeds much faster than natural selection.

A genetic algorithm is a heuristic that "mimics" the process of natural selection, which involves selecting the fittest individuals for reproduction to sire the offspring of the subsequent generation.

Let's compare and contrast the use of AI with the process of evolution in the plant and animal world, in which species adapt to their environments through the genetic operators of natural selection, reproduction, mutation, and recombination.

Genetic algorithms (GA) are a specific methodology from the general field known as evolutionary computation, which is that branch of AI wherein proposed solutions to a problem adapt much as animal creatures adapt to their environments in the real world.

In case you're interested, the following link contains some interesting details regarding genetic algorithms:

https://en.wikipedia.org/wiki/Genetic_algorithm

Knowledge Representation

The issue of representation becomes important when we consider AI-related problems. AI systems that acquire and store knowledge in order to process it and produce intelligent results also need the ability to identify and represent that knowledge. The choice of a representation is intrinsic to the nature of problem solving and understanding.

As George Polya (a famous mathematician) remarked, a good representation choice is almost as important as the algorithm or solution plan devised for a particular problem. Good and natural representations facilitate fast and comprehensible solutions.

As an example of a representation choice, consider the well-known Missionaries and Cannibals Problem, where the goal is to transfer three missionaries and three cannibals from the west bank to the east bank of a river with a boat. At any point during the transitions from west to east, you can see the solution path by selecting an appropriate representation. There are two constraints in this problem: the boat can hold no more than two people at any time and the cannibals on any bank can never outnumber the number of missionaries.

A solution for this problem (as well as the related "jealous husbands" problem) is here:

https://en.wikipedia.org/wiki/Missionaries_and_cannibals_ problem#targetText=The%20missionaries%20and%20cannibals%20 problem,an%20example%20of%20problem%20representation

Logic-based Solutions

AI researchers have used a logic-based approach for knowledge representation and problem-solving technique. A seminal example of using logic for this purpose is Terry Winograd's Blocks World (1972), in which a robot arm interacts with blocks on a tabletop. This program encompassed issues of language understanding and scene analysis as well as other aspects of AI.

In addition, production rules and production systems are used to construct many successful expert systems. The appeal of production rules and expert systems is based on the feasibility of representing heuristics clearly and concisely. Thousands of expert systems have been built incorporating this methodology.

Semantic Networks

Semantic networks are another graphical, though complex, representation of knowledge. Semantic networks precede object-oriented languages, which use inheritance (wherein an object from a particular class inherits many of the properties of a superclass).

Much of the work employing semantic networks has focused on representing the knowledge and structure of language. Examples include Stuart Shapiro SNePS (Semantic Net Processing System) and the work of Roger Schank in natural language processing.

Additional alternatives exist for knowledge representation: graphical approaches offer greater appeal to the senses, such as vision, space, and motion. Possibly the earliest graphical approaches were state-space representations, which display all the possible states of a system.

AI and Games

Since the middle of the twentieth century and the advent of computers, significant progress in computer science and proficiency in programming techniques was acquired through the challenges of training computers to play and master complex board games. Some examples of games whose play by computer have benefitted from the application of AI insights and methodologies have included chess, checkers, Go, and Othello.

Games have spurred the development and interest in AI. Early efforts were highlighted by the efforts of Arthur Samuel in 1959 on the game of checkers. His program was based on tables of fifty heuristics and was used to play against different versions of itself. The losing program in a series of matches would adopt the heuristics of the winning program. It played strong checkers, but never mastered the game.

People have been trying to train machines to play strong chess for several centuries. The infatuation with chess machines probably stems from the generally accepted view that it requires intelligence to play chess well.

In 1959, Newell, Simon, and Shaw developed the first real chess program, which followed the Shannon-Turing Paradigm. Richard Greenblatt's program was the first to play club-level chess. Computer chess programs improved steadily in the 1970s until, by the end of that decade, they reached the Expert level (equivalent to the top 1% of chess tournament players).

In 1983, Ken Thompson's Belle was the first program to officially achieve the Master level. This was followed by the success of Hitech, from Carnegie-Mellon University, which successfully accomplished a major milestone as the first Senior Master (over 2400-rated) program. Shortly thereafter the program Deep Thought (also from Carnegie-Mellon) was developed and became the first program capable of beating Grandmasters on a regular basis.

Deep Thought evolved into Deep Blue when IBM took over the project in the 1990s, and Deep Blue played a six-game match with World Champion Garry Kasparov, who saved mankind by winning a match in Philadelphia in 1996. In 1997, however, against Deeper Blue, the successor of Deep Blue, Kasparov lost, and the chess world was shaken.

In subsequent six-game matches against Kasparov, Kramnik, and other World Championship-level players, programs have fared well, but these were not World Championship Matches. Although it is generally agreed that these programs might still be slightly inferior to the best human players, most would be willing to concede that top programs play chess indistinguishably from the most accomplished humans (if one is thinking of the Turing Test).

In 1989, Jonathan Schaeffer, at the University of Alberta in Edmonton, began his long-term goal of conquering the game of checkers with his program Chinook. In a forty-game match in 1992 against longtime Checkers World Champion Marion Tinsley, Chinook lost four, with thirty-four draws. In 1994 their match was tied after six games, when Tinsley had to forfeit because of health reasons. Since that time, Schaeffer and his team have been working to solve checkers from both the end of the game (all eight-pieces and fewer endings) as well as from the beginning.

Other games that use AI techniques include backgammon, poker, bridge, Othello, and Go (often called the new drosophila).

The Success of AlphaZero

Google created AlphaZero, which is an AI-based software program that used self-play to learn how to play games. AlphaZero is the successor to Alpha Go that defeated the world's best human Go player in 2016. AlphaZero easily defeated Alpha Go in the game of Go.

Moreover, after learning the rules of chess, AlphaZero trained itself (again using self-play) and within a single day became the top chess player in the world. AlphaZero can defeat any human chess player as well as any chess-playing computer program.

The really interesting point is that AlphaZero developed its own strategy for playing chess, which not only differs from humans, but also involves chess moves that are considered counterintuitive.

Unfortunately, AlphaZero is unable to tell us how it developed a strategy that is superior to any previously developed approach for playing chess. Since AlphaZero is 100% self-taught and is the top-ranked chess player in the world, does AlphaZero qualify as intelligent?

Expert Systems

Expert systems are one of the areas that have been investigated for almost as long as AI itself has existed. It is one discipline that AI can claim as a great success. Expert systems have many characteristics that make them desirable for AI research and development. These include separation of the knowledge base from the inference engine, being more than the sum of any or all of their experts, relationship of knowledge to search techniques, reasoning, and uncertainty.

One of the earliest and most often referenced systems was heuristic DENDRAL. Its purpose was to identify unknown chemical compounds on the basis of their mass spectrographs. DENDRAL was developed at Stanford University with the goal of performing a chemical analysis of the Martian soil. It was one of the first systems to illustrate the feasibility of encoding domain-expert knowledge in a particular discipline.

Perhaps the most famous expert system is MYCIN, also from Stanford University (1984). Mycin was developed to facilitate the investigation of infectious blood diseases. Even more important than its domain, however, was the example that Mycin established for the design of all subsequent knowledge-based systems. It had over 400 rules, which were eventually used to provide a training dialogue for residents at the Stanford hospital.

In the 1970s, PROSPECTOR (also at Stanford University) was developed for mineral exploration. PROSPECTOR was also an early and valuable example of the use of inference networks.

Other famous and successful systems that followed in the 1970s were XCON (with some 10,000 rules), which was developed to help configure electrical circuit boards on VAX computers; GUIDON, a tutoring system that was an offshoot of Mycin; TEIRESIAS, a knowledge acquisition tool for Mycin; and HEARSAY I and II, the premier examples of speech understanding using the Blackboard Architecture.

The AM (Artificial Mathematician) system of Doug Lenat was another important result of research and development efforts in the 1970s, as well as the Dempster-Schafer Theory for reasoning under uncertainty, together with Zadeh's work in fuzzy logic.

Since the 1980s, thousands of expert systems have been developed in such areas as configuration, diagnosis, instruction, monitoring, planning, prognosis, remedy, and control. Today, in addition to stand-alone expert systems, many expert systems have been embedded into other software systems for control purposes, including those in medical equipment and automobiles (for example, when should traction control engage in an automobile?).

In addition, many expert systems shells, such as Emycin, OPS, EXSYS, and CLIPS, have become industry standards. Many knowledge representation languages have also been developed. Today, numerous expert systems work behind the scenes to enhance day-to-day experiences, such as the online shopping cart.

Neural Computing

McCulloch and Pitts conducted early research in neural computing because they were trying to understand the behavior of animal nervous systems. Their model of artificial neural networks (ANN) had one serious drawback: it did not include a mechanism for learning.

Frank Rosenblatt developed an iterative algorithm known as the Perceptron Learning Rule for finding the appropriate weights in a single-layered network (a network in which all neurons are directly connected to inputs). Research in this burgeoning discipline might have been severely hindered by the pronouncement by Minsky and Papert that certain problems could not be solved by single-layer perceptrons, such as the exclusive OR (XOR) function. Federal funding for neural network research was severely curtailed immediately after this proclamation.

The field witnessed a second flurry of activity in the early 1980s with the work of Hopfield. His asynchronous network model (Hopfield networks) used an energy function to approximate solutions to NP-complete problems.

The mid-1980s also witnessed the discovery of back propagation (usually called *backprop*), a learning algorithm appropriate for multilayered networks. Back propagation-based networks are routinely employed to predict Dow Jones averages and to read printed material in optical character recognition systems.

Neural networks are also used in control systems. ALVINN was a project at Carnegie Mellon University in which a back propagation network senses the highway and assists in the steering of a Navlab vehicle.

One immediate application of this work was to warn a driver impaired by lack of sleep, excess of alcohol, or other conditions whenever the vehicle strayed from its highway lane. Looking toward the future, it is hoped that, someday, similar systems will drive vehicles so that we are free to read newspapers and talk on our cell phones to take advantage of the extra free time.

Evolutionary Computation

Genetic algorithms are more generally classified as evolutionary computation. Genetic algorithms use probability and parallelism to solve combinatorial problems (also called optimization problems), which is an approach developed by John Holland.

However, evolutionary computation is not solely concerned with optimization problems. Rodney Brooks was formerly the director of the MIT Computer Science and AI Laboratory. His approach to the successful creation of a human-level Artificial Intelligence, which he aptly cites as the holy grail of AI research, renounces reliance on the symbol-based approach. This latter approach relies upon the use of heuristics and representational paradigms.

In his view, intelligent systems can be designed in multiple layers in which higher leveled layers rely upon those layers beneath them. For example, if you wanted to build a robot capable of avoiding obstacles, the obstacle avoidance routine would be built upon a lower layer, which would merely be responsible for robotic locomotion.

Brooks maintains that intelligence emerges through the interaction of an agent with its environment. He is perhaps most well known for the insectlike robots built in his lab that embody this philosophy of intelligence, wherein a community of autonomous robots interact with their environment and with each other.

Natural Language Processing

If we wish to build intelligent systems, it seems natural to ask that our systems possess a language-understanding facility. This is an axiom that was well understood by many early practitioners. Eliza is one well-known early application program, which was developed by Joseph Weizenbaum, an MIT computer scientist who worked with Kenneth Colby (a Stanford University psychiatrist).

Eliza was intended to imitate the role played by a psychiatrist of the Carl Rogers School. For instance, if the user typed in "I feel tired," Eliza was a back propagation application that learned the correct pronunciation for English text. It was claimed to pronounce English sounds with 95% accuracy. Obviously, problems arose because of inconsistencies inherent in the pronunciation of English words, such as *rough* and *through*, and the pronunciation of words derived from other languages, such as *pizza* and *fizzy*.

Terry Winograd wrote another well-known program that was named after the second set of these letters of the pair ETAOIN SHRDLU, which are the most frequently used letters in the English language on linotype machines. Winograd's program might respond with, "You say you feel tired. Tell me more." The "conversation" would continue in this manner, with the machine contributing little or nothing in terms of originality to the dialogue. A live psychoanalyst might behave in this fashion in the hope that the patient would discover their true (perhaps hidden) feelings and frustrations. Meanwhile, Eliza is merely using pattern matching to feign human-like interaction.

Curiously, Weizenbaum was disturbed by the avid interest that his students (and the public in general) took in interacting with Eliza, even though they were fully aware that Eliza was only a program. Meanwhile, Colby remained dedicated to the project and went on to author a successful program called DOCTOR.

Although Eliza has contributed little to natural language processing (NLP), it is software that pretends to possess what is perhaps our last vestige of specialness, our ability to feel emotions. What will happen when the line between a human and machine (example: android) becomes less clear, perhaps in some fifty years, and these androids will be less mortal and more like immortals?

More recently, several MIT robots, including Cog, Kismet, and Paro, have been developed with the uncanny ability to feign human emotions and evoke emotional responses from those with whom they interact. Turkle has studied the relationships that children and older persons in nursing homes have formed with these robots; relationships that involve genuine emotion and caring. Turkle speaks of the need to perhaps redefine the word *relationship* to include the encounters that people have with these so-called relational artifacts. She remains confident, however, that such relationships will never replace the bonds that can only occur between human beings who must confront their mortality on a daily basis.

Winograd's Blocks World involved a robot arm that was able to achieve various goals. For example, if SHRDLU was asked to lift a red block upon which there was a small green block, it knew that it must remove the green block before it could lift the red one. Unlike Eliza, SHRDLU was able to understand English commands and respond to them appropriately.

HEARSAY, an ambitious program in speech recognition, employed a blackboard architecture wherein independent knowledge sources (agents) for various components of language, such as phonetics and phrases, could freely communicate. Both syntax and semantics were used to prune improbable word combinations.

The HWIM (pronounced "whim" and short for Hear What I Mean) Project used augmented transition networks to understand spoken language. It had a vocabulary of 1,000 words dealing with travel budget management. Perhaps this project was too ambitious in scope because it did not perform as well as HEARSAY II.

Parsing played an integral part in the success of these natural language programs. SHRDLU employed a context-free grammar to help parse English commands. Context-free grammars provide a syntactic structure for dealing with strings of symbols. However, to effectively process natural languages, semantics must be considered as well.

A *parse tree* provides the relationship between the words that compose a sentence. For example, many sentences can be broken down into both a subject and a predicate. Subjects can be broken down perhaps into a noun phrase followed by a prepositional phrase and so on. Essentially, a parse tree gives the semantics that is the meaning of the sentence.

Each of the these early language processing systems employed world knowledge to some extent. However, in the late 1980s the greatest stumbling block for progress in NLP was the problem of common sense knowledge. For example, although many successful programs were built in particular areas of NLP and AI, these were often criticized as microworlds, meaning that the programs did not have general, real-world knowledge or common sense. For example, a program might know a lot about a particular scenario, such as ordering food in a restaurant, but it would have no knowledge of whether the waiter or waitress was alive or whether they would ordinarily be wearing any clothing. During the past twenty-five years, Douglas Lenat of MCC in Austin, Texas, has been building the largest repository of common-sense knowledge to address this issue.

NLP has undergone some interesting developments. After its initial stage (as described earlier in this section), NLP relied on statistics to govern the parse trees for sentences. Charniak describes how context-free grammars (CFGs) can be augmented such that each rule has an associated probability. These associated probabilities could be taken from the Penn Treebank, which contains more than one million words of English text that have been parsed manually, mostly from the *Wall Street Journal*. Charniak demonstrated how this statistical approach successfully obtained a parse for a sentence from the front page of the *New York Times* (no trivial feat, even for most humans).

The next step in the evolution of NLP involves deep-learning architectures called RNNs, LSTMs, and bidirectional LSTMs, which are discussed in Chapter 5. The most recent architecture is called a *transformer*, which was developed by Google in 2017. BERT is based on transformers (as well as "attention") and is one of the most powerful open-source systems currently available for solving NLP tasks. Yet another approach for NLP involves Deep Reinforcement Learning (discussed briefly in Chapter 6).

Bioinformatics

Bioinformatics is the nascent discipline that concerns the application of the algorithms and techniques of computer science to molecular biology. It is mainly concerned with the management and analysis of biological data. In structural genomics, one attempts to specify a structure for each observed protein. Automated discovery and data mining could help in this pursuit.

Juristica and Glasgow demonstrate how case-based reasoning could assist in the discovery of the representative structure for each protein. In their 2004 survey article in the AAAI special issue on *AI and Bioinformatics*, Glasgow, Jurisica, and Rost note: "Possibly the most rapidly growing area of recent activity in bioinformatics is the analysis of microarray data."

Microbiologists are overwhelmed with both the variety and quantity of data available to them. They are being asked to comprehend molecular sequence, structure, and data based solely on huge databases. Many researchers believe that AI techniques from knowledge representation and machine learning will prove beneficial as well.

The next portion of this chapter provides a quick introduction to the major parts of AI, which include machine learning and deep learning.

Major Parts of AI

The subsequent chapters in this book delve into various important parts of AI, which include:

- ML (Machine Learning)
- DL (Deep Learning)
- NLP (Natural Language Processing)
- RL (Reinforcement Learning)
- DRL (Deep Reinforcement Learning)

Traditional AI (twentieth century) is based on collections of rules, which led to expert systems in the 1980s. Traditional AI also involved LISP, which was created by John McCarthy (one of the members of the first official AI meeting in 1956).

Traditional AI is primarily a set of rules in conjunction with conditional logic, which is also true for the powerful expert systems that were developed in the 1980s. However, a rule-based system for making decisions can involve thousands of rules. Even simple objects require many rules: try to come up with a set of rules that define a chair, a table, or even just an apple. Traditional AI has some significant limitations, mainly because of the number of rules that are required.

Machine Learning

Around the middle of the twentieth century machine learning (a subset of AI) relied primarily on data to optimize and "learn" how to perform tasks, often accompanied by new or improved algorithms, such as linear regression, k-NN, decision trees, random forests, and SVMs; with the exception of linear regression, all the other algorithms are classifiers.

As you will see, machine learning is a diverse and vibrant field that includes other subfields.

Since data (instead of rules) is so important in machine learning, it's typically one of the following types:

- Supervised learning (lots of labeled data)
- Semi-supervised learning (lots of partially labeled data)
- Unsupervised learning: lots of data, clustering
- Reinforcement learning: trial, feedback, and improvement

According to Andrew Ng (the cofounder of Coursera), "99% of all machine learning is supervised."

In addition to categorizing data, machine learning algorithms can be categorized into the following major types:

- Classifiers (for images, spam, fraud, etc.)
- Regression (stock price, housing price, etc.)
- Clustering (unsupervised classifiers)

Deep Learning

One important subfield of machine learning is deep learning, which also has its roots in the middle of the twentieth century. Deep-learning architectures rely on the *perceptron* as the basis of neural networks, often involving large or massive datasets. Such architectures also involve heuristics and empirical results. Nowadays deep learning can surpass humans for some image classification.

While machine learning involves MLPs (multilayer perceptrons), deep learning introduces deep neural networks, with new algorithms and new architectures (e.g., convolutional neural networks, RNNs, and LSTMs).

Reinforcement Learning

Reinforcement learning (also a subset of machine learning) involves trial-and-error in order to maximize a reward for a so-called agent. Deep reinforcement learning combines the strengths of deep learning with reinforcement learning. In particular, the agent in reinforcement learning is replaced with a neural network.

Deep reinforcement learning has applications in many diverse fields, and three of the most popular are:

- Games (Go, Chess, etc.)
- Robotics
- NLP

Some well-known and successful examples of the use of reinforcement learning in games include:

- Alpha Go (hybrid RL)
- Alpha Zero (complete RL)
- Often involve Greedy algorithms
- Deep RL: Combines Deep Learning and RL

Robotics

Robots have entered our personal and professional lives in myriad ways, including:

- Surgery (assisting surgeons)
- Radiology (detecting cancer)
- Drug mismanagement
- Comparative theories of religion
- Law/real estate/military/science
- Comedy (including stand-up)
- Music (conducting orchestras)
- Restaurants (gourmet meals)
- Coordinated dancing teams
- Many other fields

Robot truck drivers are displacing jobs, but they also have advantages: their only cost is the upkeep of the machinery. In addition, robots aren't distracted the way that humans are, they don't engage in activities that contribute to accidents, and they don't require salaries or any sort of time off. Yet despite the surprising achievements of robots, *Star Trek*'s character Data is still just a dream.

NLP is an area of computer science and AI that involves interaction between computers and human languages. In the early days, NLP involved rule-based techniques or statistical techniques. NLP and machine learning can process/analyze volumes of natural language data, where computer programs perform that processing.

There are many NLP tasks that are solved with machine learning techniques. Some areas of interest that involve NLP include:

- Translating between languages

- Finding meaningful information from text

- Summarizing documents

- Detecting hate speech

Despite all the advances and advantages of machine learning, et al., there are issues that need to be resolved. One issue is occupational bias: an AI system inferred that white males were doctors and white females were housewives. Another issue involves detecting gender bias. For example, in Wikipedia (circa 2018) 18% of its biographies are of women, while 84% to 90% of Wikipedia editors are male.

Yet another issue, analyzed in the following article, involves data bias versus algorithmic bias:

https://www.forbes.com/sites/charlestowersclark/2018/09/19/can-we-make-artificial-intelligence-accountable

Finally, there is the question of the interaction of AI and ethics, which includes some thought-provoking questions (such as unemployment and robot rights). The following article contains an extensive list of ethical questions:

https://www.weforum.org/agenda/2016/10/top-10-ethical-issues-in-artificial-intelligence/

Code Samples

The companion disc contains the following files:

- `RubiksCube.py`

- `Board.java`

- `Search.java`

The Python file is a solution for Rubik's Cube, and the two Java files are for the solution to the Red Donkey problem.

In order to run a Java program, download the Java Runtime Environment (JRE) here:

http://www.oracle.com/technetwork/java/javase/downloads/index.html

In order to compile and run a Java program, download the Java SDK here:

https://www.java.com/en/

If you do not have Python installed, the Python-related download is here:

http://www.python.org/getit/

If you do not have Java installed, you can find online for instructions doing so, as well as instructions for compiling and launching Java code.

Summary

In this chapter, you learned about AI, strong versus weak AI, and the Turing Test for intelligence. Then you learned about heuristics and their usefulness in algorithms, followed by genetic algorithms, and knowledge representation. Next you saw how AI was initially applied to diverse areas such as games and expert systems.

You also learned about the early approaches to neural computing, evolutionary computation, NLP, and bioinformatics. In addition, you got an introduction to the major subfields of AI, which include natural language processing, machine learning, deep learning, reinforcement learning, and deep reinforcement learning.

## CHAPTER 2

INTRODUCTION TO MACHINE LEARNING

This chapter introduces numerous concepts in machine learning, such as feature selection, feature engineering, data cleaning, training sets, and test sets.

The first part of this chapter briefly discusses machine learning and the sequence of steps that are typically required in order to prepare a dataset. These steps include "feature selection" or "feature extraction" that can be performed using various algorithms.

The second section describes the types of data that you can encounter, issues that can arise with the data in datasets, and how to rectify them. You will also learn about the difference between "hold out" and "k-fold" when you perform the training step.

The third part of this chapter briefly discusses the basic concepts involved in linear regression. Although linear regression was developed more than 200 years ago, this technique is still one of the "core" techniques for solving (albeit simple) problems in statistics and machine learning. In fact, the technique known as "Mean Squared Error" (MSE) for finding a best-fitting line for data points in a 2D plane (or a hyperplane for higher dimensions) is implemented in Python and TensorFlow in order to minimize so-called "cost" functions that are discussed later.

The fourth section in this chapter contains additional code samples involving linear regression tasks using standard techniques in NumPy. Hence, if you are comfortable with this topic, you can probably skim quickly through the first two sections of this chapter. The third section shows you how to solve linear regression using `Keras`.

One point to keep in mind is that some algorithms are mentioned without delving into details about them. For instance, the section pertaining to supervised learning contains a list of algorithms that appear later in the chapter in the section that pertains to classification algorithms. The algorithms that are displayed in bold in a list are the algorithms that are of greater interest for this book. In some cases the algorithms are discussed in greater detail in the next chapter; otherwise, you can perform an online search for additional information about the algorithms that are not discussed in detail in this book.

What is Machine Learning?

In high level terms, machine learning is a subset of AI that can solve tasks that are infeasible or too cumbersome with "traditional" programming languages. A spam filter for email is an early example of machine learning. Machine learning generally supersedes the accuracy of older algorithms.

Despite the variety of machine learning algorithms, the data is arguably more important than the selected algorithm. Many issues can arise with data, such as insufficient data, poor quality of data, incorrect data, missing data, irrelevant data, duplicate data values, and so forth. Later in this chapter you will see techniques that address many of these data-related issues.

If you are unfamiliar with machine learning terminology, a dataset is a collection of data values, which can be in the form of a CSV file or a spreadsheet. Each column is called a feature, and each row is a datapoint that contains a set of specific values for each feature. If a dataset contains information about customers, then each row pertains to a specific customer.

Types of Machine Learning

There are three main types of machine learning (combinations of these are also possible) that you will encounter:

- Supervised learning
- Unsupervised learning
- Semi-supervised learning

Supervised learning means that the datapoints in a dataset have a label that identifies its contents. For example, the MNIST dataset contains 28x28 PNG files, each of which contains a single hand-drawn digit (i.e. 0 through 9 inclusive). Every image with the digit 0 has the label 0; every image with the digit 1 has the label 1; all other images are labeled according to the digit that is displayed in those images.

As another example, the columns in the Titanic dataset are features about passengers, such as their gender, the cabin class, the price of their ticket, whether or not the passenger survived, and so forth. Each row contains information about a single passenger, including the value 1 if the passenger survived. *The MNIST dataset and the Titanic dataset involve classification tasks: the goal is to train a model based on a training dataset and then predict the class of each row in a test dataset.*

In general, the datasets for classification tasks have a small number of possible values: one of nine digits in the range of 0 through 9, one of four animals (dog, cat, horse, giraffe), one of two values (survived versus perished, purchased versus not purchased). As a rule of thumb, if the number of outcomes can be displayed "reasonably well" in a drop-down list, then it's probably a classification task.

In the case of a dataset that contains real estate data, each row contains information about a specific house, such as the number of bedrooms, the square feet of the house, the number of bathrooms, the price of the house, and so forth. In this dataset the price of the house is the label for each row. Notice that the range of possible prices is too large to fit "reasonably well" in a drop-down list. *A real estate dataset involves a regression task: the goal is to train a model based on a training dataset and then predict the price of each house in a test dataset.*

Unsupervised learning involves unlabeled data, which is typically the case for clustering algorithms (discussed later). Some important unsupervised learning algorithms that involve *clustering* are listed below:

- k-Means
- Hierarchical Cluster Analysis (HCA)
- Expectation Maximization

Some important unsupervised learning algorithms that involve *dimensionality reduction* (discussed in more detail later) are listed below:

- PCA (Principal Component Analysis)
- Kernel PCA
- LLE (Locally Linear Embedding)
- t-SNE (t-distributed Stochastic Neighbor Embedding)

There is one more very important unsupervised task called anomaly detection. This task is relevant for fraud detection and detecting outliers (discussed later in more detail).

Semi-supervised learning is a combination of supervised and unsupervised learning: some datapoints are labeled and some are unlabeled. One technique involves using the labeled data in order to classify (i.e., label) the unlabeled data, after which you can apply a classification algorithm.

Types of Machine Learning Algorithms

There are three main types of machine learning algorithms:

- Regression (ex: linear regression)
- Classification (ex: k-Nearest-Neighbor)
- Clustering (ex: kMeans)

Regression is a supervised learning technique to predict numerical quantities. An example of a regression task is predicting the value of a particular stock. Note that this task is different from predicting whether the value of a particular stock will increase or decrease tomorrow (or some other future time period). Another example of a regression task involves predicting the cost of a house in a real estate dataset. Both of these tasks are examples of a regression task.

Regression algorithms in machine learning include linear regression and generalized linear regression (also called multivariate analysis in traditional statistics).

Classification is also a supervised learning technique, but it's for predicting categorical quantities. An example of a classification task is detecting the occurrence of spam, fraud, or determining the digit in a PNG file (such as the `MNIST` dataset). In this case, the data is already labeled, so you can compare the prediction with the label that was assigned to the given PNG.

Classification algorithms in machine learning include the following list of algorithms (they are discussed in greater detail in the next chapter):

- Decision Trees (a single tree)
- Random Forests (multiple trees)
- kNN (k Nearest Neighbor)
- Logistic regression (despite its name)
- Naïve Bayes
- SVM (Support Vector Machines)

Some machine learning algorithms (such as SVMs, random forests, and kNN) support regression as well as classification. In the case of SVMs, the scikit-learn implementation of this algorithm provides two APIs: SVC for classification and SVR for regression.

Each of the preceding algorithms involves a model that is trained on a dataset, after which the model is used to make a prediction. By contrast, a random forest consists of *multiple* independent trees (the number is specified by you), and each tree makes a prediction regarding the value of a feature. If the feature is numeric, take the mean or the mode (or perform some other calculation) in order to determine the "final" prediction. If the feature is categorical, use the mode (i.e., the most frequently occurring class) as the result; in the case of a tie you can select one of them in a random fashion.

Incidentally, the following link contains more information regarding the kNN algorithm for classification as well as regression:

http://saedsayad.com/k_nearest_neighbors_reg.htm

Clustering is an unsupervised learning technique for grouping similar data together. Clustering algorithms put data points in different clusters without knowing the nature of the data points. After the data has been separated into different clusters, you can use the SVM (Support Vector Machine) algorithm to perform classification.

Clustering algorithms in machine learning include the following (some of which are variations of each other):

- k-Means
- Meanshift
- Hierarchical Cluster Analysis (HCA)
- Expectation Maximization

Keep in mind the following points. First, the value of k in k-Means is a hyper parameter, and it's usually an odd number to avoid ties between two classes. Next, the meanshift algorithm is a variation of the k-Means algorithm that does *not* require you to specify a value for k. In fact, the meanshift algorithm determines the optimal number of clusters. However, this algorithm does not scale well for large datasets.

Machine Learning Tasks

Unless you have a dataset that has already been sanitized, you need to examine the data in a dataset to make sure that it's in a suitable condition. The data preparation phase involves 1) examining the rows ("data cleaning") to ensure that they contain valid data (which might require domain-specific knowledge), and 2) examining the columns (feature selection or feature extraction) to determine if you can retain only the most important columns.

A high-level list of the sequence of machine learning tasks (some of which might not be required) is shown below:

- Obtain a dataset
- Data cleaning
- Feature selection
- Dimensionality reduction
- Algorithm selection
- Train-versus-test data
- Training a model
- Testing a model

- Fine-tuning a model
- Obtain metrics for the model

First, you obviously need to obtain a dataset for your task. In the ideal scenario, this dataset already exists; otherwise, you need to cull the data from one or more data sources (e.g., a CSV file, a relational database, a no-SQL database, a Web service, and so forth).

Second, you need to perform *data cleaning*, which you can do via the following techniques:

- Missing Value Ratio
- Low Variance Filter
- High Correlation Filter

In general, data cleaning involves checking the data values in a dataset in order to resolve one or more of the following:

- Fix incorrect values
- Resolve duplicate values
- Resolve missing values
- Decide what to do with outliers

Use the Missing Value Ratio technique if the dataset has too many missing values. In extreme cases, you might be able to drop features with a large number of missing values. Use the Low Variance filter technique to identify and drop features with constant values from the dataset. Use the High Correlation filter technique to find highly correlated features, which increase multicollinearity in the dataset: such features can be removed from a dataset (but check with your domain expert before doing so).

Depending on your background and the nature of the dataset, you might need to work with a domain expert, which is a person who has a deep understanding of the contents of the dataset.

For example, you can use a statistical value (mean, mode, and so forth) to replace incorrect values with suitable values. Duplicate values can be handled in a similar fashion. You can replace missing numeric values with zero, the minimum, the mean, the mode, or the maximum value in a numeric column. You can replace missing categorical values with the mode of the categorical column.

If a row in a dataset contains a value that is an outlier, you have three choices:

- Delete the row
- Keep the row
- Replace the outlier with some other value (mean?)

When a dataset contains an outlier, you need to make a decision based on domain knowledge that is specific to the given dataset.

Suppose that a dataset contains stock-related information. As you know, there was a stock market crash in 1929, which you view as an outlier. Such an occurrence is rare, but it can contain meaningful information. Incidentally, the source of wealth for some families in the 20th century was based on buying massive amounts of stock are very low prices during the Great Depression.

Feature Engineering, Selection, and Extraction

In addition to creating a dataset and "cleaning" its values, you also need to examine the features in that dataset to determine whether or not you can reduce the dimensionality (i.e., the number of columns) of the dataset. The process for doing so involves three main techniques:

- Feature engineering
- Feature selection
- Feature extraction (aka feature projection)

Feature engineering is the process of determining a new set of features that are based on a combination of existing features in order to create a meaningful dataset for a given task. Domain expertise is often required for this process, even in cases of relatively simple datasets. Feature engineering can be tedious and expensive, and in some cases you might consider using automated feature learning. After you have created a dataset, it's a good idea to perform feature selection or feature extraction (or both) to ensure that you have a high quality dataset.

Feature selection is also called variable selection, attribute selection or variable subset selection. Feature selection involves selecting the subset of relevant features in a dataset. In essence, feature selection involves selecting the "most important" features in a dataset, which provides these advantages:

- Reduced training time
- Simpler models are easier to interpret
- Avoidance of the curse of dimensionality
- Better generalization due to a reduction in overfitting ("reduction of variance")

Feature selection techniques are often used in domains where there are many features and comparatively few samples (or data points). Keep in mind that a low-value feature can be redundant or irrelevant, which are two different concepts. For instance, a relevant feature might be redundant when it's combined with another strongly correlated feature.

Feature selection can involve three strategies: the filter strategy (e.g. information gain), the wrapper strategy (e.g. search guided by accuracy), and the embedded strategy (prediction errors are used to determine whether features are included or excluded while developing a model). One other interesting point is that feature selection can also be useful for regression as well as classification tasks.

Feature extraction creates new features from functions that produce combinations of the original features. By contrast, feature selection involves determining a subset of the existing features.

Feature selection and feature extraction both result in *dimensionality reduction* for a given dataset, which is the topic of the next section.

Dimensionality Reduction

Dimensionality Reduction refers to algorithms that reduce the number of features in a dataset: hence the term "dimensionality reduction." As you will see, there are many techniques available, and they involve either feature selection or feature extraction.

Algorithms that use feature selection to perform dimensionality reduction are listed here:

- Backward Feature Elimination
- Forward Feature Selection

- Factor Analysis

- Independent Component Analysis

Algorithms that use feature extraction to perform dimensionality reduction are listed here:

- Principal component analysis (PCA)

- Non-negative matrix factorization (NMF)

- Kernel PCA

- Graph-based kernel PCA

- Linear discriminant analysis (LDA)

- Generalized discriminant analysis (GDA)

- Autoencoder

The following algorithms combine feature extraction and dimensionality reduction:

- Principal component analysis (PCA)

- Linear discriminant analysis (LDA)

- Canonical correlation analysis (CCA)

- Non-negative matrix factorization (NMF)

These algorithms can be used during a pre-processing step before using clustering or some other algorithm (such as kNN) on a dataset.

One other group of algorithms involves methods based on projections, which includes t-Distributed Stochastic Neighbor Embedding (t-SNE) as well as UMAP.

This chapter discusses PCA, and you can perform an online search to find more information about the other algorithms.

PCA

Principal Components are new components that are linear combinations of the initial variables in a dataset. In addition, these components are uncorrelated and the most meaningful or important information is contained in these new components.

There are two advantages to PCA: 1) reduced computation time due to far fewer features and 2) the ability to graph the components when there are at most three components. If you have four or five components, you won't be able to display them visually, but you could select subsets of three components for visualization, and perhaps gain some additional insight into the dataset.

PCA uses the variance as a measure of information: the higher the variance, the more important the component. In fact, just to jump ahead slightly: PCA determines the eigenvalues and eigenvectors of a covariance matrix (discussed later), and constructs a new matrix whose columns are eigenvectors, ordered from left-to-right based on the maximum eigenvalue in the left-most column, decreasing until the right-most eigenvector also has the smallest eigenvalue.

Covariance Matrix

As a reminder, the statistical quantity called the variance of a random variable X is defined as follows:

```
variance(x) = [SUM (x - xbar)*(x-xbar)]/n
```

A covariance matrix C is an nxn matrix whose values on the main diagonal are the variance of the variables X1, X2, . . ., Xn. The other values of C are the covariance values of each pair of variables Xi and Xj.

The formula for the covariance of the variables X and Y is a generalization of the variance of a variable, and the formula is shown here:

```
covariance(X, Y) = [SUM (x - xbar)*(y-ybar)]/n
```

Notice that you can reverse the order of the product of terms (multiplication is commutative), and therefore the covariance matrix C is a symmetric matrix:

```
covariance(X, Y) = covariance(Y,X)
```

PCA calculates the eigenvalues and the eigenvectors of the covariance matrix A.

Working with Datasets

In addition to data cleaning, there are several other steps that you need to perform, such as selecting training data versus test data, and deciding whether to use "hold out" or cross-validation during the training process. More details are provided in the subsequent sections.

Training Data Versus Test Data

After you have performed the tasks described earlier in this chapter (i.e., data cleaning and perhaps dimensionality reduction), you are ready to split the dataset into two parts. The first part is the *training set*, which is used to train a model, and the second part is the *test set*, which is used for "inferencing" (another term for making predictions). Make sure that you conform to the following guidelines for your test sets:

- The set is large enough to yield statistically meaningful results
- It's representative of the data set as a whole
- Never train on test data
- Never test on training data

What Is Cross-validation?

The purpose of cross-validation is to test a model with non- overlapping test sets, which is performed in the following manner:

- Step 1) Split the data into k subsets of equal size
- Step 2) Select one subset for testing and the others for training
- Step 3) Repeat step 2 for the other k-1 subsets

This process is called *k-fold cross-validation*, and the overall error estimate is the average of the error estimates. A standard method for evaluation involves ten-fold cross-validation. Extensive experiments have shown that 10 subsets is the best choice to obtain an accurate estimate. In fact, you can repeat ten-fold cross-validation ten times and compute the average of the results, which helps to reduce the variance.

The next section discusses regularization, which is an important yet optional topic if you are primarily interested in TF 2 code. If you plan to become proficient in machine learning, you will need to learn about regularization.

What Is Regularization?

Regularization helps to solve overfitting problem, which occurs when a model performs well on training data but poorly on validation or test data.

Regularization solves this problem by adding a penalty term to the cost function, thereby controlling the model complexity with this penalty term.

Regularization is generally useful for:

- Large number of variables

- Low ratio of (# observations)/(# of variables)

- High multi-collinearity

There are two main types of regularization: L1 Regularization (which is related to MAE, or the absolute value of differences) and L2 Regularization (which is related to MSE, or the square of differences). In general, L2 performs better than L1, and it's efficient in terms of computation.

ML and Feature Scaling

Feature Scaling standardizes the range of features of data. This step is performed during the data preprocessing step, in part because gradient descent benefits from feature scaling.

The assumption is that the data conforms to a standard normal distribution, and standardization involves subtracting the mean and divide by the standard deviation for every data point, which results in a $N(0,1)$ normal distribution.

Data Normalization vs Standardization

Data normalization is a linear scaling technique. Let's assume that a dataset has the values $\{X1, X2, \ldots, Xn\}$ along with the following terms:

```
Minx = minimum of Xi values

Maxx = maximum of Xi values
```

Now calculate a set of new Xi values as follows:

```
Xi = (Xi - Minx)/[Maxx - Minx]
```

The new `Xi` values are now scaled so that they are between 0 and 1.

The Bias-Variance Tradeoff

Bias in machine learning can be due to an error from wrong assumptions in a learning algorithm. High bias might cause an algorithm to miss relevant relations between features and target outputs (underfitting). Prediction bias can occur because of "noisy" data, an incomplete feature set, or a biased training sample.

Error due to bias is the difference between the expected (or average) prediction of your model and the correct value that you want to predict. Repeat the model building process multiple times, and gather new data each time, and also perform an analysis to produce a new model. The resulting models have a range of predictions because the underlying data sets have a degree of randomness. Bias measures the extent to the predictions for these models are from the correct value.

Variance in machine learning is the expected value of the squared deviation from the mean. High variance can/might cause an algorithm to model the random noise in the training data, rather than the intended outputs (aka overfitting).

Adding parameters to a model increases its complexity, increases the variance, and decreases the bias. Dealing with bias and variance is dealing with underfitting and overfitting.

Error due to variance is the variability of a model prediction for a given data point. As before, repeat the entire model building process, and the variance is the extent to which predictions for a given point vary among different "instances" of the model.

Metrics for Measuring Models

One of the most frequently used metrics is R-squared, which measures how close the data is to the fitted regression line (regression coefficient). The R-squared value is always a percentage between 0 and 100%. The value 0% indicates that the model explains none of the variability of the response data around its mean. The value 100% indicates that the model explains all the variability of the response data around its mean. In general, a higher R-squared value indicates a better model.

Limitations of R-Squared

Although high R-squared values are preferred, they are not necessarily always good values. Similarly, low R-squared values are not always bad. For example, an R-squared value for predicting human behavior is often less than 50%. Moreover, R-squared cannot determine whether the coefficient estimates and predictions are biased. In addition, an R-squared value does not indicate whether a regression model is adequate. Thus, it's possible to have a low R-squared value for a good model, or a high R-squared value for a poorly fitting model. Evaluate R-squared values in conjunction with residual plots, other model statistics, and subject area knowledge.

Confusion Matrix

In its simplest form, a confusion matrix (also called an error matrix) is a type of contingency table with two rows and two columns that contains the # of false positives, false negatives, true positives, and true negatives. The four entries in a 2x2 confusion matrix can be labeled as follows:

```
TP: True Positive
FP: False Positive
TN: True Negative
FN: False Negative
```

The diagonal values of the confusion matrix are correct, whereas the off-diagonal values are incorrect predictions. In general a lower FP value is better than a FN value. For example, an FP indicates that a healthy person was incorrectly diagnosed with a disease, whereas an FN indicates that an unhealthy person was incorrectly diagnosed as healthy.

Accuracy vs Precision vs Recall

A 2x2 confusion matrix has four entries that that represent the various combinations of correct and incorrect classifications. Given the definitions in the preceding section, the definitions of precision, accuracy, and recall are given by the following formulas:

```
precision = TP/(TN + FP)
accuracy  = (TP + TN)/[P + N]
recall    = TP/[TP + FN]
```

Accuracy can be an unreliable metric because it yields misleading results in unbalanced data sets. When the number of observations in different classes are significantly different, it gives equal importance to both false positive and false negative classifications. For example, declaring cancer as benign is worse than incorrectly informing patients that they are suffering from cancer. Unfortunately, accuracy won't differentiate between these two cases.

Keep in mind that the confusion matrix can be an nxn matrix and not just a 2x2 matrix. For example, if a class has 5 possible values, then the confusion matrix is a 5x5 matrix, and the numbers on the main diagonal are the "true positive" results.

The ROC Curve

The ROC (receiver operating characteristic) curve is a curve that plots the TPR, which is the true positive rate (i.e., the recall) against the FPR, which is the false positive rate). Note that the TNR (the true negative rate) is also called the specificity.

The following link contains a Python code sample using SKLearn and the Iris dataset, and also code for plotting the ROC:

https://scikit-learn.org/stable/auto_examples/model_selection/plot_roc.html

The following link contains an assortment of Python code samples for plotting the ROC:

https://stackoverflow.com/questions/25009284/how-to-plot-roc-curve-in-python

Other Useful Statistical Terms

Machine learning relies on a number of statistical quantities in order to assess the validity of a model, some of which are listed here:

- RSS
- TSS
- R^2
- F1 score
- p-value

The definitions of RSS, TSS, and R^2 are shown below, where $y^\wedge$ is the y-coordinate of a point on a best-fitting line and $y\_$ is the mean of the y-values of the points in the dataset:

```
RSS = sum of squares of residuals (y - y^)**2
TSS = toal sum of squares       (y - y_)**2
R^2 = 1 - RSS/TSS
```

What Is an F1 Score?

The F1 score is a measure of the accuracy of a test, and it's defined as the harmonic mean of precision and recall. Here are the relevant formulas, where p is the precision and r is the recall:

```
p = (# of correct positive results)/(# of all
        positive results)
```

```
r = (# of correct positive results)/(# of all
        relevant samples)
F1-score = 1/[((1/r) + (1/p))/2]
         = 2*[p*r]/[p+r]
```

The best value of an F1 score is 0 and the worse value is 0. Keep in mind that an F1 score tends to be used for categorical classification problems, whereas the R^2 value is typically for regression tasks (such as linear regression).

What Is a p-value?

The p-value is used to reject the null hypothesis if the p-value is small enough (< 0.005) which indicates a higher significance. Recall that the null hypothesis states that there is no correlation between a dependent variable (such as y) and an independent variable (such as x). The threshold value for p is typically 1% or 5%.

There is no straightforward formula for calculating p-values, which are values that are always between 0 and 1. In fact, p-values are statistical quantities to evaluate the so-called "null hypothesis," and they are calculated by means of p-value tables or via spreadsheet/statistical software.

What Is Linear Regression?

The goal of linear regression is to find the best fitting line that "represents" a dataset. Keep in mind two key points. First, the best fitting line does not necessarily pass through all (or even most of) the points in the dataset. The purpose of a best fitting line is to minimize the vertical distance of that line from the points in dataset. Second, linear regression does not determine the best-fitting polynomial: the latter involves finding a higher-degree polynomial that passes through many of the points in a dataset.

Moreover, a dataset in the plane can contain two or more points that lie on the same *vertical* line, which is to say that those points have the same x value. However, a function *cannot* pass through such a pair of points: if two points (x1,y1) and (x2,y2) have the same x value then they must have the same y value (i.e., y1=y2). On the other hand, a function can have two or more points that lie on the same *horizontal* line.

Now consider a scatter plot with many points in the plane that are sort of "clustered" in an elongated cloud-like shape: a best-fitting line will probably intersect only limited number of points (in fact, a best-fitting line might not intersect *any* of the points).

One other scenario to keep in mind: suppose a dataset contains a set of points that lie on the same line. For instance, let's say the x values are in the set $\{1,2,3,\ldots,10\}$ and the y values are in the set $\{2,4,6,\ldots,20\}$. Then the equation of the best-fitting line is $y=2*x+0$. In this scenario, all the points are *collinear*, which is to say that they lie on the same line.

Linear Regression vs Curve-Fitting

Suppose a dataset consists of n data points of the form (x, y), and no two of those data points have the same x value. Then according to a well-known result in mathematics, there is a polynomial of degree less than or equal to n-1 that passes through those n points (if you are really interested, you can find a mathematical proof of this statement in online articles). For example, a line is a polynomial of degree one and it can intersect any pair of non-vertical points in the plane. For any triple of points (that are not all on the same line) in the plane, there is a quadratic equation that passes through those points.

In addition, sometimes a lower degree polynomial is available. For instance, consider the set of 100 points in which the x value equals the y value: in this case, the line $y = x$ (which is a polynomial of degree one) passes through all 100 points.

However, keep in mind that the extent to which a line "represents" a set of points in the plane depends on how closely those points can be approximated by a line, which is measured by the *variance* of the points (the variance is a statistical quantity). The more collinear the points, the smaller the variance; conversely, the more "spread out" the points are, the larger the variance.

When Are Solutions Exact Values?

Although statistics-based solutions provide closed-form solutions for linear regression, neural networks provide *approximate* solutions. This is due to the fact that machine learning algorithms for linear regression involve a sequence of approximations that "converges" to optimal values, which means that machine learning algorithms produce estimates of the exact values. For example, the slope m and y-intercept b of a best-fitting line for a set of points a 2D plane have a closed-form solution in statistics, but they can only be approximated via machine learning algorithms (exceptions do exist, but they are rare situations).

Keep in mind that even though a closed-form solution for "traditional" linear regression provides an exact value for both m and b, sometimes you can only use an approximation of the exact value. For instance, suppose that the slope m of a best-fitting line equals the square root of 3 and the y-intercept b is the square root of 2. If you plan to use these values in source code, you can only work with an approximation of these two numbers. In the same scenario, a Neural Network computes approximations for m and b, regardless of whether or not the exact values for m and b are irrational, rational, or integer values. However, machine learning algorithms are better suited for complex, non-linear, multi-dimensional datasets, which is beyond the capacity of linear regression.

As a simple example, suppose that the closed form solution for a linear regression problem produces integer or rational values for both m and b. Specifically, let's suppose that a closed form solution yields the values 2.0 and 1.0 for the slope and y-intercept, respectively, of a best-fitting line. The equation of the line looks like this:

```
y = 2.0 * x + 1.0
```

However, the corresponding solution from training a neural network might produce the values 2.0001 and 0.9997 for the slope m and the y-intercept b, respectively, as the values of m and b for a best-fitting line. Always keep this point in mind, especially when you are training a Neural Network.

What Is Multivariate Analysis?

Multivariate analysis generalizes the equation of a line in the Euclidean plane to higher dimensions, and it's called a *hyper plane* instead of a line. The generalized equation has the following form:

```
y = w1*x1 + w2*x2 + . . . + wn*xn + b
```

In the case of 2D linear regression, you only need to find the value of the slope (m) and the y-intercept (b), whereas in multivariate analysis you need to find the values for w1, w2, . . ., wn. Note that multivariate analysis is a term from statistics, and in machine learning it's often referred to as "generalized linear regression."

Keep in mind that most of the code samples in this book that pertain to linear regression involve 2D points in the Euclidean plane.

Other Types of Regression

Linear regression finds the best fitting line that "represents" a dataset, but what happens if a line in the plane is not a good fit for the dataset? This is a relevant question when you work with datasets.

Some alternatives to linear regression include quadratic equations, cubic equations, or higher-degree polynomials. However, these alternatives involve trade-offs, as we'll discuss later.

Another possibility is a sort of hybrid approach that involves piece-wise linear functions, which comprises a set of line segments. If contiguous line segments are connected then it's a piece-wise linear continuous function; otherwise it's a piece-wise linear discontinuous function.

Thus, given a set of points in the plane, regression involves addressing the following questions:

- What type of curve fits the data well? How do we know?

- Does another type of curve fit the data better?

- What does "best fit" mean?

One way to check if a line fits the data involves a visual check, but this approach does not work for data points that are higher than two dimensions. Moreover, this is a subjective decision, and some sample datasets are displayed later in this chapter. By visual inspection of a dataset, you might decide that a quadratic or cubic (or even higher degree) polynomial has the potential of being a better fit for the data. However, visual inspection is probably limited to points in a 2D plane or in three dimensions.

Let's defer the non-linear scenario and let's make the assumption that a line would be a good fit for the data. There is a well-known technique for finding the "best fitting" line for such a dataset that involves minimizing the Mean Squared Error (MSE) that we'll discuss later in this chapter.

The next section provides a quick review of linear equations in the plane, along with some images that illustrate examples of linear equations.

Working with Lines in the Plane (optional)

This section contains a short review of lines in the Euclidean plane, so you can skip this section if you are comfortable with this topic. A minor point that's often overlooked is that lines in the Euclidean plane have infinite length. If you select two distinct points of a line, then all the points between those two selected points is a *line segment*. A *ray* is a "half infinite" line: when you select one point as an endpoint, then all the points on one side of the line constitutes a ray.

For example, the points in the plane whose y-coordinate is 0 is a line and also the x-axis, whereas the points between (0,0) and (1,0) on the x-axis form a line segment. In addition, the points on the x-axis that are to the right of (0,0) form a ray, and the points on the x-axis that are to the left of (0,0) also form a ray.

For simplicity and convenience, in this book we'll use the terms "line" and "line segment" interchangeably, and now let's delve into the details of lines in the Euclidean plane. Just in case you're a bit fuzzy on the details, here is the equation of a (non-vertical) line in the Euclidean plane:

```
y = m*x + b
```

The value of m is the slope of the line and the value of b is the y-intercept (i.e., the place where the line intersects the y-axis).

If need be, you can use a more general equation that can also represent vertical lines, as shown here:

```
a*x + b*y + c = 0
```

However, we won't be working with vertical lines, so we'll stick with the first formula.

Figure 2.1 displays three horizontal lines whose equations (from top to bottom) are y = 3, y = 0, and y = -3, respectively.

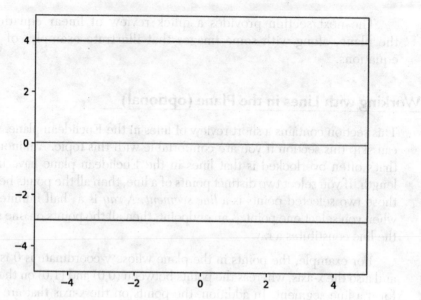

FIGURE 2.1 A Graph of Three Horizontal Line Segments.

Figure 2.2 displays two slanted lines whose equations are $y = x$ and $y = -x$, respectively.

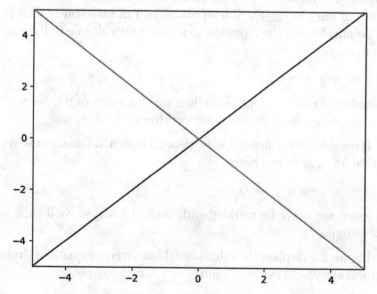

FIGURE 2.2 A Graph of Two Diagonal Line Segments.

Figure 2.3 displays two slanted parallel lines whose equations are $y = 2*x$ and $y = 2*x + 3$, respectively.

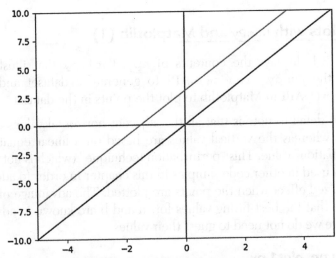

FIGURE 2.3 A Graph of Two Slanted Parallel Line Segments.

Figure 2.4 displays a piece-wise linear graph consisting of connected line segments.

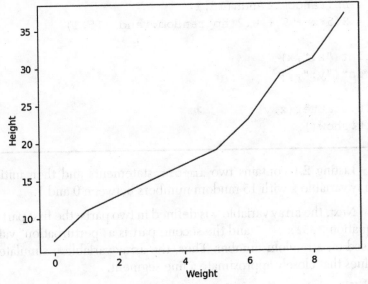

FIGURE 2.4 A Piece-wise Linear Graph of Line Segments.

Now let's turn our attention to generating quasi-random data using a NumPy API, and then we'll plot the data using Matplotlib.

Scatter Plots with NumPy and Matplotlib (1)

Listing 2.1 displays the contents of np_plot1.py that illustrates how to use the Numpy randn() API to generate a dataset and then the scatter() API in Matplotlib to plot the points in the dataset.

One detail to note is that all the adjacent horizontal values are equally spaced, whereas the vertical values are based on a linear equation plus a "perturbation" value. This "perturbation technique" (which is not a standard term) is used in other code samples in this chapter in order to add a slightly randomized effect when the points are plotted. The advantage of this technique is that the best-fitting values for m and b are known in advance, and therefore we do not need to guess their values.

Listing 2.1: np_plot1.py

```python
import numpy as np
import matplotlib.pyplot as plt

x = np.random.randn(15,1)
y = 2.5*x + 5 + 0.2*np.random.randn(15,1)

print("x:",x)
print("y:",y)

plt.scatter(x,y)
plt.show()
```

Listing 2.1 contains two import statements and then initializes the array variable x with 15 random numbers between 0 and 1.

Next, the array variable y is defined in two parts: the first part is a linear equation 2.5*x + 5 and the second part is a "perturbation" value that is based on a random number. Thus, the array variable y simulates a set of values that closely approximate a line segment.

This technique is used in code samples that simulate a line segment, and then the training portion approximates the values of m and b for the best-fitting line. Obviously we already *know* the equation of the best fitting-line: the purpose of this technique is to compare the trained values for the slope m and y-intercept b with the known values (which in this case are 2.5 and 5).

A partial output from Listing 2.1 is here:

```
x: [[-1.42736308]
 [ 0.09482338]
 [-0.45071331]
 [ 0.19536304]
 [-0.22295205]
 // values omitted for brevity
y: [[1.12530514]
 [5.05168677]
 [3.93320782]
 [5.49760999]
 [4.46994978]
 // values omitted for brevity
```

Figure 2.5 displays a scatter plot of points based on the values of x and y.

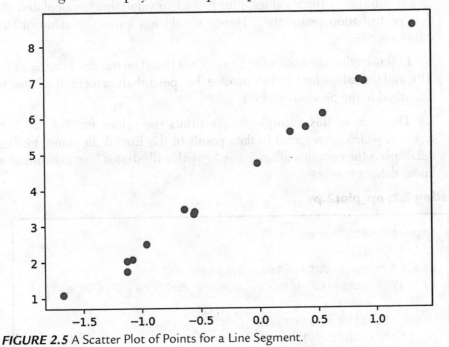

FIGURE 2.5 A Scatter Plot of Points for a Line Segment.

Why the "Perturbation Technique" Is Useful

You already saw how to use the "perturbation technique" and by way of comparison, consider a dataset with the following points that are defined in the Python array variables X and Y:

```
X = [0,0.12,0.25,0.27,0.38,0.42,0.44,0.55,0.92,1.0]
Y = [0,0.15,0.54,0.51, 0.34,0.1,0.19,0.53,1.0,0.58]
```

If you need to find the best fitting line for the preceding dataset, how would you guess the values for the slope m and the y-intercept b? In most cases, you probably cannot guess their values. On the other hand, the "perturbation technique" enables you to "jiggle" the points on a line whose value for the slope m (and optionally the value for the y-intercept b) is specified in advance.

Keep in mind that the "perturbation technique" only works when you introduce small random values that do not result in different values for m and b.

Scatter Plots with NumPy and Matplotlib (2)

The code in Listing 2.1 assigned random values to the variable x, whereas a hard-coded value is assigned to the slope m. The y values are a hard-coded multiple of the x values, plus a random value that is calculated via the "perturbation technique". Hence we do not know the value of the y-intercept b.

In this section the values for trainX are based on the np.linspace() API, and the values for trainY involve the "perturbation technique" that is described in the previous section.

The code in this example simply prints the values for trainX and trainY, which correspond to data points in the Euclidean plane. Listing 2.2 displays the contents of np_plot2.py that illustrates how to simulate a linear dataset in NumPy.

Listing 2.2: np_plot2.py

```
import numpy as np

trainX = np.linspace(-1, 1, 11)
trainY = 4*trainX + np.random.randn(*trainX.shape)*0.5

print("trainX: ",trainX)
print("trainY: ",trainY)
```

Listing 2.6 initializes the `NumPy` array variable `trainX` via the `NumPy` `linspace()` API, followed by the array variable `trainY` that is defined in two parts. The first part is the linear term `4*trainX` and the second part involves the "perturbation technique" that is a randomly generated number. The output from Listing 2.6 is here:

```
trainX:  [-1.  -0.8 -0.6 -0.4 -0.2  0.   0.2  0.4
          0.6  0.8  1. ]
trainY:  [-3.60147459 -2.66593108 -2.26491189
          -1.65121314 -0.56454605  0.22746004
          0.86830728  1.60673482  2.51151543
          3.59573877  3.05506056]
```

The next section contains an example that is similar to Listing 2.2, using the same "perturbation technique" to generate a set of points that approximate a quadratic equation instead of a line segment.

A Quadratic Scatterplot with `NumPy` and Matplotlib

Listing 2.3 displays the contents of np_plot_quadratic.py that illustrates how to plot a quadratic function in the plane.

Listing 2.3: np_plot_quadratic.py

```
import numpy as np
import matplotlib.pyplot as plt

#see what happens with this set of values:
#x = np.linspace(-5,5,num=100)

x = np.linspace(-5,5,num=100)[:,None]
y = -0.5 + 2.2*x +0.3*x**2 + 2*np.random.
    randn(100,1)
print("x:",x)

plt.plot(x,y)
plt.show()
```

Listing 2.3 initializes the array variable x with the values that are generated via the np.linspace() API, which in this case is a set of 100 equally spaced decimal numbers between -5 and 5. Notice the snippet [:,None] in the initialization of x, which results in an array of elements, each of which is an array consisting of a single number.

The array variable y is defined in two parts: the first part is a quadratic equation -0.5 + 2.2*x +0.3*x**2 and the second part is a "perturbation" value that is based on a random number (similar to the code in Listing 2.1). Thus, the array variable y simulates a set of values that approximates a quadratic equation. The output from Listing 2.3 is here:

```
x:
[[-5.        ]
 [-4.8989899 ]
 [-4.7979798 ]
 [-4.6969697 ]
 [-4.5959596 ]
 [-4.49494949]
// values omitted for brevity
 [ 4.8989899 ]
 [ 5.        ]]
```

Figure 2.6 displays a scatter plot of points based on the values of x and y, which have an approximate shape of a quadratic equation.

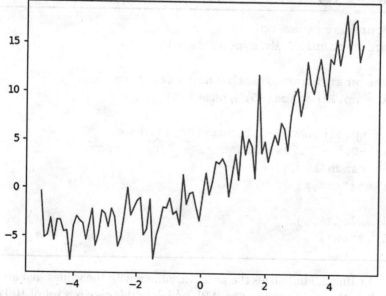

FIGURE 2.6 A Scatter Plot of Points for a Quadratic Equation.

The Mean Squared Error (MSE) Formula

In plain English, the MSE is the sum of the squares of the difference between an actual y value and the predicted y value, divided by the number of points. Notice that the predicted y value is the y value that each point would have if that point were actually on the best-fitting line.

Although the MSE is popular for linear regression, there are other error types available, some of which are discussed briefly in the next section.

A List of Error Types

Although we will only discuss MSE for linear regression in this book, there are other types of formulas that you can use for linear regression, some of which are listed here:

- MSE
- RMSE
- RMSPROP
- MAE

The MSE is the basis for the preceding error types. For example, RMSE is "Root Mean Squared Error," which is the square root of MSE.

On the other hand, MAE is "Mean Absolute Error," which is the sum of *the absolute value of the differences of the y terms* (*not* the square of the differences of the y terms), which is then divided by the number of terms.

The RMSProp optimizer utilizes the magnitude of recent gradients to normalize the gradients. Specifically, RMSProp maintain a moving average over the RMS (root mean squared) gradients, and then divides that term by the current gradient.

Although it's easier to compute the derivative of MSE, it's also true that MSE is more susceptible to outliers, whereas MAE is less susceptible to outliers. The reason is simple: a squared term can be significantly larger than the absolute value of a term. For example, if a difference term is 10, then a squared term of 100 is added to MSE, whereas only 10 is added to MAE. Similarly, if a difference term is -20, then a squared term 400 is added to MSE, whereas only 20 (which is the absolute value of -20) is added to MAE.

Non-linear Least Squares

When predicting housing prices, where the dataset contains a wide range of values, techniques such as linear regression or random forests can cause the model to overfit the samples with the highest values in order to reduce quantities such as mean absolute error.

In this scenario, you probably want an error metric, such as relative error, that reduces the importance of fitting the samples with the largest values. This technique is called *non-linear least squares*, which may use a log-based transformation of labels and predicted values.

The next section contains several code samples, the first of which involves calculating the MSE manually, followed by an example that uses NumPy formulas to perform the calculations. Finally, we'll look at a Tensor-Flow example for calculating the MSE.

Calculating the MSE Manually

This section contains two line graphs, both of which contain a line that approximates a set of points in a scatter plot.

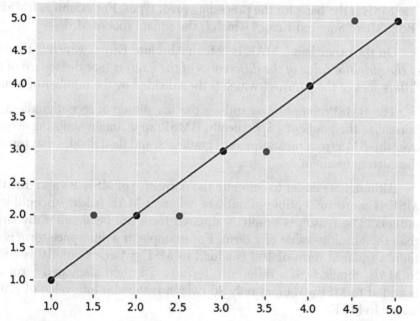

FIGURE 2.7 A Line Graph that Approximates Points of a Scatter Plot.

Figure 2.7 displays a line segment that approximates a scatter plot of points (some of which intersect the line segment). The MSE for the line in Figure 2.7 is computed as follows:

```
MSE = (1*1 + (-1)*(-1) + (-1)*(-1) + 1*1)/7 = 4/7
```

Figure 2.8 displays a set of points and a line that is a potential candidate for best-fitting line for the data. The MSE for the line in Figure 2.8 is computed as follows:

```
MSE = ((-2)*(-2) + 2*2)/7 = 8/7
```

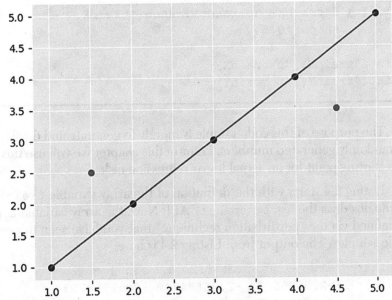

FIGURE 2.8 A Line Graph that Approximates Points of a Scatter Plot.

Thus, the line in Figure 2.7 has a smaller MSE than the line in Figure 2.8, which might have surprised you (or did you guess correctly?)

In these two figures we calculated the MSE easily and quickly, but in general it's significantly more difficult. For instance, if we plot 10 points in the Euclidean plane that do not closely fit a line, with individual terms that involve non-integer values, we would probably need a calculator.

A better solution involves NumPy functions, such as the np.linspace() API, as discussed in the next section.

Approximating Linear Data with `np.linspace()`

Listing 2.4 displays the contents of `np_linspace1.py` that illustrates how to generate some data with the `np.linspace()` API in conjunction with the "perturbation technique."

Listing 2.4: np_linspace1.py

```
import numpy as np

trainX = np.linspace(-1, 1, 6)
trainY = 3*trainX+ np.random.randn(*trainX.
        shape)*0.5

print("trainX: ", trainX)
print("trainY: ", trainY)
```

The purpose of this code sample is merely to generate and display a set of randomly generated numbers. Later in this chapter we will use this code as a starting point for an actual linear regression task.

Listing 2.4 starts with the definition of the array variable `trainX` that is initialized via the `np.linspace()` API. Next, the array variable `trainY` is defined via the "perturbation technique" that you have seen in previous code samples. The output from Listing 2.4 is here:

```
trainX:  [-1.  -0.6 -0.2  0.2  0.6  1. ]
trainY:  [-2.9008553  -2.26684745 -0.59516253
         0.66452207  1.82669051  2.30549295]
trainX:  [-1.  -0.6 -0.2  0.2  0.6  1. ]
trainY:  [-2.9008553  -2.26684745 -0.59516253
         0.66452207  1.82669051  2.30549295]
```

Now that we know how to generate (x, y) values for a linear equation, let's learn how to calculate the MSE, which is discussed in the next section.

The next example generates a set of data values using the `np.linspace()` method and the `np.random.randn()` method in order to introduces some randomness in the data points.

Calculating MSE with `np.linspace()` API

The code sample in this section differs from many of the earlier code samples in this chapter: it uses a hard-coded array of values for X and also for Y instead of the "perturbation" technique. Hence, you will *not* know the correct value for the slope and y-intercept (and you probably will not be able to guess their correct values). Listing 2.5 displays the contents of `plain_linreg1.py` that illustrates how to compute the MSE with simulated data.

Listing 2.5: plain_linreg1.py

```
import numpy as np
import matplotlib.pyplot as plt

X = [0,0.12,0.25,0.27,0.38,0.42,0.44,0.55,0.92,1.0]
Y = [0,0.15,0.54,0.51,
     0.34,0.1,0.19,0.53,1.0,0.58]

costs = []
#Step 1: Parameter initialization
W = 0.45
b = 0.75

for i in range(1, 100):
  #Step 2: Calculate Cost
  Y_pred = np.multiply(W, X) + b
  Loss_error = 0.5 * (Y_pred - Y)**2
  cost = np.sum(Loss_error)/10

  #Step 3: Calculate dW and db
  db = np.sum((Y_pred - Y))
  dw = np.dot((Y_pred - Y), X)
  costs.append(cost)

  #Step 4: Update parameters:
  W = W - 0.01*dw
  b = b - 0.01*db

  if i%10 == 0:
    print("Cost at", i,"iteration = ", cost)
```

(Continued)

```
#Step 5: Repeat via a for loop with 1000 iterations

#Plot cost versus # of iterations
print("W = ", W,"& b = ",  b)
plt.plot(costs)
plt.ylabel('cost')
plt.xlabel('iterations (per tens)')
plt.show()
```

Listing 2.5 initializes the array variables X and Y with hard-coded values, and then initializes the scalar variables W and b. The next portion of Listing 2.5 contains a for loop that iterates 100 times. After each iteration of the loop, the variables Y_pred, Loss_error, and cost are calculated. Next, the values for dw and db are calculated, based on the sum of the terms in the array Y_pred-Y, and the inner product of Y_pred-y and X, respectively.

Notice how W and b are updated: their values are decremented by the term 0.01*dw and 0.01*db, respectively. This calculation ought to look somewhat familiar: the code is programmatically calculating an approximate value of the gradient for W and b, both of which are multiplied by the learning rate (the hard-coded value 0.01), and the resulting term is decremented from the current values of W and b in order to produce a new approximation for W and b. Although this technique is very simple, it does calculate reasonable values for W and b.

The final block of code in Listing 2.5 displays the intermediate approximations for W and b, along with a plot of the cost (vertical axis) versus the number of iterations (horizontal axis). The output from Listing 2.5 is here:

```
Cost at 10 iteration =  0.04114630674619492
Cost at 20 iteration =  0.026706242729839392
Cost at 30 iteration =  0.024738889446900423
Cost at 40 iteration =  0.023850565034634254
Cost at 50 iteration =  0.0231499048706651
Cost at 60 iteration =  0.02255361434242207
Cost at 70 iteration =  0.0220425055291673
Cost at 80 iteration =  0.021604128492245713
Cost at 90 iteration =  0.02122811750568435
W =  0.4725647353193927 & b =  0.19578262688662174
```

Figure 2.9 displays a scatter plot of points generated by the code in Listing 2.5.

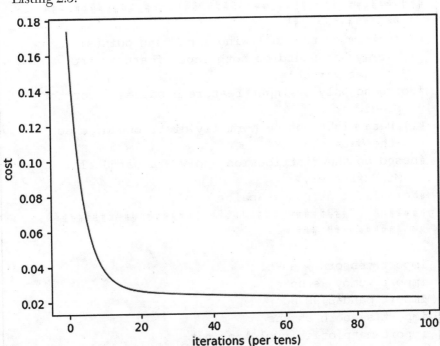

FIGURE 2.9 MSE Values With Linear Regression.

The code sample `plain-linreg2.py` is similar to the code in Listing 2.5: the difference is that instead of a single loop with 100 iterations, there is an outer loop that execute 100 times, and during each iteration of the outer loop, the inner loop also execute 100 times.

Linear Regression with `Keras`

The code sample in this section contains primarily `Keras` code in order to perform linear regression. If you have read the previous examples in this chapter, this section will be easier for you to understand because the steps for linear regression are the same.

Listing 2.6 displays the contents of `keras_linear_regression.py` that illustrates how to perform linear regression in `Keras`.

Listing 2.6: keras_linear_regression.py

```
###################################################
    ##############
#Keep in mind the following important points:
#1) Always standardize both input features and
    target variable:
#doing so only on input feature produces incorrect
    predictions
#2) Data might not be normally distributed: check
    the data and
#based on the distribution apply StandardScaler,
    MinMaxScaler,
#Normalizer or RobustScaler
###################################################
    ##############

import tensorflow as tf
import numpy as np
import pandas as pd
import seaborn as sns
import matplotlib.pyplot as plt
from sklearn.preprocessing import MinMaxScaler
from sklearn.model_selection import train_test_
    split

df = pd.read_csv('housing.csv')
X = df.iloc[:,0:13]
y = df.iloc[:,13].values

mmsc = MinMaxScaler()
X = mmsc.fit_transform(X)
y = y.reshape(-1,1)
y = mmsc.fit_transform(y)

X_train, X_test, y_train, y_test = train_test_
    split(X, y, test_size=0.3)
```

```python
# this Python method creates a Keras model
def build_keras_model():
  model = tf.keras.models.Sequential()
  model.add(tf.keras.layers.Dense(units=13,
    input_dim=13))
  model.add(tf.keras.layers.Dense(units=1))

  model.compile(optimizer='adam',loss='mean_
    squared_error',metrics=['mae','accuracy'])
  return model

batch_size=32
epochs = 40

# specify the Python method 'build_keras_model'
    to create a Keras model
# using the implementation of the scikit-learn
    regressor API for Keras
model = tf.keras.wrappers.scikit_learn.
        KerasRegressor(build_fn=build_
        keras_model, batch_size=batch_
        size,epochs=epochs)

# train ('fit') the model and then make
    predictions:
model.fit(X_train, y_train)
y_pred = model.predict(X_test)
#print("y_test:",y_test)
#print("y_pred:",y_pred)

# scatter plot of test values-vs-predictions
fig, ax = plt.subplots()
ax.scatter(y_test, y_pred)
ax.plot([y_test.min(), y_test.max()], [y_test.
    min(), y_test.max()], 'r*--')
ax.set_xlabel('Calculated')
ax.set_ylabel('Predictions')
plt.show()
```

Listing 2.6 starts with multiple `import` statements and then initializes the dataframe `df` with the contents of the CSV file `housing.csv` (a portion of which is shown in Listing 2.7). Notice that the training set X is initialized with the contents of the first 13 columns of the dataset `housing.csv`, and the variable y contains the rightmost column of the dataset housing.csv.

The next section in Listing 2.6 uses the `MinMaxScaler` class to calculate the mean and standard deviation, and then invokes the `fit_transform()` method in order to update the X values and the y values so that they have a mean of 0 and a standard deviation of 1.

Next, the `build_keras_mode()` Python method creates a `Keras`-based model with two dense layers. Notice that the input layer has size 13, which is the number of columns in the dataframe X. The next code snippet compiles the model with an `adam` optimizer, the MSE loss function, and also specifies the MAE and accuracy for the metrics. The compiled model is then returned to the caller.

The next portion of Listing 2.6 initializes the `batch_size` variable to 32 and the epochs variable to 40, and specifies them in the code snippet that creates the model, as shown here:

```
model =
tf.keras.wrappers.scikit_learn.
   KerasRegressor(build_fn=build_keras_model,
   batch_size=batch_size,epochs=epochs)
```

The short comment block that appears in Listing 2.6 explains the purpose of the preceding code snippet, which constructs our `Keras` model.

The next portion of Listing 2.6 invokes the `fit()` method to train the model and then invokes the `predict()` method on the X_test data to calculate a set of predictions and initialize the variable y_pred with those predictions.

The final portion of Listing 2.6 displays a scatter plot in which the horizontal axis is the values in `y_test` (the actual values from the CSV file housing.csv) and the vertical axis is the set of predicted values.

Figure 2.5 displays a scatter plot of points based on the test values and the predictions for those test values.

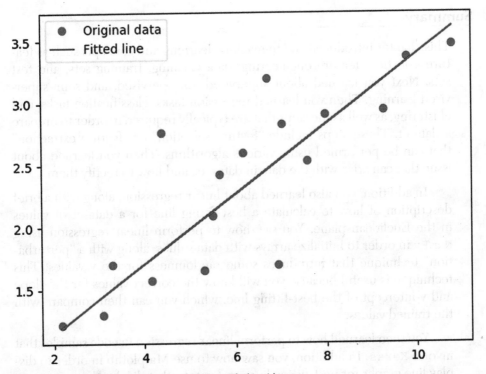

FIGURE 2.10 A Scatter Plot and a Best-Fitting Line.

Listing 2.7 displays the first four rows of the CSV file `housing.csv` that is used in the Python code in Listing 2.6.

Listing 2.7: housing.csv

```
0.00632,18,2.31,0,0.538,6.575,65.2,4.09,1,296,15.3,
    396.9,4.98,24
0.02731,0,7.07,0,0.469,6.421,78.9,4.9671,2,242,17
    .8,396.9,9.14,21.6
0.02729,0,7.07,0,0.469,7.185,61.1,4.9671,2,242,17
    .8,392.83,4.03,34.7
0.03237,0,2.18,0,0.458,6.998,45.8,6.0622,3,222,18
    .7,394.63,2.94,33.4
```

Summary

This chapter introduced you to machine learning and concepts such as feature selection, feature engineering, data cleaning, training sets, and test sets. Next you learned about supervised, unsupervised, and semi-supervised learning. Then you learned regression tasks, classification tasks, and clustering, as well as the steps that are typically required in order to prepare a dataset. These steps include "feature selection" or "feature extraction" that can be performed using various algorithms. Then you learned about issue that can arise with the data in datasets, and how to rectify them.

In addition, you also learned about linear regression, along with a brief description of how to calculate a best-fitting line for a dataset of values in the Euclidean plane. You saw how to perform linear regression using NumPy in order to initialize arrays with data values, along with a "perturbation" technique that introduces some randomness for the y values. This technique is useful because you will know the correct values for the slope and y-intercept of the best-fitting line, which you can then compare with the trained values.

You then learned how to perform linear regression in code samples that involve Keras. In addition, you saw how to use Matplotlib in order to display line graphs for best-fitting lines and graphs that display the cost versus the number of iterations during the training-related code blocks.

CHAPTER 3

CLASSIFIERS IN MACHINE LEARNING

This chapter presents numerous classification algorithms in machine learning. This includes algorithms such as the kNN (k Nearest Neighbor) algorithm, logistic regression (despite its name it *is* a classifier), decision trees, random forests, SVMs, and Bayesian classifiers. The emphasis on algorithms is intended to introduce you to machine learning, which includes a tree-based code sample that relies on `scikit-learn`. The latter portion of this chapter contains `Keras`-based code samples for standard datasets.

Due to space constraints, this chapter does not cover other well-known algorithms, such as Linear Discriminant Analysis and the kMeans algorithm (which is for unsupervised learning and clustering). However, there are many online tutorials available that discuss these and other algorithms in machine learning.

With these points in mind, the first section of this chapter briefly discusses the classifiers that are mentioned in the introductory paragraph. The second section of this chapter provides an overview of activation functions, which will be very useful if you decide to learn about deep neural networks. In this section you will learn how and why they are used in neural networks. This section also contains a list of the TensorFlow APIs for activation functions, followed by a description of some of their merits.

The third section introduces logistic regression, which relies on the sigmoid function, which is also used in RNNs (Recurrent Neural

Networks) and LSTMs (Long Short Term Memory). The fourth part of this chapter contains a code sample involving Logistic Regression and the `MNIST` dataset.

In order to give you some context, classifiers are one of three major types of algorithms: regression algorithms (such as linear regression in Chapter 4), classification algorithms (discussed in this chapter), and clustering algorithms (such as kMeans, which is not discussed in this book).

Another point: the section pertaining to activation functions does involve a basic understanding of hidden layers in a neural network. Depending on your comfort level, you might benefit from reading some preparatory material before diving into this section (there are many articles available online).

What Is Classification?

Given a dataset that contains observations whose class membership is known, classification is the task of determining the class to which a new datapoint belongs. *Classes* refer to categories and are also called *targets* or *labels*. For example, spam detection in email service providers involves binary classification (only two classes). The `MNIST` dataset contains a set of images, where each image is a single digit, which means there are ten labels. Some applications in classification include credit approval, medical diagnosis, and target marketing.

What Are Classifiers?

In the previous chapter you learned that linear regression uses supervised learning in conjunction with numeric data: the goal is to train a model that can make numeric predictions (e.g., the price of stock tomorrow, the temperature of a system, its barometric pressure, and so forth). By contrast, classifiers use supervised learning in conjunction with various classes of data: the goal is to train a model that can make categorical predictions.

For instance, suppose that each row in a dataset is a specific wine, and each column pertains to a specific wine feature (tannin, acidity, and so forth). Suppose further that there are five classes of wine in the dataset: for simplicity, let's label them A, B, C, D, and E. Given a new data point, which is to say a new row of data, a classifier for this dataset attempts to determine the label for this wine.

Some of the classifiers in this chapter can perform categorical classification and make numeric predictions (i.e., they can be used for regression as well as classification).

Common Classifiers

Some of the most popular classifiers for machine learning are listed here (in no particular order):

- Linear classifiers
- kNN
- Logistic regression
- Decision trees
- Random forests
- SVMs
- Bayesian classifiers
- CNNs (deep learning)

Keep in mind that different classifiers have different advantages and disadvantages, which often involve a trade-off between complexity and accuracy, similar to algorithms in fields that are outside of AI.

In the case of deep learning, CNNs (Convolutional Neural Networks) perform image classification, which makes them classifiers (they can also be used for audio and text processing).

The next sections provide a brief description of these ML classifiers.

Binary vs MultiClass Classification

Binary classifiers work with datasets that have two classes, whereas multiclass classifiers (sometimes called multinomial classifiers) distinguish more than two classes. Random forest classifiers and naïve Bayes classifiers support multiple classes, whereas SVMs and linear classifiers can only be used as binary classifiers (but multi-class extensions for SVM exist).

In addition, there are techniques for multiclass classification that are based on binary classifiers: One-versus-All (OvA) and One-versus-One (OvO).

The OvA technique (also called one-versus-the-rest) involves multiple binary classifiers that are equal to the number of classes. For example, if a dataset has five classes, then OvA uses five binary classifiers, each of which detects one of the five classes. In order to classify a datapoint in this dataset, select the binary classifier that has output the highest score.

The OvO technique also involves multiple binary classifiers, but in this case a binary classifier is used to train on a pair of classes. For instance, if the classes are A, B, C, D, and E, then ten binary classifiers are required: one for A and B, one for A and C, one for A and D, and so forth, until the last binary classifier for D and E.

In general, if there are n classes, then $n*(n-1)/2$ binary classifiers are required. Although the OvO technique requires considerably more binary classifiers (e.g., 190 are required for 20 classes) than the OvA technique (e.g., a mere 20 binary classifiers for 20 classes), the OvO technique has the advantage that each binary classifier is only trained on the portion of the dataset that pertains to its two chosen classes.

MultiLabel Classification

Multilabel classification involves assigning multiple labels to an instance from a dataset. Hence, multilabel classification generalizes multiclass classification (discussed in the previous section), where the latter involves assigning a single label to an instance belonging to a dataset that has multiple classes. An article involving multilabel classification that contains Keras-based code is here:

https://medium.com/@vijayabhaskar96/multi-label-image-classification-tutorial-with-keras-imagedatagenerator-cd541f8eaf24

You can also perform an online search for articles that involve SKLearn or PyTorch for multilabel classification tasks.

What Are Linear Classifiers?

A linear classifier separates a dataset into two classes. A linear classifier is a line for 2D points, a plane for 3D points, and a hyper plane (a generalization of a plane) for higher dimensional points.

Linear classifiers are often the fastest classifiers, so they are often used when the speed of classification is of high importance. Linear classifiers usually work well when the input vectors are sparse (i.e., mostly zero values) or when the number of dimensions is large.

What Is kNN?

The kNN (k Nearest Neighbor) algorithm is a classification algorithm. In brief, data points that are near each other are classified as belonging to the same class. When a new point is introduced, it's added to the class of the majority of its nearest neighbor. For example, suppose that k equals 3, and a new data point is introduced. Look at the class of its three nearest neighbors: let's say they are A, A, and B. Then by majority vote, the new data point is labeled as a data point of class A.

The kNN algorithm is essentially a heuristic and not a technique with complex mathematical underpinnings, and yet it's still an effective and useful algorithm.

Try the kNN algorithm if you want to use a simple algorithm or when you believe that the nature of your dataset is highly unstructured. The kNN algorithm can produce highly nonlinear decisions despite being very simple. You can use kNN in search applications where you are searching for similar items.

Measure similarity by creating a vector representation of the items, and then compare the vectors using an appropriate distance metric (such as Euclidean distance).

Some concrete examples of kNN search include searching for semantically similar documents.

How to Handle a Tie in kNN

An odd value for k is less likely to result in a tie vote, but it's not impossible. For example, suppose that k equals 7, and when a new data point is introduced, its seven nearest neighbors belong to the set {A,B,A,B,A,B,C}. As you can see, there is no majority vote, because there are 3 points in class A, 3 points in class B, and 1 point in class C.

There are several techniques for handling a tie in kNN:

- Assign higher weights to closer points
- Increase the value of k until a winner is determined
- Decrease the value of k until a winner is determined
- Randomly select one class

If you reduce k until it equals 1, it's still possible to have a tie vote: there might be two points that are equally distant from the new point, so you need a mechanism for deciding which of those two points to select as the 1-neighbor.

If there is a tie between classes A and B, then randomly select either class A or class B. Another variant is to keep track of the tie votes, and alternate round-robin style to ensure a more even distribution.

What Are Decision Trees?

Decision trees are another type of classification algorithm that involves a treelike structure. In a generic tree, the placement of a data point is determined by simple conditional logic. As a simple illustration, suppose that a dataset contains a set of numbers that represent ages of people, and let's also suppose that the first number is 50. This number is chosen as the root of the tree, and all numbers that are smaller than 50 are added on the left branch of the tree, whereas all numbers that are greater than 50 are added on the right branch of the tree.

For example, suppose we have the sequence of numbers is {50, 25, 70, 40}. Then we can construct a tree as follows: 50 is the root node; 25 is the left child of 50; 70 is the right child of 50; and 40 is the right child of 20. Each additional numeric value that we add to this dataset is processed to determine which direction to proceed (left or right) at each node in the tree.

Listing 3.1 displays the contents of `sklearn_tree2.py` that defines a set of 2D points in the Euclidean plane, along with their labels, and then predicts the label (i.e., the class) of several other 2D points in the Euclidean plane.

Listing 3.1: sklearn_tree2.py

```
from sklearn import tree

# X = pairs of 2D points and Y = the class of each
    point
X = [[0, 0], [1, 1], [2,2]]
Y = [0, 1, 1]

tree_clf = tree.DecisionTreeClassifier()
tree_clf = tree_clf.fit(X, Y)

#predict the class of samples:
print("predict class of [-1., -1.]:")
print(tree_clf.predict([[-1., -1.]]))

print("predict class of [2., 2.]:")
print(tree_clf.predict([[2., 2.]]))

# the percentage of training samples of the same
    class
# in a leaf note equals the probability of each
    class
print("probability of each class in [2.,2.]:")
print(tree_clf.predict_proba([[2., 2.]]))
```

Listing 3.1 imports the tree class from sklearn and then initializes the arrays X and y with data values. Next, the variable tree_clf is initialized as an instance of the DecisionTreeClassifier class, after which it is trained by invoking the fit() method with the values of X and y.

Now launch the code in Listing 3.3 and you will see the following output:

```
predict class of [-1., -1.]:
[0]
predict class of [2., 2.]:
[1]
probability of each class in [2.,2.]:
[[0. 1.]]
```

As you can see, the points [-1,-1] and [2,2] are correctly labeled with the values 0 and 1, respectively, which is probably what you expected.

Listing 3.2 displays the contents of sklearn_tree3.py that extends the code in Listing 3.1 by adding a third label, and also by predicting the label of three points instead of two points in the Euclidean plane (the modifications are shown in bold).

Listing 3.2: sklearn_tree3.py

```
from sklearn import tree

# X = pairs of 2D points and Y = the class of each
    point
X = [[0, 0], [1, 1], [2,2]]
Y = [0, 1, 2]

tree_clf = tree.DecisionTreeClassifier()
tree_clf = tree_clf.fit(X, Y)

#predict the class of samples:
print("predict class of [-1., -1.]:")
print(tree_clf.predict([[-1., -1.]]))

print("predict class of [0.8, 0.8]:")
print(tree_clf.predict([[0.8, 0.8]]))

print("predict class of [2., 2.]:")
print(tree_clf.predict([[2., 2.]]))

# the percentage of training samples of the same
    class
# in a leaf note equals the probability of each
    class
print("probability of each class in [2.,2.]:")
print(tree_clf.predict_proba([[2., 2.]]))
```

Now launch the code in Listing 3.2 and you will see the following output:

```
predict class of [-1., -1.]:
[0]
predict class of [0.8, 0.8]:
[1]
predict class of [2., 2.]:
[2]
probability of each class in [2.,2.]:
[[0. 0. 1.]]
```

As you can see, the points [-1,-1], [0.8, 0.8], and [2,2] are correctly labeled with the values 0, 1, and 2, respectively, which again is probably what you expected.

Listing 3.3 displays a portion of the dataset partial_wine.csv, which contains two features and a label column (there are three classes). The total row count for this dataset is 178.

Listing 3.3: partial_wine.csv

```
Alcohol, Malic acid, class
14.23,1.71,1
13.2,1.78,1
13.16,2.36,1
14.37,1.95,1
13.24,2.59,1
14.2,1.76,1
```

Listing 3.4 displays contents of tree_classifier.py that uses a decision tree in order to train a model on the dataset partial_wine.csv.

Listing 3.4: tree_classifier.py

```
import numpy as np
import matplotlib.pyplot as plt
import pandas as pd

# Importing the dataset
dataset = pd.read_csv('partial_wine.csv')
```

(Continued)

```
X = dataset.iloc[:, [0, 1]].values
y = dataset.iloc[:, 2].values

# split the dataset into a training set and a test set
from sklearn.model_selection import train_test_
    split
X_train, X_test, y_train, y_test = train_test_
    split(X, y, test_size = 0.25, random_state = 0)

# Feature Scaling
from sklearn.preprocessing import StandardScaler
sc = StandardScaler()
X_train = sc.fit_transform(X_train)
X_test = sc.transform(X_test)

# ====> INSERT YOUR CLASSIFIER CODE HERE <====
from sklearn.tree import DecisionTreeClassifier
classifier = DecisionTreeClassifier(criterion='entropy
    ',random_state=0)
classifier.fit(X_train, y_train)
# ====> INSERT YOUR CLASSIFIER CODE HERE <====

# predict the test set results
y_pred = classifier.predict(X_test)

# generate the confusion matrix
from sklearn.metrics import confusion_matrix
cm = confusion_matrix(y_test, y_pred)
print("confusion matrix:")
print(cm)
```

Listing 3.4 contains some import statements and then populates the Pandas DataFrame dataset with the contents of the CSV file partial_wine.csv. Next, the variable X is initialized with the first two columns (and all the rows) of dataset, and the variable y is initialized with the third column (and all the rows) of dataset.

Next, the variables X_train, X_test, y_train, y_test are populated with data from X and y using a 75/25 split proportion. Notice that the variable sc (which is an instance of the StandardScalar class) performs a scaling operation on the variables X_train and X_test.

The code block shown in bold in Listing 3.4 is where we create an instance of the DecisionTreeClassifier class and then train the instance with the data in the variables X_train and X_test.

The next portion of Listing 3.4 populates the variable y_pred with a set of predictions that are generated from the data in the X_test variable. The last portion of Listing 3.4 creates a confusion matrix based on the data in y_test and the predicted data in y_pred.

Remember that all the diagonal elements of a confusion matrix are correct predictions (such as true positive and true negative); all the other cells contain a numeric value that specifies the number of predictions that are incorrect (such as false positive and false negative).

Now launch the code in Listing 3.4 and you will see the following output for the confusion matrix in which there are thirty-six correct predictions and nine incorrect predictions (with an accuracy of 80%):

```
confusion matrix:
[[13  1  2]
 [ 0 17  4]
 [ 1  1  6]]
from sklearn.metrics import confusion_matrix
```

There is a total of forty-five entries in the preceding 3x3 matrix, and the diagonal entries are correctly identified labels. Hence the accuracy is 36/45 = 0.80.

What Are Random Forests?

Random Forests are a generalization of decision trees: this classification algorithm involves multiple trees (the number is specified by you). If the data involves making a numeric prediction, the average of the predictions of the trees is computed. If the data involves a categorical prediction, the mode of the predictions of the trees is determined.

By way of analogy, random forests operate in a manner similar to financial portfolio diversification: the goal is to balance the losses with higher gains. Random forests use a majority vote to make predictions, which operates under the assumption that selecting the majority vote is more likely to be correct (and more often) than any individual prediction from a single tree.

You can easily modify the code in Listing 3.4 to use a random forest by replacing the two lines shown in bold with the following code:

```
from sklearn.ensemble import RandomForestClassifier
classifier = RandomForestClassifier(n_estimators = 10,
    criterion='entropy', random_state = 0)
```

Make this code change, launch the code, and examine the confusion matrix to compare its accuracy with the accuracy of the decision tree in Listing 3.4.

What Are SVMs?

Support Vector Machines involve a supervised ML algorithm and can be used for classification or regression problems. SVM can work with nonlinearly separable data as well as linearly separable data. SVM uses a technique called the *kernel trick* to transform data and then finds an optimal boundary the transform involves higher dimensionality. This technique results in a separation of the transformed data, after which it's possible to find a hyperplane that separates the data into two classes.

SVMs are more common in classification tasks than regression tasks. Some use cases for SVMs include:

- Text classification tasks: category assignment

- Detecting spam/sentiment analysis

- Image recognition: aspect-based recognition, color-based classification

- Handwritten digit recognition (postal automation)

Tradeoffs of SVMs

Although SVMs are extremely powerful, there are tradeoffs involved. Some of the advantages of SVMs are:

- has high accuracy

- works well on smaller cleaner datasets

- can be more efficient because it uses a subset of training points
- can be an alternative to CNNs in cases of limited datasets
- captures more complex relationships between data points

Despite the power of SVMS, there are some disadvantages of SVMs:

- not suited to larger datasets: training time can be high
- less effective on noisier datasets with overlapping classes

SVMs involve more parameters than decision trees and random forests

Suggestion: modify Listing 3.4 to use an SVM by replacing the two lines shown in bold with the following two lines shown in bold:

```
from sklearn.svm import SVC
classifier = SVC(kernel = 'linear',
            random_state = 0)
```

You now have an SVM-based model, simply by making the previous code update! Make the code change, then launch the code and examine the confusion matrix in order to compare its accuracy with the accuracy of the decision tree model and the random forest model earlier in this chapter.

What Is Bayesian Inference?

Bayesian inference is an important technique in statistics that involves statistical inference and Bayes' theorem to update the probability for a hypothesis as more information becomes available. Bayesian inference is often called *Bayesian probability*, and it's important in dynamic analysis of sequential data.

Bayes Theorem

Given two sets A and B, let's define the following numeric values (all of them are between 0 and 1):

```
P(A) = probability of being in set A
P(B) = probability of being in set B
P(Both) = probability of being in A intersect B
P(A|B) = probability of being in A (given you're in B)
P(B|A) = probability of being in B (given you're in A)
```

Then the following formulas are also true:

```
P(A|B) = P(Both)/P(B) (#1)
P(B|A) = P(Both)/P(A) (#2)
```

Multiply the preceding pair of equations by the term that appears in the denominator and we get these equations:

```
P(B)*P(A|B) = P(Both) (#3)
P(A)*P(B|A) = P(Both) (#4)
```

Now set the left-side of equations #3 and #4 equal to each another and that gives us this equation:

```
P(B)*P(A|B) = P(A)*P(B|A) (#5)
```

Divide both sides of #5 by P(B) and we get this well-known equation:

```
P(A|B) = P(A)*P(A|B)/P(B) (#6)
```

Some Bayesian Terminology,

In the previous section, we derived the following relationship:

```
P(h|d) = (P(d|h) * P(h)) / P(d)
```

There is a name for each of the four terms in the preceding equation:

First, the *posterior probability* is P(h|d), which is the probability of hypothesis d given the data d.

Second, P(d|h) is the probability of data d given that the hypothesis h was true.

Third, the *prior probability* of h is P(h), which is the probability of hypothesis h being true (regardless of the data).

Finally, P(d) is the probability of the data (regardless of the hypothesis)

We are interested in calculating the posterior probability of P(h|d) from the prior probability p(h) with P(d) and P(d|h).

What Is MAP?

The maximum a posteriori (MAP) hypothesis is the hypothesis with the highest probability, which is the maximum probable hypothesis. This can be written as follows:

```
MAP(h) = max(P(h|d))
```
or:
```
MAP(h) = max((P(d|h) * P(h)) / P(d))
```
or:
```
MAP(h) = max(P(d|h) * P(h))
```

Why Use Bayes' Theorem?

Bayes Theorem describes the probability of an event based on the prior knowledge of the conditions that might be related to the event. If we know the conditional probability, we can use Bayes rule to find out the reverse probabilities. The previous statement is the general representation of the Bayes rule.

What Is a Bayesian Classifier?

A Naive Bayes Classifier is a probabilistic classifier inspired by the Bayes theorem. An NB classifier assumes the attributes are conditionally independent and it works well even when assumption is not true. This assumption greatly reduces computational cost, and it's a simple algorithm to implement that only requires linear time. Moreover, a NB classifier easily scalable to larger datasets and good results are obtained in most cases. Other advantages of a NB classifier include that it:

- can be used for Binary & Multiclass classification
- provides different types of NB algorithms
- is good choice for Text Classification problems
- is a popular choice for spam email classification
- can be easily trained on small datasets

As you can probably surmise, NB classifiers do have some disadvantages, such as:

- All features are assumed unrelated
- It cannot learn relationships between features
- It can suffer from the "zero probability problem"

The "zero probability problem" refers to the case when the conditional probability is zero for an attribute, it fails to give a valid prediction. However, can be fixed explicitly using a Laplacian estimator.

Types of Naïve Bayes Classifiers

There are three major types of NB classifiers:

- Gaussian Naive Bayes
- MultinomialNB Naive Bayes
- Bernoulli Naive Bayes

Details of these classifiers are beyond the scope of this chapter, but you can perform an online search for more information.

Training Classifiers

Some common techniques for training classifiers are:

- Holdout method
- k-fold cross-validation

The *holdout method* is the most common method, which starts by dividing the dataset into two partitions called *train* and *test* (80% and 20%, respectively). The train set is used for training the model, and the test data tests its predictive power.

The *k-fold cross-validation* technique is used to verify that the model is not over-fitted. The dataset is randomly partitioned into k mutually exclusive subsets, where each partition has equal size. One partition is for testing and the other partitions are for training. Iterate throughout the whole of the k folds.

Evaluating Classifiers

Whenever you select a classifier for a dataset, it's obviously important to evaluate the accuracy of that classifier. Some common techniques for evaluating classifiers are:

- Precision and Recall
- ROC curve (Receiver Operating Characteristics)

Precision and recall are discussed in Chapter 2 and reproduced here for your convenience. Let's define the following variables:

```
TP = the number of true positive results
FP = the number of false positive results
TN = the number of true negative results
FN = the number of false negative results
```

Then the definitions of precision, accuracy, and recall are given by the following formulas:

```
precision = TP/(TN + FP)
accuracy  = (TP + TN)/[P + N]
recall    = TP/[TP + FN]
```

The *ROC curve (Receiver Operating Characteristics)* is used for visual comparison of classification models that shows the trade-off between the true positive rate and the false positive rate. The area under the ROC curve is a measure of the accuracy of the model. When a model is closer to the diagonal, it is less accurate, and the model with perfect accuracy will have an area of 1.0.

The ROC curve plots True Positive Rate versus False Positive Rate. Another type of curve is the PR curve that plots Precision versus Recall. When dealing with highly skewed datasets (strong class imbalance), Precision-Recall (PR) curves give better results.

Later in this chapter you will see many of the Keras-based classes (located in the tf.keras.metrics namespace) that correspond to common statistical terms, which includes some of the terms in this section.

This concludes the portion of the chapter pertaining to statistical terms and techniques for measuring the validity of a dataset. Now let's look at activation functions in machine learning.

What Are Activation Functions?

A one-sentence description: an activation function is (usually) a nonlinear function that introduces nonlinearity into a neural network, thereby preventing a "consolidation" of the hidden layers in neural network. Specifically, suppose that every pair of adjacent layers in a neural network involves just a matrix transformation and no activation function. *Such a network is a linear system, which means that its layers can be consolidated into a much smaller system.*

First, the weights of the edges that connect the input layer with the first hidden layer can be represented by a matrix: let's call it W1. Next, the weights of the edges that connect the first hidden layer with the second hidden layer can also be represented by a matrix: let's call it W2. Repeat this process until we reach the edges that connect the final hidden layer with the output layer: let's call this matrix Wk. Since we do not have an activation function, we can simply multiply the matrices W1, W2, ..., Wk together and produce one matrix: let's call it W. We have now replaced the original neural network with an equivalent neural network that contains one input layer, a single matrix of weights W, and an output layer. In other words, we no longer have our original multi-layered neural network!

Fortunately, we can prevent the previous scenario from happening when we specify an activation function between every pair of adjacent layers. In other words, *an activation function at each layer prevents this "matrix consolidation."* Hence, we can maintain all the intermediate hidden layers during the process of training the neural network.

For simplicity, let's assume that we have the same activation function between every pair of adjacent layers (we'll remove this assumption shortly). The process for using an activation function in a neural network is a *two step*, described as follows:

- Step 1. Start with an input vector x1 of numbers

- Step 2. Multiply x1 by the matrix of weights W1 that represents the edges that connect the input layer with the first hidden layer: the result is a new vector x2

- Step 3. Apply the activation function to each element of x2 to create another vector x3

Now repeat steps 2 and 3, except that we use the starting vector x3 and the weights matrix W2 for the edges that connect the first hidden layer with the second hidden layer (or just the output layer if there is only one hidden layer).

After completing the preceding process, we have preserved the neural network, which means that it can be trained on a dataset. One other thing: instead of using the same activation function at each step, you can replace each activation function by a different activation function (the choice is yours).

Why Do We Need Activation Functions?

The previous section outlines the process for transforming an input vector from the input layer and then through the hidden layers until it reaches the output layer. The purpose of activation functions in neural networks is vitally important, so it's worth repeating here: activation functions "maintain" the structure of neural networks and prevent them from being reduced to an input layer and an output layer. In other words, if we specify a nonlinear activation function between every pair of consecutive layers, then the neural network cannot be replaced with a neural network that contains fewer layers unless you explicitly remove them.

Without a nonlinear activation function, we simply multiply a weight matrix for a given pair of consecutive layers with the output vector that is produced from the previous pair of consecutive layers. We repeat this simple multiplication until we reach the output layer of the neural network. After reaching the output layer, we have effectively replaced multiple matrices with a single matrix that "connects" the input layer with the output layer.

How Do Activation Functions Work?

If this is the first time you have encountered the concept of an activation function, it's probably confusing, so here's an analogy that might be helpful. Suppose you're driving your car late at night and there's nobody else on the highway. You can drive at a constant speed for as long as there are no obstacles (stop signs, traffic lights, and so forth). On the other hand, suppose you drive into the parking lot of a large grocery store. When you approach a speed bump you must slow down, cross the speed bump, and increase speed again, and repeat this process for every speed bump.

Think of the nonlinear activation functions in a neural network as the counterpart to the speed bumps: you simply cannot maintain a constant speed, which (by analogy) means that you cannot first multiply all the weight matrices together and "collapse" them into a single weight matrix. Another analogy involves a road with multiple toll booths: you must slow down, pay the toll, and then resume driving until you reach the next toll booth. These are only analogies (and hence imperfect) to help you understand the need for nonlinear activation functions.

Common Activation Functions

Although there are many activation functions (and you can define your own if you know how to do so), here is a list of common activation functions, followed by brief descriptions:

- Sigmoid
- Tanh
- ReLU
- ReLU6
- ELU
- SELU

The `sigmoid` activation function is based on Euler's constant e, with a range of values between 0 and 1, and its formula is shown here:

```
1/[1+e^(-x)]
```

The `tanh` activation function is also based on Euler's constant e, and its formula is shown here:

```
[e^x - e^(-x)]/[e^x+e^(-x)]
```

One way to remember the preceding formula is to note that the numerator and denominator have the same pair of terms: they are separated by a "-" sign in the numerator and a "+" sign in the denominator. The `tanh` function has a range of values between -1 and 1.

The ReLU (Rectified Linear Unit) activation function is straightforward: if x is negative then ReLU(x) is 0; for all other values of x, ReLU(x) equals x. ReLU6 is specific to TensorFlow, and it's a variation of ReLU(x): the additional constraint is that ReLU(x) equals 6 when x >= 6 (hence its name).

ELU is Exponential Linear Unit and it's the exponential "envelope" of ReLU, which replaces the two linear segments of ReLU with an exponential activation function that is differentiable for all values of x (including x = 0).

SELU is an acronym for Scaled Exponential Linear Unit, and it's slightly more complicated than the other activation functions (and used less frequently). For a thorough explanation of these and other activation functions (along with graphs that depict their shape), navigate to the following Wikipedia link:

https://en.wikipedia.org/wiki/Activation_function

This link provides a long list of activation functions as well as their derivatives.

Activation Functions in Python

Listing 3.5 displays contents of the file `activations.py` that contains the formulas for various activation functions.

Listing 3.5: activations.py

```
import numpy as np

# Python sigmoid example:
z = 1/(1 + np.exp(-np.dot(W, x)))

# Python tanh example:
z = np.tanh(np.dot(W,x))

# Python ReLU example:
z = np.maximum(0, np.dot(W, x))
```

Listing 3.5 contains Python code that use `NumPy` methods in order to define a sigmoid function, a `tanh` function, and a ReLU function. Note that you need to specify values for `x` and `W` in order to launch the code in Listing 3.5.

Keras Activation Functions

TensorFlow (and many other frameworks) provide implementations for many activation functions, which saves you the time and effort from writing your own implementation of activation functions.

Here is a list of TF 2/Keras APIs activation functions that are located in the tf.keras.layers namespace:

- tf.keras.layers.leaky_relu
- tf.keras.layers.relu
- tf.keras.layers.relu6
- tf.keras.layers.selu
- tf.keras.layers.sigmoid
- tf.keras.layers.sigmoid_cross_entropy_with_logits
- tf.keras.layers.softmax
- tf.keras.layers.softmax_cross_entropy_with_logits_v2
- tf.keras.layers.softplus
- tf.keras.layers.softsign
- tf.keras.layers.softmax_cross_entropy_with_logits
- tf.keras.layers.tanh
- tf.keras.layers.weighted_cross_entropy_with_logits

The following subsections provide additional information regarding some of the activation functions in the preceding list. Keep the following point in mind: for simple neural networks, use ReLU as your first preference.

The ReLU and ELU Activation Functions

Currently ReLU is often the "preferred" activation function: previously the preferred activation function was tanh (and before tanh it was sigmoid). ReLU behaves close to a linear unit and provides the best training accuracy and validation accuracy.

ReLU is like a switch for linearity: it's "off" if you don't need it, and its derivative is 1 when it's active, which makes ReLU the simplest of all the current activation functions. Note that the second derivative of the function is 0 everywhere: it's a very simple function that simplifies optimization. In addition, the gradient is large whenever you need large values, and it never "saturates" (i.e., it does not shrink to zero on the positive horizontal axis).

Rectified linear units and generalized versions are based on the principle that linear models are easier to optimize. Use the ReLU activation function or one of its related alternatives (discussed later).

The Advantages and Disadvantages of ReLU

The following list contains the advantages of the ReLU activation function:

- Does not saturate in the positive region
- Very efficient in terms of computation
- Models with ReLU typically converge faster those with other activation functions

However, ReLU does have a disadvantage when the activation value of a ReLU neuron becomes 0: then the gradients of the neuron will also be 0 during back-propagation. You can mitigate this scenario by judiciously assigning the values for the initial weights as well as the learning rate.

ELU

ELU is an acronym for *exponential linear unit* that is based on ReLU: the key difference is that ELU is differentiable at the origin (ReLU is a continuous function but *not* differentiable at the origin). However, keep in mind several points. First, ELUs trade computational efficiency for *immortality* (immunity to dying): read the following paper for more details: arxiv.org/abs/1511.07289. Secondly, RELUs are still popular and preferred over ELU because the use of ELU introduces an additional new hyper-parameter.

Sigmoid, Softmax, and Hardmax Similarities

The `sigmoid` activation function has a range in $(0,1)$, and it saturates and kills gradients. Unlike the `tanh` activation function, `sigmoid` outputs are not zero-centered. In addition, both `sigmoid` and `softmax` (discussed later) are discouraged for vanilla feed forward implementation (see Chapter 6 of the online book, *Deep Learning* by Ian Goodfellow et al.). However, the `sigmoid` activation function is still used in LSTMs (specifically for the forget gate, input gate, and the output gate), GRUs (Gated Recurrent Units), and probabilistic models. Moreover, some autoencoders have additional requirements that preclude the use of piecewise linear activation functions.

Softmax

The `softmax` activation function maps the values in a dataset to another set of values that are between 0 and 1, and whose sum equals 1. Thus, `softmax` creates a probability distribution. In the case of image classification with Convolutional Neural Networks (CNNs), the `softmax` activation function maps the values in the final hidden layer to the ten neurons in the output layer. The index of the position that contains the largest probability is matched with the index of the number 1 in the one-hot encoding of the input image. If the index values are equal, then the image has been classified, otherwise it's considered a mismatch.

Softplus

The `softplus` activation function is a smooth (i.e., differentiable) approximation to the ReLU activation function. Recall that the origin is the only nondifferentiable point of the ReLU function, which is smoothed by the `softmax` activation whose equation is:

```
f(x) = ln(1 + e^x)
```

Tanh

The `tanh` activation function has a range in $(-1,1)$, whereas the `sigmoid` function has a range in $(0,1)$. Both of these activations saturate, but unlike the `sigmoid` neuron the `tanh` output is zero-centered. Therefore, in practice the `tanh` nonlinearity is always preferred to the `sigmoid` nonlinearity.

The `sigmoid` and `tanh` activation functions appear in LSTMs (sigmoid for the three gates and tanh for the internal cell state) as well as GRUs (Gated Recurrent Units) during the calculations pertaining to input gates, forget gates, and output gates (discussed in more detail in the next chapter).

Sigmoid, Softmax, and HardMax Differences

This section briefly discusses some of the differences among these three functions. First, the `sigmoid` function is used for binary classification in logistic regression model, as well as the gates in LSTMs and GRUs. The `sigmoid` function is used as activation function while building neural networks, but keep in mind that the sum of the probabilities is *not* necessarily equal to 1.

Second, the `softmax` function generalizes the `sigmoid` function: it's used for multiclassification in logistic regression model. The `softmax` function is the activation function for the *fully connected layer* in CNNs, which is the rightmost hidden layer and the output layer. Unlike the sigmoid function, the sum of the probabilities *must* equal 1. You can use either the sigmoid function or `softmax` for binary (n=2) classification.

Third, the so-called `hardmax` function assigns 0 or 1 to output values (similar to a step function). For example, suppose that we have three classes {c1, c2, c3} whose scores are [1, 7, 2], respectively. The `hardmax` probabilities are [0, 1, 0], whereas the `softmax` probabilities are [0.1, 0.7, 0.2]. Notice that the sum of the `hardmax` probabilities is 1, which is also true of the sum of the `softmax` probabilities. However, the `hardmax` probabilities are all-or-nothing, whereas the `softmax` probabilities are analogous to receiving "partial credit."

What Is Logistic Regression?

Despite its name, logistic regression is a classifier and a linear model with a binary output. Logistic regression works with multiple independent variables and involves a sigmoid function for calculating probabilities. Logistic regression is essentially the result of applying the `sigmoid` activation function to linear regression in order to perform binary classification.

Logistic regression is useful in a variety of unrelated fields. Such fields include machine learning, various medical fields, and social sciences. Logistic regression can be used to predict the risk of developing a given disease, based on various observed characteristics of the patient. Other fields that use logistic regression include engineering, marketing, and economics.

Logistic regression can be binomial (only two outcomes for a dependent variable), multinomial (three or more outcomes for a dependent variable), or ordinal (dependent variables are ordered). For instance, suppose that a dataset consists of data that belong either to class A or to class B. If you are given a new data point, logistic regression predicts whether that new data point belongs to class A or to class B. By contrast, linear regression predicts a numeric value, such as the next-day value of a stock.

Setting a Threshold Value

The threshold value is a numeric value that determines which data points belong to class A and which points belong to class B. For instance, a pass/fail threshold might be 0.70. A pass/fail threshold for passing a writing driver's test in California is 0.85.

As another example, suppose that p = 0.5 is the *cutoff* probability. Then we can assign class A to the data points that occur with probability > 0.5 and assign class B to data points that occur with probability <= 0.5. Since there are only two classes, we do have a classifier.

A similar (yet slightly different) scenario involves tossing a well-balanced coin. We know that there is a 50% chance of throwing heads (let's label this outcome as class A) and a 50% chance of throwing tails (let's label this outcome as class B). If we have a dataset that consists of labeled outcomes, then we have the expectation that approximately 50% of them are class A and class B.

On the other hand, we have no way to determine (in advance) what percentage of people will pass their written driver's test, or the percentage of people who will pass their course. Datasets containing outcomes for these types of scenarios need to be trained, and logistic regression can be a suitable technique for doing so.

Logistic Regression: Important Assumptions

Logistic regression requires the observations to be independent of each other. In addition, logistic regression requires little or no multi collinearity among the independent variables. Logistic regression handles numeric, categorical, and continuous variables and also assumes linearity of independent variables and log odds, which is defined as:

```
odds = p/(1-p) and logit = log(odds)
```

This analysis does not require the dependent and independent variables to be related linearly; however, another requirement is that independent variables are linearly related to the log odds.

Logistic regression is used to obtain odds ratio in the presence of more than one explanatory variable. The procedure is quite similar to multiple linear regression, with the exception that the response variable is binomial. The result is the impact of each variable on the odds ratio of the observed event of interest.

Linearly Separable Data

Linearly separable data is data that can be separated by a line (in 2D), a plane (in 3D), or a hyperplane (in higher dimensions). Linearly nonseparable data is data (clusters) that cannot be separated by a line or a hyperplane. For example, the XOR function involves datapoints that cannot be separated by a line. If you create a truth table for an XOR function with two inputs, the points (0,0) and (1,1) belong to class 0, whereas the points (0,1) and (1,0) belong to class 1 (draw these points in a 2D plane to convince yourself). The solution involves transforming the data in a higher dimension so that it becomes linearly separable, which is the technique used in SVMS (discussed earlier in this chapter).

Keras, Logistic Regression, and Iris Dataset

Listing 3.6 displays the contents of tf2-keras-iris.py that defines a Keras-based model to perform logistic regression.

Listing 3.6: tf2-keras-iris.py

```python
import tensorflow as tf
import matplotlib.pyplot as plt

from sklearn.datasets import load_iris
from sklearn.model_selection import train_test_
    split
from sklearn.preprocessing import OneHotEncoder,
    StandardScaler

iris = load_iris()
X = iris['data']
y = iris['target']

#you can view the data and the labels:
#print("iris data:",X)
#print("iris target:",y)

# scale the X values so they are between 0 and 1
scaler = StandardScaler()
X_scaled = scaler.fit_transform(X)

X_train, X_test, y_train, y_test = train_test_
    split(X_scaled, y, test_size = 0.2)

model = tf.keras.models.Sequential()
model.add(tf.keras.layers.
    Dense(activation='relu', input_dim=4,
          units=4, kernel_initializer='uniform'))

model.add(tf.keras.layers.
    Dense(activation='relu', units=4,
                    kernel_initializer='uniform'))
```

```
model.add(tf.keras.layers.
    Dense(activation='sigmoid', units=1,
                    kernel_initializer='uniform'))
#model.add(tf.keras.layers.Dense(1,
    activation='softmax'))

model.compile(optimizer='adam', loss='mean_
    squared_error', metrics=['accuracy'])

model.fit(X_train, y_train, batch_size=10,
    epochs=100)

# Predicting values from the test set
y_pred = model.predict(X_test)

# scatter plot of test values-vs-predictions
fig, ax = plt.subplots()
ax.scatter(y_test, y_pred)
ax.plot([y_test.min(), y_test.max()], [y_test.
    min(), y_test.max()], 'r*--')
ax.set_xlabel('Calculated')
ax.set_ylabel('Predictions')
plt.show()
```

Listing 3.6 starts with an assortment of import statements, and then initializes the variable iris with the Iris dataset. The variable X contains the first three columns (and all the rows) of the Iris dataset, and the variable y contains the fourth column (and all the rows) of the Iris dataset.

The next portion of Listing 3.6 initializes the training set and the test set using an 80/20 data split. Next, the Keras-based model contains three Dense layers, where the first two specify the relu activation function and the third layer specifies the sigmoid activation function.

The next portion of Listing 3.6 compiles the model, trains the model, and then calculates the accuracy of the model via the test data. Launch the code in Listing 3.6 and you will see the following output:

```
Train on 120 samples
Epoch 1/100
120/120 [==============================] - 0s
   980us/sample - loss: 0.9819 - accuracy: 0.3167
Epoch 2/100
120/120 [==============================] - 0s
   162us/sample - loss: 0.9789 - accuracy: 0.3083
Epoch 3/100
120/120 [==============================] - 0s
   204us/sample - loss: 0.9758 - accuracy: 0.3083
Epoch 4/100
120/120 [==============================] - 0s
   166us/sample - loss: 0.9728 - accuracy: 0.3083
Epoch 5/100
120/120 [==============================] - 0s
   160us/sample - loss: 0.9700 - accuracy: 0.3083
// details omitted for brevity
Epoch 96/100
120/120 [==============================] - 0s
   128us/sample - loss: 0.3524 - accuracy: 0.6500
Epoch 97/100
120/120 [==============================] - 0s
   184us/sample - loss: 0.3523 - accuracy: 0.6500
Epoch 98/100
120/120 [==============================] - 0s
   128us/sample - loss: 0.3522 - accuracy: 0.6500
Epoch 99/100
120/120 [==============================] - 0s
   187us/sample - loss: 0.3522 - accuracy: 0.6500
Epoch 100/100
120/120 [==============================] - 0s
   167us/sample - loss: 0.3521 - accuracy: 0.6500
```

Figure 3.1 displays a scatter plot of points based on the test values and the predictions for those test values.

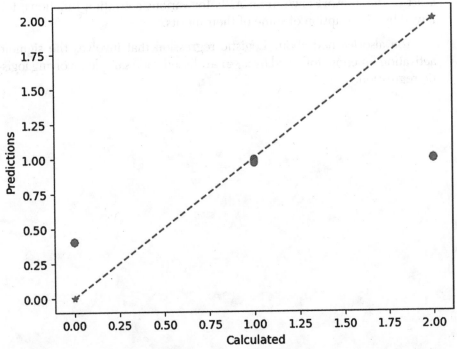

FIGURE 3.1 A Scatter Plot and a Best-Fitting Line.

The accuracy is admittedly poor (abysmal?), and yet it's quite possible that you will encounter this type of situation. Experiment with a different number of hidden layers and replace the final hidden layer with a Dense layer that specifies a softmax activation function—or some other activation function—to see if this change improves the accuracy.

Summary

This chapter started with an explanation of classification and classifiers, followed by a brief explanation of commonly used classifiers in machine learning.

Next you learned about activation functions, why they are important in neural networks, and how they are used in neural networks. Then you saw a list of the TensorFlow/Keras APIs for various activation functions, followed by a description of some of their merits.

You also learned about Logistic regression that involves the sigmoid activation function, followed by a Keras-based code sample involving logistic regression.

## CHAPTER 4

DEEP LEARNING INTRODUCTION

This chapter introduces you to deep learning, which includes MLPs (Multilayer Perceptrons), CNNs (Convolutional Neural Networks). Other deep learning architectures, such as RNNs (Recurrent Neural Networks), and LSTMs (Long Short Term Memory), are discussed in Chapter 5.

Most of the material in this chapter is descriptive content, along with some Keras-based code samples that assume you have read the Keras material in the previous chapters. *This chapter is meant to be a cursory introduction to a diverse set of topics, along with suitable links to additional information.*

If you are new to deep learning, many topics in this chapter will probably require additional study in order to become comfortable with them: think of this chapter as a modest step toward your mastery of deep learning.

The first portion of this chapter briefly discusses deep learning, the problems it can solve, and the challenges for the future. The second part of this chapter briefly introduces Perceptrons, which is essentially a core building block for neural networks. In fact, ANNs, MLPs, RNNs, LSTMs, VAEs are all based on multiple layers that contain multiple Perceptrons, along with additional processing steps.

The third part of this chapter provides an introduction of CNNs, followed by an example of training a Keras-based CNN with the MNIST dataset: this code sample will make more sense if you have read the section pertaining to activation functions in Chapter 5.

Keras and the XOR Function

The XOR function is a well-known function that is not linear separable in the plane. The truth table for the XOR ("exclusive OR") function is straightforward: given two binary inputs, the output is 1 if at most one input is a 1; otherwise, the output is 0. If we treat XOR as the name of a function with two binary inputs, here are the outputs:

```
XOR(0,0) = 0
XOR(1,0) = 1
XOR(0,1) = 1
XOR(1,1) = 0
```

We can treat the output values as labels that are associated with the input values. Specifically, the points (0,0) and (1,1) are in class 0 and the points (1,0) and (0,1) are in class 1. Draw these points in the plane, and you will have the four vertices of a unit square whose lower-left vertex is the origin. Moreover, each pair of diagonal elements belongs to the same class, and you cannot separate the points in class 0 from the points in class 1 with a straight line in the Euclidean plane. Hence, the XOR function is not linearly separable in the plane. If you're skeptical, try to find a linear separator for the XOR function in the Euclidean plane.

Listing 4.1 displays the contents of tf2_keras_xor.py that illustrates how to create a Keras-based neural network to train the XOR function.

Listing 4.1: tf2_keras_xor.py

```
import tensorflow as tf
import numpy as np

# Logical XOR operator and "truth" values:
x = np.array([[0., 0.],[0., 1.],[1., 0.],[1.,
    1.]])
y = np.array([[0.], [1.], [1.], [0.]])

model = tf.keras.models.Sequential()
model.add(tf.keras.layers.Dense(2, input_dim=2,
    activation='relu'))
model.add(tf.keras.layers.Dense(1))
```

```
print("compiling model...")
model.compile(loss='mean_squared_error',
    optimizer='adam')
print("fitting model...")
model.fit(x,y,verbose=0,epochs=1000)
pred = model.predict(x)

# Test final prediction
print("Testing XOR operator")
p1 = np.array([[0., 0.]])
p2 = np.array([[0., 1.]])
p3 = np.array([[1., 0.]])
p4 = np.array([[1., 1.]])

print(p1,":", model.predict(p1))
print(p2,":", model.predict(p2))
print(p3,":", model.predict(p3))
print(p4,":", model.predict(p4))
```

Listing 4.1 initializes the `NumPy` array x with 4 pairs of numbers that are the four combinations of 0 and 1, followed by the `NumPy` array y that contains the logical OR of each pair of numbers in x.

The next portion of Listing 4.1 defines a `Keras`-based model with two `Dense` layers. Next, the model is compiled, trained, and then the variable `pred` is populated with a set of predictions based on the trained model.

The next code block initializes the points p1, p2, p3, and p4 and then displays the values that are predicted for those points. The output from launching the code in Listing 4.1 is here:

```
compiling model...
fitting model...
Testing XOR operator
[[0. 0.]] : [[0.36438465]]
[[0. 1.]] : [[1.0067574]]
[[1. 0.]] : [[0.36437267]]
[[1. 1.]] : [[0.15084022]]
```

Experiment with different values for `epochs` and see how that affects the predictions. Use the code in Listing 4.1 as a template for other logical functions. The only modification to Listing 4.1 that is required is the replacement of the variable y in Listing 4.1 with the variable y that is specified as the labels for several other logic gates that are listed below.

The labels for the NOR function:

```
y = np.array([[1.], [0.], [0.], [1.]])
```

The labels for the OR function:

```
y = np.array([[0.], [1.], [1.], [1.]])
```

The labels for the XOR function:

```
y = np.array([[0.], [1.], [1.], [0.]])
```

The labels for the ANDR function:

```
y = np.array([[0.], [0.], [0.], [1.]])
mnist = tf.keras.datasets.mnist
```

The preceding code snippets are the only required code changes to Listing 4.1 in order to train a model for a different logical function. For your convenience, the companion disc contains the following `Keras`-based code samples for the preceding functions:

```
tf2_keras-nor.py
tf2_keras-or.py
tf2_keras-xor.py
tf2_keras-and.py
```

After you have finished working with the preceding samples, try the NAND function, or create more complex combinations of these basic functions.

Now that you have seen an example of the limitations of a neural network with a single hidden layer, the usefulness of architectures with multiple hidden layers makes more sense, as discussed in the next section.

What Is Deep Learning?

Deep learning is a subset of machine learning that focuses on neural networks and algorithms for training neural networks. As you learned in the introduction to this chapter, deep learning comprises many types of neural networks, such as CNNs, RNNs, LSTMs, GRUs, Variational Autoencoders (VAEs), and GANs. A deep learning model requires at least two hidden layers in a neural network (*very deep learning* involves neural networks with at least ten hidden layers).

From a high-level perspective, deep learning with supervised learning involves defining a model (a.k.a. neural network) as well as:

- Making an estimate for a datapoint

- Calculating the loss or error of each estimate

- Reducing the error via gradient descent

In Chapter 3, you learned about linear regression in the context of machine learning, which starts with initial values for m and b:

```
m = tf.Variable(0.)

b = tf.Variable(0.)
```

The training process involves finding the optimal values for m and b in the following equation:

```
y = m*x + b
```

We want to calculate the dependent variable y given a value for the independent variable x. In this case, the calculation is handled by the following Python function:

```
def predict(x):

    y = m*x + b

    return y
```

The loss is another name for the error of the current estimate, which can be calculated via the following Python function that determines the MSE value:

```
def squared_error(y_pred, y_actual):

    return tf.reduce_mean(tf.square(y_pred-y_actual))
```

We also need to initialize variables for the training data (often named x_train and y_train) and the test-related data (often named x_test and y_test), which is typically an 80/20 or 75/25 split between training data and test data. Then the training process invokes the preceding Python functions in the following manner:

```
loss = squared_error(predict(x_train), y_train)
print("Loss:", loss.numpy())
```

Although the Python functions in this section are simple, they can be generalized to handle complex models, such as the models that are described later in this chapter.

You can also solve linear regression via deep learning, which involves the same code that you saw earlier in this section.

What Are Hyper Parameters?

Deep learning involves *hyper parameters*, which are sort of like knobs and dials whose values are initialized by you prior to the actual training process. For instance, the number of hidden layers and the number of neurons in hidden layers are examples of hyper parameters. You will encounter many hyper parameters in deep learning models, some of which are listed here:

- Number of hidden layers
- Number of neurons in hidden layers
- Weight initialization
- An activation function
- A cost function
- An optimizer
- A learning rate
- A dropout rate

The first three hyper parameters in the preceding list are required for the initial set-up of a neural network. The fourth hyper parameter is required for forward propagation. The next three hyper parameters (i.e., the cost function, optimizer, and learning rate) are required in order to perform backward error propagation (often called simply *backprop*) during supervised learning tasks. This step calculates a set of numbers that are used to update the values of the weights in the neural network in order to improve the accuracy of the neural network. The final hyper parameter is useful if you need to reduce overfitting in your model. In general, the cost function is the most complex of all these hyper parameters.

During back propagation, *the vanishing gradient* problem can occur (i.e., the gradient value is very close to zero), after which some weights are no longer updated, in which case the neural network is essentially inert (and debugging this problem is generally nontrivial). Another consideration: deciding whether or not a local minima is "good enough" and preferable to expending the additional time and effort that is required to find an absolute minima.

Deep Learning Architectures

As discussed previously, deep learning supports various architectures, including MLPs, CNNs, RNNs, and LSTMs. Although there is overlap in terms of the types of tasks that these architectures can solve, each one has a specific reason for its creation. As you progress from MLPs to LSTMs, the architectures become more complex. Sometimes combinations of these architectures are well suited for solving tasks. For example, capturing video and making predictions typically involves a CNN (for processing each input image in a video sequence) and an LSTM to make predictions of the position of objects that are in the video stream.

In addition, neural networks for NLP can contain one or more CNNs, RNNs, LSTMs, and biLSTMs (bidirectional LSTMs). In particular, the combination of reinforcement learning with these architectures is called deep reinforcement learning.

Although MLPs have been popular for a long time, they suffer from two disadvantages: they are not scalable for computer vision tasks, and they are somewhat difficult to train. On the other hand, CNNs do not require adjacent layers to be fully connected. Another advantage of CNNs is something called *translation invariance*, which means that an image (such as a digit, cat, dog, and so forth) is recognized as such, regardless of where it appears in a bitmap.

Problems that Deep Learning Can Solve

As you know, back propagation involves updating the weights of the edges between consecutive layers, which is performed in a right-to-left fashion (i.e., from the output layer toward the input layer). The updates involve the chain rule (a rule for computing derivatives) and an arithmetic product of parameters and gradient values. There are two anomalous results that can occur: the product of terms approaches zero (which is called the *vanishing gradient* problem) or the product of terms becomes arbitrarily large (which is called the *exploding gradient* problem). These problems arise with the sigmoid activation function.

Deep learning can mitigate both problems via LSTMs. Deep learning models usually replace the sigmoid activation function with the ReLU activation function. ReLU is a very simple continuous function that is differentiable (with a value of 1 to the right of the y-axis and a value of -1 to the left of the y-axis) everywhere except the origin. Hence, it's necessary to perform some tweaking to make things work nicely at the origin.

Challenges in Deep Learning

Although deep learning is powerful and has produced impressive results in many fields, there are some important ongoing challenges that are being explored, including:

- Bias in algorithms
- Susceptibility to adversarial attacks
- Limited ability to generalize
- Lack of explainability
- Correlation but not causality

Algorithms can contain unintentional bias, and even if the bias is removed, there can be unintentional bias in data. For example, one neural network was trained on a dataset containing pictures of Caucasian males and females. The outcome of the training process "determined" that males were physicians and that females were housewives and did so with a high probability. The reason was simple: the dataset depicted males and females almost exclusively in those two roles. The following article contains more information regarding bias in algorithms:

https://www.technologyreview.com/s/612876/this-is-how-ai-bias-really-happensand-why-its-so-hard-to-fix

Deep learning focuses on finding patterns in datasets, and generalizing those results is a more difficult task. There are some initiatives that attempt to provide explainability for the outcomes of neural networks, but such work is still in its infancy. Deep learning finds patterns and can determine correlation, but it's incapable of determining causality.

Now that you have a bird's eye view of deep learning, let's rewind and discuss an important cornerstone of machine learning called the Perceptron, which is the topic of the next section.

What Are Perceptrons?

Recall from Chapter 4 that a model for linear regression involves an output layer that contains a single neuron, whereas a multineuron output layer is for classifiers (discussed in Chapter 3). DNNs (Deep Neural Networks) contain at least two hidden layers, and they can solve logistic regression problems and as well as classification problems. In fact, the output layer of a model for classification problems consists of a set of probabilities (one for each class in the dataset) whose sum equals 1.

Figure 4.1 displays a Perceptron with incoming edges that have numeric weights.

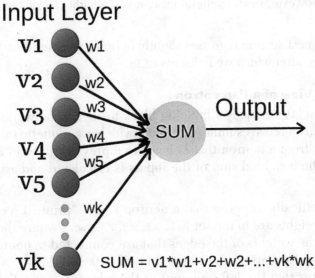

FIGURE 4.1 An Example of a Perceptron.

Image adapted from [Arunava Chakraborty, Source: *https://towardsda-tascience.com/the-perceptron-3af34c84838c*]

The next section delves into the details of a perceptron, and how they form the backbone of MLPs.

Definition of the Perceptron Function

A Perceptron involves a function f(x) where the following holds:

```
f(x) = 1 if w*x + b > 0 (otherwise f(x) = 0)
```

In the previous expression, w is a vector of weights, x is an input vector, b is a vector of biases. The product w*x is the inner product of the vectors w and x, and activating a Perceptron is an all-or-nothing decision (e.g., a light bulb is either on or off, with no intermediate states).

Notice that the function f(x) checks the value of the linear term w*x+b, which is also specified in the sigmoid function for logistic regression. The same term appears as part of the calculation of the sigmoid value, as shown here:

```
1/[1 + e^(w*x+b)]
```

Given a value for w*x+b, the preceding expression generates a numeric value. However, in the general case, W is a weight matrix, and x and b are vectors.

The next section digresses slightly in order to describe artificial neural networks, after which we'll discuss MLPs.

A Detailed View of a Perceptron

A neuron is essentially a building block for neural networks. In general, each neuron receives multiple inputs (which are numeric values), each of which is from a neuron that belongs to a previous layer in a neural network. The weighted sum of the inputs is calculated and assigned to the neuron.

Specifically, suppose that a neuron N' (N "prime") receives inputs whose weights are in the set {w1, w2, w3, ..., wn}, where these numbers specify the weights of the edges that are connected to neuron N'. Since forward propagation involves a flow of data in a left-to-right fashion, this means that the left endpoint of the edges is connected to neurons

{N1, N2, . . ., Nk} in a preceding layer, and the right endpoint of these edges is N'. The weighted sum is calculated as follows:

```
x1*w1 + x2*w2 + . . . + xn*wn
```

After the weighted sum is calculated, it's fed to an activation function that calculates a second value. This step is required for artificial neural networks, and it's explained later in the chapter. This process of calculating a weighted sum is repeated for every neuron in a given layer, and then the same process is repeated on the neurons in the next layer of a neural network.

The entire process is called *forward propagation*, which is complemented by the *backward error propagation* step (also called *backprop*). During the backward error propagation step, new weight values are calculated for the entire neural network. The combination of forward prop and backward prop is repeated for each data point (e.g., each row of data in a CSV file). The goal is to finish this training process so that the finalized neural network (also called a *model*) accurately represents the data in a dataset and can also accurately predict values for the test data. Of course, the accuracy of a neural network depends on the dataset in question, and the accuracy can be higher than 99%.

The Anatomy of an Artificial Neural Network (ANN)

An ANN consists of an input layer, an output layer, and one or more hidden layers. For each pair of adjacent layers in an ANN, neurons in the left layer are connected with neurons in the right layer via an edge that has a numeric weight. If all neurons in the left-side layer are connected to all neurons in the right-side layer, it's called an MLP (discussed later).

Keep in mind that the Perceptrons in an ANN are "stateless:" they do *not* retain any information about previously processed data. Furthermore, an ANN does not contain cycles (hence ANNs are acyclic). By contrast, RNNs and LSTMs *do* retain state and they do have cycle-like behavior, as you will see later in this chapter.

Incidentally, if you have a mathematics background, you might be tempted to think of an ANN as a set of contiguous bipartite graphs in which data flows from the input layer (think "multiple sources") toward the output layer ("the sink"). Unfortunately, this viewpoint doesn't prove useful for understanding ANNs. A better way to understand ANNs is to think of their structure as a combination of the hyper parameters in the following list:

- The number of hidden layers
- The number of neurons in each hidden layer
- The initial weights of edges connecting pairs of neurons
- The activation function
- A cost (a.k.a. loss) function
- An optimizer (used with the cost function)
- The learning rate (a small number)
- The dropout rate (optional)

Figure 4.2 displays the contents of an ANN (there are many variations: this is simply one example).

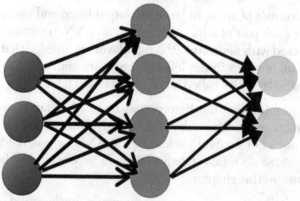

FIGURE 4.2 An Example of an ANN.

Image adapted from [Cburnett, Source: *https://commons.wikimedia. org/wiki/File:Artificial_neural_network.svg*]

Since the output layer of the ANN in Figure 4.2 contains more than one neuron, we know that it's a model for a classification task.

Initializing Hyperparameters of a Model

The first three parameters in the list of bullet items in the previous section are required for initializing the neural network. The hidden layers are intermediate computational layers, each of which is composed of neurons. The number of edges between each pair of adjacent layers is flexible and determined by you. More information about network initialization is here:

http://www.deeplearning.ai/ai-notes/initialization/

The edges that connect neurons in each pair of adjacent layers (including the input layer and the output layer) have numeric weights. The initial values of these weights are often small random numbers between 0 and 1. Keep in mind that the connections between adjacent layers can affect the complexity of a model. *The purpose of the training process is to fine-tune edge weights in order to improve the accuracy of a model.*

An ANN is not necessarily fully connected, which is to say that some edges between pairs of neurons in adjacent layers might be missing. By contrast, neural networks such as CNNs share edges (and their weights), which can make them more computationally feasible (but even CNNs can require significant training time). Note that the Keras `tf.keras.layers.Dense()` class handles the task of fully connecting two adjacent layers. As discussed later, MLPs are fully connected, which can greatly increase the training time for such a neural network.

The Activation Hyperparameter

The fourth parameter is the activation function that is applied to weights between each pair of consecutive layers. Neural networks with many layers typically involve different activation functions. For instance, CNNs use the ReLU activation function on feature maps (created by applying filters to an image), whereas the penultimate layer is connected to the output layer via the softmax function (which is a generalization of the sigmoid function).

The Loss Function Hyperparameter

The fifth, sixth, and seventh hyper parameters are required for backward error propagation that starts from the output layer and move in a right-to-left toward the input layer. These hyper parameters perform the heavy lifting of machine learning frameworks: they compute the updates to the weights of the edges in neural networks.

The *loss function* is a function in multidimensional Euclidean space. For example, the MSE loss function is a bowl-shaped loss function that has a global minimum. In general, the goal is to minimize the MSE function in order to minimize the loss, which in turn will help us maximize the accuracy of a model (but this is not guaranteed for other loss functions). However, sometimes a local minimum might be considered "good enough" instead of finding a global minimum: you must make this decision (i.e., it's not a purely programmatic decision).

Alas, loss functions for larger datasets tend to be very complex, which is necessary in order to detect potential patterns in datasets. Another loss function is the cross-entropy function, which involves maximizing the likelihood function (contrast this with MSE). Search for online articles (such as Wikipedia) for more details about loss functions.

The Optimizer Hyperparameter

An *optimizer* is an algorithm that is chosen in conjunction with a loss function, and its purpose is to converge to the minimum value of the cost function during the training phase (see the comment in the previous section regarding a local minimum). Different optimizers make different assumptions regarding the way new approximations are calculated during the training process. Some optimizers involve only the most recent approximation, whereas other optimizers use a *rolling average* that takes into account several previous approximations.

There are several well-known optimizers, including SGD, RMSprop, Adagrad, Adadelta, and Adam. Check online for details regarding the advantages and trade-offs of these optimizers.

The Learning Rate Hyperparameter

The *learning rate* is a small number, often between 0.001 and 0.05, which affects the magnitude of number that is added to the current weight of an edge in order to train the model with these updated weights. The learning rate has a sort of throttling effect. If the value is too large, the new approximation might overshoot the optimal point; if it's too small, the training time can increase significantly. By analogy, imagine you are in a passenger jet and you're 100 miles away from an airport. The speed of the airplane decreases as you approach the airport, which corresponds to decreasing the learning rate in a neural network.

The Dropout Rate Hyperparameter

The *dropout rate* is the eighth hyper parameter, which is a decimal value between 0 and 1, typically between 0.2 and 0.5. Multiply this decimal value with 100 to determine the percentage of randomly selected neurons to ignore during each forward pass in the training process. For example, if the dropout rate is 0.2, then 20% of the neurons are selected randomly *and ignored* during each step of the forward propagation. A different set of neurons is randomly selected whenever a new datapoint is processed in the neural network. Note that the neurons are not removed from the neural network: they still exist, and ignoring them during forward propagation has the effect of thinning the neural network. In TF 2 the `tf.keras.layers.Dropout` class performs the task of thinning a neural network.

There are additional hyper parameters that you can specify, but they are optional and not required in order to understand ANNs.

What Is Backward Error Propagation?

An ANN is typically drawn in a *left-to-right* fashion, where the left-most layer is the input layer. The output from each layer becomes the input for the next layer. The term forward propagation refers to supplying values to the input layer and progress through the hidden layers toward the output layer. The output layer contains the results (which are estimated numeric values) of the forward pass through the model.

Here is a key point: *backward error propagation involves the calculation of numbers that are used to update the weights of the edges in the neural network.* The update process is performed by means of a loss function (and an optimizer and a learning rate), starting from the output layer (the right-most layer) and then moving in a *right-to-left* fashion in order to update the weights of the edges between consecutive layers. This procedure trains the neural network, which involves reducing the loss between the estimated values at the output layer and the true values (in the case of supervised learning). This procedure is repeated for each data point in the training portion of the dataset. Processing the dataset is called an epoch, and many times a neural network is trained via multiple epochs.

The previous paragraph did not explain what the loss function is or how it's chosen: that's because the loss function and the optimizer and the learning rate are hyper parameters that are discussed in previous sections. However, two commonly used loss functions are MSE and cross entropy; a commonly used optimizer is Adam optimizer (and SGD and RMSprop and others); and a common value for the learning rate is 0.01.

What Is a Multilayer Perceptron (MLP)?

A multilayer perceptron (MLP) is a feed forward artificial neural network that consists of at least three layers of nodes: an input layer, a hidden layer, and an output layer. An MLP is fully connected: given a pair of adjacent layers, every node in the left layer is connected to every node in the right layer. Apart from the nodes in the input layer, each node is a neuron and each layer of neurons involves a nonlinear activation function. In addition, MLPs use a technique called *backward error propagation* (or simply *back prop*) for training, which is also true for CNNs (Convolutional Neural Networks).

Figure 4.3 displays the contents of an MLP with two hidden layers.

One point to keep in mind: the nonlinear activation function of an MLP differentiates an MLP from a linear perceptron. In fact, an MLP can handle data that is not linearly separable. For instance, the OR function and the AND function involve linearly separable data, so they can be represented via a linear perceptron. On the other hand, the XOR function involves data that is not linearly separable, and therefore requires a neural network such as an MLP.

MLP (Two Hidden Layers)

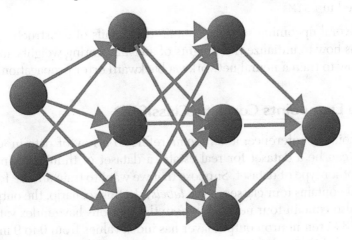

FIGURE 4.3 An Example of an MLP.

Activation Functions

An MLP without an activation function between any adjacent pair of layers is a linear system: at each layer, simply multiply the vector from the previous layer with the current matrix (which connects the current layer to the next layer) to produce another vector.

On the other hand, it's straightforward to multiply a set of matrices to produce a *single* matrix. Since a neural network without activation functions is a linear system, we can multiply those matrices (one matrix for each pair of adjacent layers) together to produce a single matrix: the original neural network is thereby reduced to a two-layer neural network consisting of an input layer and an output layer, which defeats the purpose of having a multilayered neural network.

In order to prevent such a reduction of the layers of a neural network, an MLP must include a nonlinear activation function between adjacent layers (this is also true of any other deep neural network). The choice of nonlinear activation function is typically sigmoid, tanh (which is a hyperbolic tangent function), or ReLU (Rectified Linear Unit).

The output of the sigmoid function ranges from 0 to 1, which has the effect of "squashing" the data values. Similarly, the output of the tanh function ranges from -1 to 1. However, the ReLU activation function (or one of its variants) is preferred for ANNs and CNNs, whereas sigmoid and tanh are used in LSTMs.

Several upcoming sections contain the details of constructing an MLP, such as how to initialize the weights of an MLP, storing weights and biases, and how to train a neural network via backward error propagation.

How Are Datapoints Correctly Classified?

As a point of reference: a *datapoint* refers to a row of data in a dataset, which can be a dataset for real estate, a dataset of thumbnail images, or some other type of dataset. Suppose that we want to train an MLP for a dataset that contains four classes (a.k.a. *labels*). In this scenario, the output layer must also contain four neurons, where the neurons have index values 0, 1, 2, and 3 (a ten-neuron output layer has index values from 0 to 9 inclusive). The sum of the probabilities in the output layer always equals 1 because of the softmax activation function that is used when transitioning from the penultimate layer to the output layer.

The *index* value that has the largest probability is compared with the *index* value one-hot encoding of the label of the current datapoint from the dataset. If the index values are equal, then the NN has correctly classified the current datapoint (otherwise it's a mismatch).

For example, the MNIST dataset contains images of hand-drawn digits from 0 through 9 inclusive, which means that a NN for the MNIST dataset has ten outputs in the final layer, one for each digit. Suppose that an image containing the digit 3 is currently being passed through the NN. The one-hot encoding for 3 is [0,0,0,1,0,0,0,0,0,0], and the index value with the largest value in the one-hot encoding is also 3. Now suppose that output layer of the neural network after processing the digit 3 is the following vector of values: [0.05,0.05,0.2,0.6,0.2,0.2,0.1,0.1,0.238]. As you can see, the index value with the maximum value (which is 0.6) is also 3. In this scenario, the neural network has correctly identified the input image.

A *binary* classifier involves two outcomes for handling tasks such as determining spam/not-spam, fraud/not-fraud, stock increase/decrease (or temperature, or barometric pressure), and so forth. *Predicting the future value of a stock price is a regression task, whereas predicting whether the price will increase or decrease is a classification task.*

In machine learning, the multilayer perceptron is a neural network for supervised learning of binary classifiers (and it's a type of linear classifier). However, single layer Perceptrons are only capable of learning linearly separable patterns. In fact, a famous book entitled *Perceptrons* by Marvin Minsky and Seymour Papert (written in 1969) showed that it was impossible for these classes of network to learn an XOR function. However, an XOR function can be "learned" by a two-layer Perceptron.

A High-Level View of CNNs

CNNs are deep NNs (with one or more convolutional layers) that are well suited for image classification, along with other use cases, such as audio and NLP (Natural Language Processing).

Although MLPs were successfully used for image recognition, they do not scale well because every pair of adjacent layers is fully connected, which in turn can result in massive neural networks. For large images (or other large inputs) the complexity becomes significant and adversely affects performance.

Figure 4.4 displays the contents of a CNN (there are many variations: this is simply one example).

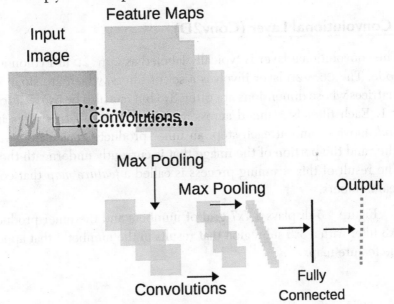

FIGURE 4.4 An Example of a CNN.

Adapted from [Source: *https://commons.wikimedia.org/w/index.php?curid=45679374*]

A Minimalistic CNN

A production quality CNN can be very complex, comprising many hidden layers. However, in this section we're going to look at a minimalistic CNN (essentially a "toy" neural network), which consists of the following layers:

- Conv2D (a convolutional layer)

- ReLU (activation function)

- Max Pooling (reduction technique)

- Fully Connected (FC) Layer

- Softmax activation function

The next subsections briefly explain the purpose of each bullet point in the preceding list of items.

The Convolutional Layer (Conv2D)

The convolutional layer is typically labeled as Conv2D in Python and TF code. The Conv2D layer involves a set of filters, which are small square matrices whose dimensions are often 3x3 but can also be 5x5, 7x7, or even 1x1. Each filter is scanned across an image (think of tricorders in *Star Trek* movies), and at each step, an inner product is calculated with the filter and the portion of the image that is currently underneath the filter. The result of this scanning process is called a *feature map* that contains real numbers.

Figure 4.5 displays a 7x7 grid of numbers and the inner product of a 3x3 filter with a 3x3 subregion that results in the number 4 that appears in the feature map.

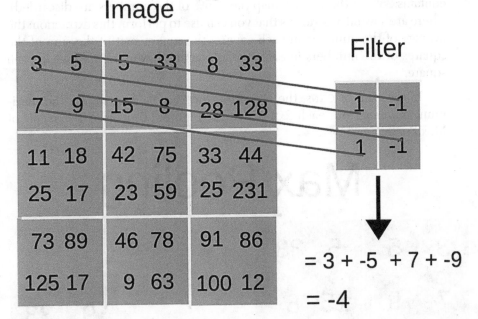

FIGURE 4.5 Performing a Convolution.

The ReLU Activation Function

After each feature map is created, it's possible that some of the values in the feature map are negative. The purpose of the ReLU activation function is to replace negative values (if any) with zero. Recall the definition of the ReLU function:

```
ReLU(x) = x if x >=0 and ReLU(x) = 0 if x < 0
```

If you draw a 2D graph of ReLU, it consists of two parts: the horizontal axis for x less than zero and the identity function (which is a line) in the first quadrant for x greater than or equal to 0.

The Max Pooling Layer

The third step involves *max pooling*, which is simple to perform: after processing the feature map with the ReLU activation function in the previous step, partition the updated feature map into 2x2 rectangles, and select the largest value from each of those rectangles. The result is a smaller array that contains 25% of the feature map (i.e., 75% of the numbers are discarded). There are several algorithms that you can use to perform this extraction: the average of the numbers in each square; the square root of the sum of the squares of the numbers in each square; or the maximum number in each square.

In the case of CNNs, the algorithm for Max Pooling selects the maximum number from each 2x2 rectangle. Figure 4.6 displays the result of Max Pooling in a CNN.

Max Pooling

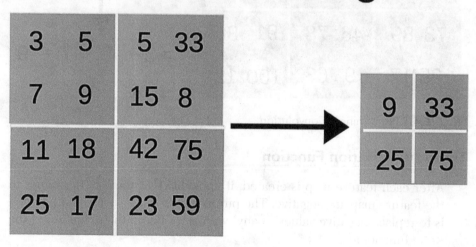

FIGURE 4.6 An Example of Max Pooling in a CNN.

As you can see, the result is a small square array whose size is only 25% of the previous feature map. This sequence is performed for each filter in the set of filters that were chosen in the Conv2D layer. This set can have 8, 16, 32, or more filters.

If you feel puzzled or skeptical about this technique, consider the analogy involving compression algorithms, which can be divided into two types: lossy and lossless. In case you didn't already know, JPEG is a lossy algorithm (i.e., data is lost during the compression process), and yet it works just fine for compressing images. If it's helpful, think of max pooling as the counterpart to lossy compression algorithms, and perhaps that will persuade you of the efficacy of this algorithm.

At the same time, your skepticism is valid. In fact, Geoffrey Hinton (often called the godfather of deep learning) proposed a replacement for max pooling called *capsule networks*. This architecture is more complex and more difficult to train, and beyond the scope of this book (you can find online tutorials that discuss capsule networks in detail). However, capsule networks tend to be more resistant to GANs (Generative Adversarial Networks).

Repeat the previous sequence of steps (as in LeNet), and then perform a rather nonintuitive action: flatten all these small arrays so that they are one-dimensional vectors, and concatenate these vectors into one (very long) vector. The resulting vector is then fully connected with the output layer, where the latter consists of 10 "buckets." In the case of `MNIST`, these placeholders are for the digits from 0 to 9 inclusive. Note that the `Keras` class `tf.keras.layers.Flatten` performs this flattening process.

The `softmax` activation function is applied to the long vector of numbers in order to populate the 10 buckets of the output layer. The result: the 10 buckets are populated with a set of non-zero (and non-negative) numbers whose sum equals one. Find the *index* of the bucket containing the largest number and compare this number with the *index* of the one-hot encoded label associated with the image that was just processed. If the index values are equal, then the image was successfully identified.

More complex `CNN`s involve multiple `Conv2D` layers, multiple `FC` (fully connected) layers, different filter sizes, and techniques for combining previous layers (such as `ResNet`) to boost the data values' current layer. Additional information about `CNN`s is here: *https://en.wikipedia.org/wiki/Convolutional_neural_network*.

Now that you have a high-level understanding of `CNN`s, let's look at a code sample that illustrates an image in the `MNIST` dataset (and the pixel values of that image), followed by two code samples that use `Keras` to train a model on the `MNIST` dataset.

Displaying an Image in the MNIST Dataset

Listing 4.2 displays the contents of `tf2_keras_mnist_digit.py` that illustrates how to create a neural network in TensorFlow that processes the MNIST dataset.

Listing 4.2: tf2_keras_mnist_digit.py

```
import tensorflow as tf

mnist = tf.keras.datasets.mnist

(X_train, y_train), (X_test, y_test) = mnist.
    load_data()

print("X_train.shape:",X_train.shape)
print("X_test.shape: ",X_test.shape)

first_img = X_train[0]

# uncomment this line to see the pixel values
#print(first_img)

import matplotlib.pyplot as plt
plt.imshow(first_img, cmap='gray')
plt.show()
```

Listing 4.2 starts with some `import` statements and then populates the training data and test data from the MNIST dataset. The variable `first_img` is initialized as the first entry in the `X_train` array, which is the first image in the training dataset. The final block of code in Listing 4.2 displays the pixel values for the first image. The output from Listing 4.2 is here:

```
X_train.shape: (60000, 28, 28)

X_test.shape:  (10000, 28, 28)
```

Figure 4.7 displays the contents of the first image in the MNIST dataset.

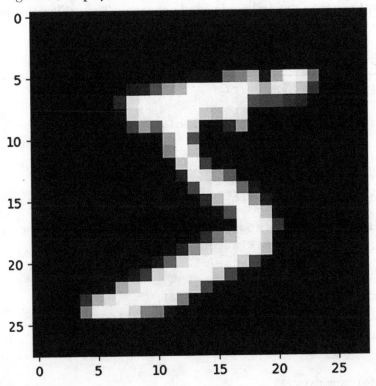

FIGURE 4.7 The First Image in the MNIST Dataset.

Keras and the MNIST Dataset

When you read code samples that contain Keras-based models that use the MNIST dataset, the models use a different API in the input layer.

Specifically, a model that is not a CNN flattens the input images into a one-dimensional vector via the tf.keras.layers.Flatten() API, an example of which is here (see Listing 4.3 for details):

```
tf.keras.layers.Flatten(input_shape=(28,28))
```

On the other hand, a CNN uses the tf.keras.layers.Conv2D() API, an example of which is here (see Listing 4.4 for details):

```
tf.keras.layers.Conv2D(32,(3,3),activation='relu',in
    put_shape=(28,28,1))
```

Listing 4.3 displays the contents of `keras_mnist.py` that illustrates how to create a `Keras`-based neural network in TensorFlow that processes the `MNIST` dataset.

Listing 4.3: keras_mnist.py

```
import tensorflow as tf

mnist = tf.keras.datasets.mnist
(x_train, y_train),(x_test, y_test) = mnist.load_
   data()

x_train, x_test = x_train / 255.0, x_test / 255.0

model = tf.keras.models.Sequential([
  tf.keras.layers.Flatten(input_shape=(28, 28)),
  tf.keras.layers.Dense(512, activation=tf.
   nn.relu),
  tf.keras.layers.Dropout(0.2),
  tf.keras.layers.Dense(10, activation=tf.
   nn.softmax)
])

model.summary()

model.compile(optimizer='adam',
             loss='sparse_categorical_
   crossentropy',
             metrics=['accuracy'])

model.fit(x_train, y_train, epochs=5)
model.evaluate(x_test, y_test)
```

Listing 4.3 starts with some `import` statements and then initializes the variable `mnist` as a reference to the built-in `MNIST` dataset. Next, the training-related and test-related variables are initialized with their respective portions of the `MNIST` dataset, followed by a scaling transformation for `x_train` and `x_test`.

The next portion of Listing 4.3 defines a very simple `Keras`-based model with four layers that are created from classes in the `tf.keras.layers` package. The next code snippet displays a summary of the model definition, as shown here:

```
Model: "sequential"
```

Layer (type)	Output Shape	Param #
flatten (Flatten)	(None, 784)	0
dense (Dense)	(None, 512)	401920
dropout (Dropout)	(None, 512)	0
dense_1 (Dense)	(None, 10)	5130

```
Total params: 407,050
Trainable params: 407,050
Non-trainable params: 0
```

The remaining portion of Listing 4.3 compiles, fits, and evaluates the model, which produces the following output:

```
Epoch 1/5
60000/60000 [==============================] - 14s
   225us/step - loss: 0.2186 - acc: 0.9360
Epoch 2/5
60000/60000 [==============================] - 14s
   225us/step - loss: 0.0958 - acc: 0.9704
Epoch 3/5
60000/60000 [==============================] - 14s
   232us/step - loss: 0.0685 - acc: 0.9783
Epoch 4/5
60000/60000 [==============================] - 14s
   227us/step - loss: 0.0527 - acc: 0.9832
Epoch 5/5
60000/60000 [==============================] - 14s
   225us/step - loss: 0.0426 - acc: 0.9861
10000/10000 [==============================] - 1s
   59us/step
```

As you can see, the final accuracy for this model is 98.6%, which is a respectable value.

Keras, CNNs, and the MNIST Dataset

Listing 4.4 displays the contents of keras_cnn_mnist.py that illustrates how to create a Keras-based neural network in TensorFlow that processes the MNIST dataset.

Listing 4.4: keras_cnn_mnist.py

```
import tensorflow as tf
import numpy as np
import matplotlib.pyplot as plt

(train_images, train_labels), (test_images, test_
    labels) = tf.keras.datasets.mnist.load_data()

train_images = train_images.reshape((60000, 28, 28,
    1))
test_images  = test_images.reshape((10000, 28, 28, 1))

# Normalize pixel values: from the range 0-255 to
    the range 0-1
train_images, test_images = train_images/255.0,
    test_images/255.0

model = tf.keras.models.Sequential()
model.add(tf.keras.layers.Conv2D(32, (3, 3),
    activation='relu', input_shape=(28, 28, 1)))
model.add(tf.keras.layers.MaxPooling2D((2, 2)))
model.add(tf.keras.layers.Conv2D(64, (3, 3),
    activation='relu'))
model.add(tf.keras.layers.MaxPooling2D((2, 2)))
model.add(tf.keras.layers.Conv2D(64, (3, 3),
    activation='relu'))
model.add(tf.keras.layers.Flatten())
model.add(tf.keras.layers.Dense(64,
    activation='relu'))
```

```
model.add(tf.keras.layers.Dense(10,
    activation='softmax'))

model.summary()

model.compile(optimizer='adam',
        loss='sparse_categorical_crossentropy',
        metrics=['accuracy'])

model.fit(train_images, train_labels, epochs=1)
test_loss, test_acc = model.evaluate(test_images,
    test_labels)
print(test_acc)

# predict the label of one image
test_image = np.expand_dims(test_images[300],
    axis = 0)
plt.imshow(test_image.reshape(28,28))
plt.show()

result = model.predict(test_image)
print("result:", result)
print("result.argmax():", result.argmax())
```

Listing 4.4 initializes the training data and labels, as well as the test data and labels, via the `load_data()` function. Next, the images are reshaped so that they are 28x28 images, and then the pixel values are rescaled from the range 0-255 (all integers) to the range 0-1 (decimal values).

The next portion of Listing 4.4 uses the `Keras Sequential()` API to define a `Keras`-based model called `model`, which contains two pairs of `Conv2D` and `MaxPooling2D` layers, followed by the `Flatten` layer, and then two consecutive `Dense` layers.

Next, the model is compiled, trained, and evaluated via the `compile()`, `fit()`, and `evaluate()` methods, respectively. The final portion of Listing 4.4 successfully predicts the image whose label is 4, which is then displayed via `Matplotlib`. Launch the code in Listing 4.4 and you will see the following output on the command line:

```
Model: "sequential"
```

Layer (type)	Output Shape	Param #
conv2d (Conv2D)	(None, 26, 26, 32)	320
max_pooling2d (MaxPooling2D)	(None, 13, 13, 32)	0
conv2d_1 (Conv2D)	(None, 11, 11, 64)	18496
max_pooling2d_1 (MaxPooling2)	(None, 5, 5, 64)	0
conv2d_2 (Conv2D)	(None, 3, 3, 64)	36928
flatten (Flatten)	(None, 576)	0
dense (Dense)	(None, 64)	36928
dense_1 (Dense)	(None, 10)	650

```
Total params: 93,322
Trainable params: 93,322
Non-trainable params: 0

60000/60000 [==============================] - 54s
   907us/sample - loss: 0.1452 - accuracy: 0.9563
10000/10000 [==============================] - 3s
   297us/sample - loss: 0.0408 - accuracy: 0.9868
0.9868
Using TensorFlow backend.
result: [[6.2746993e-05 1.7837329e-03 3.8957372e-04
   4.6143982e-06 9.9723744e-01
   1.5522403e-06 1.9182076e-04 3.0044283e-04
   2.2602901e-05 5.3929521e-06]]
result.argmax(): 4
```

Figure 4.8 displays the image that is displayed when you launch the code in Listing 4.4.

You might be asking yourself how the model in Listing 4.4 can achieve such high accuracy when every input image is flattened into a one-dimensional vector, which loses the *adjacency* information that is available in a two-dimensional image. Before CNNs became popular, one technique involved using MLPs and another technique involved SVMs as models for images. In fact, if you don't have enough images to train a model, you can still use an SVM. Another option is to generate synthetic data using a GAN (which was its original purpose).

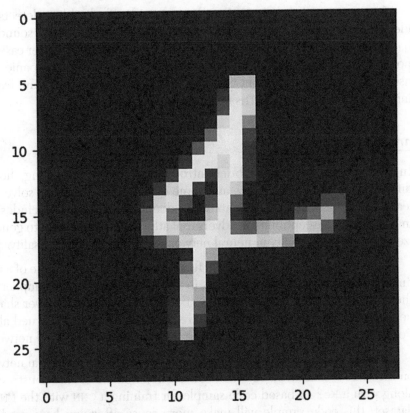

FIGURE 4.8 An Image in the MNIST Dataset.

Analyzing Audio Signals with CNNs

In addition to image classification, you can train CNNs with audio signals, which can be converted from analog to digital. Audio signals have various numeric parameters (such as decibel level and voltage level) that are described here:

https://en.wikipedia.org/wiki/Audio_signal

If you have a set of audio signals, the numeric values of their associated parameters become the dataset for a CNN. Remember that CNNs have no understanding of the numeric input values: the numeric values are processed in the same fashion, regardless of the source of the numeric values.

One use case involves a microphone outside of a building detects and identifies various sounds. Obviously it's important to identify the sound of a backfire from a vehicle versus the sound of a gunshot. In the latter case, the police would be notified about a potential crime. There are companies that use CNNs to identify different types of sounds; other companies are exploring the use of RNNs and LSTMs instead of CNNs.

Summary

In this chapter, you got a brief introduction to deep learning, how it differs from machine learning, and some of the problems it can solve. You learned about the challenges that exist in deep learning, which includes bias in algorithms, susceptibility to adversarial attacks, limited ability to generalize, lack of explainability in neural networks, and the lack of causality.

Next you learned about the XOR function, which is an example of a nonlinearly separable set of four points in the plane. Despite its simplicity in the 2D case, the XOR function cannot be solved with a single-layer shallow network: instead, two hidden layers are required. Next you learned about Perceptrons, which is essentially a core building block for neural networks.

You also saw a Keras-based code sample for training a neural network on the MNIST dataset. In addition, you learned how CNNs are constructed, along with a Keras-based code sample for training a CNN with the MNIST dataset: this code sample will make more sense after you have read the section pertaining to activation functions in Chapter 3.

DEEP LEARNING: RNNs AND LSTMs

This chapter extends the introduction from Chapter 4 by discussing RNNs (recurrent neural networks) and LSTMs (long short term memory). Although most of this chapter contains descriptive content regarding these architectures, there are Keras-based code samples. Hence, this would be a good point to read the Keras material in the associated appendix in case you haven't already done so.

The first part of this chapter introduces you to the architecture of RNNs, BPTT (back propagation through time), and a short Keras-based code sample. As you will see, RNNs can keep track of information from earlier time periods, which makes them useful for a variety of tasks, including NLP tasks.

The second part of this chapter introduces you to the architecture of LSTMs, which are more complex than RNNs. Specifically, LSTMs includes a forget gate, an input gate, and an output gate, as well as a long-term memory cell. You will also learn about the advantages of LSTMs over RNNs. In addition, you will be exposed to bidirectional LSTMs that are used in some well-known NLP-related models (see Chapter 6).

The third part of this chapter introduces you to the architecture of autoencoders and the rationale for using them, as well as an introduction to variational autoencoders.

Please keep in mind that the code samples in this chapter assume that you have some familiarity with Keras (discussed in Appendix A).

What Is an RNN?

An RNN is a Recurrent Neural Network, which is a type of architecture that was developed during the 1980s. RNNs are suitable for datasets that contain sequential data as well as for NLP tasks, such as language modeling, text generation, or autocompletion of sentences. In fact, you might be surprised to learn that you can even perform image classification (such as MNIST) via an RNN. Figure 5.1 displays the contents of a simple RNN.

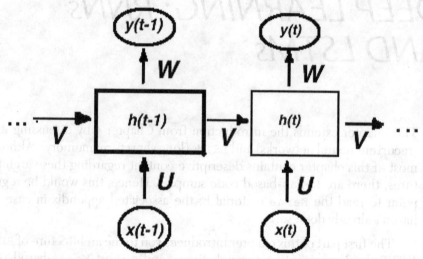

FIGURE 5.1 An Example of an RNN.

Image adapted from [Source: *https://commons.wikimedia.org/w/index. php?curid=60109157*]

In addition to simple RNNs there are more powerful constructs such as LSTMs and GRUs. A basic RNN has the simplest type of feedback mechanism (described later) and involves a sigmoid activation function.

RNNs (which includes LSTMs and GRUs) differ from ANNs in several important ways, as listed here:

- Statefulness (all RNNs)

- Feedback mechanism (all RNNs)

- A sigmoid or tanh activation function

- Multiple gates (LSTMs and GRUs)

- BPTT (Back Propagation Through Time)

- Truncated BPTT (simple RNNs)

First, ANNs and CNNs are essentially *stateless*, whereas RNNs are *stateful* because they have internal state. Hence, RNNs can process more complex sequences of inputs, which makes them suitable for tasks such as handwriting recognition and or speech recognition.

Anatomy of an RNN

Consider the RNN in Figure 5.1. Suppose that the sequence of inputs is labeled x1, x2, x3, ..., x(t), ... and also that the sequence of *hidden states* is labeled h1, h2, h3, ..., h(t). Note that each input sequence and hidden state is a 1xn vector, where n is the number of features.

At time period t, the input is based on a combination of h(t-1) and x(t), after which an activation function is applied to this combination (which can also involve adding a bias vector).

Another difference is the feedback mechanism for RNNs that occurs between consecutive time periods. Specifically, the output at a *previous* time period is combined with the new input of the *current* time period in order to calculate the new internal state. Let's use the sequence {h(0), h(1), h(2), . . . h(t-1), h(t)} to represent the set of internal states of an RNN during time periods {0, 1, 2, ..., t-1, t} and let's also suppose that the sequence {x(0), x(1), x(2), ..., x(t-1), x(t)} is the inputs during the same time periods.

The fundamental relationship for an RNN at time period t is here:

```
h(t) = f(W*x(t) + U*h(t-1))
```

In the preceding formula, W and U are weight matrices and f is typically the tanh activation function.

Here is a code snippet of a TF 2 Keras-based model that is based on the tf.keras.layers.SimpleRNN class:

```
import tensorflow as tf
...
model = tf.keras.models.Sequential()
model.add(tf.keras.layers.SimpleRNN(5, input_
    shape=(1,2), batch_input_shape=[1,1,2],
    stateful=True))
...
```

Perform an online search for more information and code samples involving `Keras` and RNNs.

What Is BPTT?

BPTT (back propagation through time) in RNNs is the counterpart to *backprop* for CNNs. The weight matrices of RNNs are updated during BPTT in order to train the neural network.

However, there is a problem called the *exploding gradient* that can occur in RNNs, which is to say that the gradient becomes arbitrary large (versus the gradient becoming arbitrary small in the so-called vanishing gradient scenario). One way to deal with the exploding gradient problem is to use a *truncated BPTT*, which means that BPTT is computed for a small number of steps instead of all time steps. Another technique is to specify a maximum value for the gradient, which involves simple conditional logic.

The good news is that there is another way to overcome both the exploding gradient and vanishing gradient problem, which involves LSTMs that are discussed later in this chapter.

Working with RNNs and `Keras`

Listing 5.1 displays the contents of `keras_rnn_model.py` that illustrates how to create a simple `Keras`-based RNN model.

Listing 5.1: keras_rnn_model.py

```
import tensorflow as tf

timesteps = 30
input_dim = 12

# number of units in RNN cell
units = 512

# number of classes to be identified
n_classes = 5
```

```
# Keras Sequential model with RNN and Dense layer
model = tf.keras.models.Sequential()
model.add(tf.keras.layers.SimpleRNN(units=units,
                 dropout=0.2,
                 input_shape=(timesteps, input_dim)))
model.add(tf.keras.layers.Dense(n_classes,
    activation='softmax'))

# model loss function and optimizer
model.compile(loss='categorical_crossentropy',
         optimizer=tf.keras.optimizers.Adam(),
         metrics=['accuracy'])

model.summary()
```

Listing 5.1 first initializes the variables `timesteps` (the number of time steps), `input_dim` (the number of elements in each input vector of numbers), `units` (the number of hidden units in the RNN neuron), and `n_classes` (the number of classes in the dataset).

The next portion of Listing 5.1 creates a `Keras`-based model that looks similar to earlier `Keras`-based models, with the exception of the code snippet for the RNN layer, as shown here:

```
model.add(tf.keras.layers.SimpleRNN(units=units,
        dropout=0.2,
        input_shape=(timesteps, input_dim)))
```

As you can see, the preceding code snippet adds an instance of the `SimpleRNN` class as well as the variables that are defined in the preceding code block.

The final portion of code invokes the `compile()` method, followed by the `summary()` method to display the structure of the model.

Launch the code in Listing 5.1 and you will see the following output:

```
Model: "sequential"
```

Layer (type)	Output Shape Shape	Param #
simple_rnn (SimpleRNN)	(None, 512)	268800
dense (Dense)	(None, 5)	2565

```
Total params: 271,365
Trainable params: 271,365
Non-trainable params: 0
```

Now that you see how easy it is to create an RNN-based model in Keras, let's look at an example of an RNN-based model in Keras that will be trained on the MNIST dataset, which is the topic of the next section.

Working with Keras, RNNs, and MNIST

Listing 5.2 displays the contents of keras_rnn_mnist.py that illustrates how to create a simple Keras-based RNN model that is trained on the MNIST dataset.

Listing 5.2: keras_rnn_mnist.py

```
#Simple RNN and MNIST dataset
import tensorflow as tf
import numpy as np

# instantiate mnist and load data:
mnist = tf.keras.datasets.mnist
(x_train, y_train), (x_test, y_test) = mnist.
   load_data()

# one-hot encoding for all labels to create 1x10
# vectors that are compared with the final layer:
y_train = tf.keras.utils.to_categorical(y_train)
y_test  = tf.keras.utils.to_categorical(y_test)
```

```
# resize and normalize the 28x28 images:
image_size = x_train.shape[1]
x_train = np.reshape(x_train,[-1, image_size,
    image_size])
x_test  = np.reshape(x_test, [-1, image_size,
    image_size])
x_train = x_train.astype('float32') / 255
x_test  = x_test.astype('float32')  / 255

# initialize some hyper- parameters:
input_shape = (image_size, image_size)
batch_size = 128
hidden_units = 128
dropout_rate = 0.3

# RNN-based Keras model with 128 hidden units:
model = tf.keras.models.Sequential()
model.add(tf.keras.layers.SimpleRNN(units=hidden_
    units,
                   dropout=dropout_rate,
                   input_shape=input_shape))
model.add(tf.keras.layers.Dense(num_labels))
model.add(tf.keras.layers.Activation('softmax'))
model.summary()

model.compile(loss='categorical_crossentropy',
            optimizer='sgd',
            metrics=['accuracy'])

# train the network on the training data:
model.fit(x_train, y_train, epochs=8, batch_
    size=batch_size)

#calculate and then display the accuracy:
loss, acc = model.evaluate(x_test, y_test, batch_
    size=batch_size)
print("\nTest accuracy: %.1f%%" % (100.0 * acc))
```

Listing 5.2 contains the usual import statements, followed by the initialization of the `mnist` variable as a reference to the `MNIST` dataset, after which the four variables for the training data and the test data are initialized.

The next portion of Listing 5.2 ensures that the training images and test images are resized as 28x28 images, after which the pixel values (which are in the range of 0 to 255) in these images are scaled down so that they are in the range of 0 to 1. The next portion of Listing 5.2 is very similar to Listing 5.1: some hyper parameters are initialized and then an RNN-based model in `Keras` is created.

At this point we have new code, starting with the code snippet that saves the model structure in the `rnn-mnist.png` file. A second new code block invokes the `compile()` method to synch up the model with the training data, followed by the `fit()` method that trains the model.

The final portion of Listing 5.2 evaluates the trained model on the test data and displays the values of `loss` and `acc` that correspond to the loss and the accuracy, respectively, of the model on the test data. Launch the code in Listing 5.2 and you will see the following output:

```
Model: "sequential"
```

Layer (type)	Output Shape	Param #
simple_rnn (SimpleRNN)	(None, 256)	72960
dense (Dense)	(None, 10)	2570
activation (Activation)	(None, 10)	0

```
Total params: 75,530
Trainable params: 75,530
Non-trainable params: 0

Epoch 1/5
60000/60000 [==============================] - 33s
   542us/sample - loss: 0.8198 - accuracy: 0.7605
```

```
Epoch 2/5
 6528/60000 [==>.........................] - ETA:
    27s - loss: 0.4661 - accuracy: 0.8627
60000/60000 [==============================] - 34s
    559us/sample - loss: 0.3724 - accuracy: 0.8917
Epoch 3/5
60000/60000 [==============================] - 33s
    545us/sample - loss: 0.2764 - accuracy: 0.9183
Epoch 4/5
60000/60000 [==============================] - 33s
    545us/sample - loss: 0.2269 - accuracy: 0.9327
Epoch 5/5
60000/60000 [==============================] - 34s
    561us/sample - loss: 0.1983 - accuracy: 0.9407
10000/10000 [==============================] - 2s
    237us/sample - loss: 0.1396 - accuracy: 0.9577
Test accuracy: 95.8%
```

Working with TensorFlow and RNNs (Optional)

The code sample in this section is optional because it's based on Tensor-Flow 1.x. As this book goes to print, Google released TensorFlow 2, after which TensorFlow 1.x becomes legacy code that will be supported for one additional year. Keep this in mind when you encounter any other code samples in this book that involve TensorFlow 1.x.

However, this code sample does provide some low-level details regarding the output and the state for each hidden layer in an RNN neuron, which can give you some insight into how the calculations are performed and the values that are generated. Keep in mind that the data for the two time steps is simulated, which is to say that the data does not reflect any meaningful use case. The purpose of the simplified data is to help you focus on the way in which calculations are performed.

Listing 5.3 displays the contents of `dynamic_rnn_2TP.py` that illustrates how to create a simple TensorFlow-based RNN model.

Listing 5.3: dynamic_rnn_2TP.py

```python
import tensorflow as tf
import numpy as np

n_steps = 2     # number of time steps
n_inputs = 3    # number of inputs per time unit
n_neurons = 5  # number of hidden units

X_batch = np.array([
  # t = 0        t = 1
  [[0, 1, 2], [9, 8, 7]], # instance 0
  [[3, 4, 5], [0, 0, 0]], # instance 1
  [[6, 7, 8], [6, 5, 4]], # instance 2
  [[9, 0, 1], [3, 2, 1]], # instance 3
])

#sequence_length <= # of elements in each batch
seq_length_batch = np.array([2, 1, 2, 2])

X = tf.placeholder(dtype=tf.float32, shape=[None,
    n_steps, n_inputs])
seq_length = tf.placeholder(tf.int32, [None])

basic_cell = tf.nn.rnn_cell.BasicRNNCell(num_
    units=n_neurons)
outputs, states = tf.nn.dynamic_rnn(basic_cell, X,
    sequence_length=seq_length, dtype=tf.float32)

with tf.Session() as sess:
  sess.run(tf.global_variables_initializer())
  outputs_val, states_val = sess.run([outputs,
    states],
                  feed_dict={X:X_batch, seq_
    length:seq_length_batch})

  print("X_batch     shape:", X_batch.shape)
        # (4,2,3)
  print("outputs_val shape:", outputs_val.shape)
        # (4,2,5)
```

```
print("states_val  shape:", states_val.shape)
     # (4,5)

print("outputs_val:",outputs_val)
print("--------------------------\n")
print("states_val: ",states_val)

##################################################
  #################
# outputs => output of ALL RNN states
# states  => output of LAST ACTUAL RNN state
  (ignores zero vector)
# state = output[1] for full sequences
# state = output[0] for short sequences
##################################################
  #################
```

Listing 5.3 starts by initializing n_steps (the number of time steps), n_inputs (the number of inputs), and n_neurons (the number of neurons) to 2, 3, and 5, respectively.

Next the NumPy array X_batch is a 4x2x3 array that is initialized with integers. As you can see from the comment line, the first column of values are for time step 0, and the second column of values are for the time step 1. You can also think of each row of data in X_batch as an instance of data for both time steps.

Next, the variable seq_length_batch is a one-dimensional vector of integers, each of which specifies that number of time steps that appear to the left of a vector consisting of purely zero values. As you can see, this vector contains the value 2 for instances number 0, 2, and 3, and the value 0 for instance number 1.

The next portion of Listing 5.3 defines the placeholder X that can hold an arbitrary number of arrays whose shape is [n_steps, n_inputs]. Now we're ready to define an RNN cell and specify its outputs and states, as shown here:

```
basic_cell = tf.nn.rnn_cell.BasicRNNCell(num_
    units=n_neurons)
outputs, states = tf.nn.dynamic_rnn(basic_cell, X,
    sequence_length=seq_length, dtype=tf.float32)
```

The key point to remember is that the final output value from the right-most hidden unit is the value that is passed to the next neuron.

Launch the code in Listing 5.3 and you will see the following output, where the value of interest is shown in bold:

```
#---------------------------
#outputs_val:
#[[[-0.09700205  0.7671716   0.6775758   0.01522888
    0.5460828 ]
#  [ 0.92776424 -0.5916748   0.67824966  0.99423325
    0.9999991 ]]
#
#  [[ 0.24040672  0.81568515  0.8890421   0.780813
    0.99762475]
#  [ 0.          0.          0.          0.          0.
     ]]
#
#  [[ 0.5282535   0.8549201   0.9647311   0.9692446
    0.99999046]
#  [ 0.9725177  -0.7165484   0.46688017  0.9411293
    0.9999323 ]]
#
#  [[ 0.81080747 -0.9926888   0.56612366  0.9561879
    0.9997731 ]
#  [ 0.48786768 -0.7099759  -0.7283263   0.76442945
    0.9971904 ]]]
#---------------------------
#states_val:
#[[ 0.92776424 -0.5916748   0.67824966  0.99423325
    0.9999991 ]
#  [ 0.24040672  0.81568515  0.8890421   0.780813
    0.99762475]
#  [ 0.9725177  -0.7165484   0.46688017  0.9411293
    0.9999323 ]
#  [ 0.48786768 -0.7099759  -0.7283263   0.76442945
    0.9971904 ]]
#---------------------------
```

In the preceding output, notice that the row count of the rows shown in bold are 2, 1, 2, 2, *which is exactly the same as the values in* `seq_length_batch`. As you can see, these highlighted rows appear (also in bold) in the array labeled `states_val`.

Listing 5.3 is a very small and artificial example of an RNN, and hopefully this example gives you a better understanding of the inner workings of an RNN. There are many variants of RNNs, and you can read about some of them here:

https://en.wikipedia.org/wiki/Recurrent_neural_network

What Is an LSTM?

LSTMs are a special type of RNN, and they are well suited for many use cases, including NLP, speech recognition, and handwriting recognition. LSTMs are well suited for handling something called *long term dependency*, which refers to the distance gap between relevant information and the location where that information is required. This situation arises when information in one section of a document needs to be linked to information that is in a more distant location of the document.

LSTMs were developed in 1997 and went on to exceed the accuracy performance of state-of-the-art algorithms. LSTMs also began revolutionizing speech recognition (circa 2007). Then in 2009 an LSTM won pattern recognition contests, and in 2014, Baidu used RNNs to exceed speech recognition records. Navigate to the following link in order to see an example of an LSTM: *https://commons.wikimedia.org/w/index.php?curid=60149410*

Anatomy of an LSTM

LSTMs are *stateful* and they contain three gates (forget gate, input gate, and an output gate) that involve a sigmoid function, and also a cell state that involves the `tanh` activation function. At time period `t` the input to an LSTM is based on a combination of the two vectors `h(t-1)` and `x(t)`. This pair of inputs is combined, after which a sigmoid activation function is applied to this combination (which can also include a bias vector) in the case of the forget gate, input gate, and the output gate.

The processing that occurs at time step `t` is the short term memory of an `LSTM`. The internal cell state of `LSTMs` maintains long term memory. Updating the internal cell state involves the `tanh` activation function, whereas the other gates use the sigmoid activation function, as mentioned in the previous paragraph. Here is a TF 2 code block that defines `Keras`-based model for an `LSTM`:

```
import tensorflow as tf
. . .
model = tf.keras.models.Sequential()
model.add(tf.keras.layers.LSTMCell(6,batch_input_
    shape=(1,1,1),kernel_initializer='ones',statefu
    l=True))
model.add(tf.keras.layers.Dense(1))
. . .
```

You can learn about the difference between an `LSTM` and an `LSTMCell` here:

> *https://stackoverflow.com/questions/48187283/whats-the-difference-between-lstm-and-lstmcell*

In case you're interested, additional information about `LSTMs` and also how to define a custom `LSTM` cell is here:

> *https://en.wikipedia.org/wiki/Recurrent_neural_network*

> *https://stackoverflow.com/questions/54231440/define-custom-lstm-cell-in-keras*

Bidirectional LSTMs

In addition to one-directional LSTMs, you can also define a *bidirectional* `LSTM` that consists of two regular `LSTMs`: one `LSTM` for the forward direction and one `LSTM` in the backward or opposite direction. You might be surprised to discover that bidirectional `LSTMs` are well suited for solving NLP tasks.

For instance, `ELMo` is a deep word representation for NLP tasks that uses bidirectional `LSTMs`. An even newer architecture in the NLP world is called a *transformer*, and bidirectional transformers are used in `BERT`, which is a very well-known system (released by Google in 2018) that can solve complex NLP problems.

The following TF 2 code block contains a `Keras`-based model that involves bidirectional LSTMs:

```
import tensorflow as tf
. . .
model = Sequential()
model.add(Bidirectional(LSTM(10, return_
    sequences=True), input_shape=(5,10)))
model.add(Bidirectional(LSTM(10)))
model.add(Dense(5))
model.add(Activation('softmax'))
model.compile(loss='categorical_crossentropy',
    optimizer='rmsprop')
. . .
```

The previous code block contains two bidirectional LSTM cells, both of which are shown in bold.

LSTM Formulas

The formulas for LSTMs are more complex than the update formula for a simple RNN, but there are some patterns that can help you understand those formulas.

Navigate to the following link in order to see the formulas for an LSTM:

https://en.wikipedia.org/wiki/Long_short-term_memory#cite_note-lstm1997-1]

The formulas show you how the new weights are calculated for the forget gate f, the input gate i, and the output gate i during time step t. In addition, the preceding link shows you how the new internal state and the hidden state (both at time step t) are calculated.

Notice the pattern for gates f, i, and o: all of them calculate the sum of two terms, each of which is a product involving x(t) and h(t), after which the sigmoid function is applied to that sum. Specifically, here's the formula for the *forget gate* at time t:

```
f(t) = sigma(W(f)*x(t) + U(f)*h(t) + b(f))
```

In the preceding formula, W(f), U(f), and b(f) are the weight matrices associated with x(t), the weight matrix associated with h(t), and the bias vector for the forget gate f, respectively.

Notice that the calculations for i(t) and o(t) have the same pattern as the calculation for f(t). The difference is that i(t) has the matrices W(i) and U(i), whereas o(t) has the matrices W(o) and U(o). Thus, f(t), i(t), and o(t) have a *parallel construction.*

The calculations for c(t), i(t), and h(t) are based on the values for f(t), i(t), and o(t), as shown here:

```
c(t)  = f(t) * c(t-1) + i(t) * tanh(c'(t))
c'(t) = sigma(W(c) * x(t) + U(c) * h(t-1))
h(t)  = o(t) * tanh(c(t))
```

The final state of an LSTM is a one-dimensional vector that contains the output from all the other layers in the LSTM. If you have a model that contains multiple LSTMs, the final state vector for a given LSTM becomes the input for the next LSTM in that model.

LSTM Hyperparameter Tuning

LSTMs are also prone to overfitting, and here is a list of things to consider if you are manually optimizing hyper parameters for LSTMs:

- Overfitting (use regularization such as L1 or L2)
- Larger networks are more prone to overfitting
- More data tends to reduce overfitting
- Train the networks over multiple epochs
- The learning rate is vitally important
- It can be helpful to stack layers
- Use softsign instead of softmax for LSTMs
- RMSprop, AdaGrad, or momentum are good choices
- Xavier weight initialization

Perform an online search to obtain more information about the optimizers in the preceding list.

Working with TensorFlow and LSTMs (Optional)

Listing 5.4 displays the contents of dynamic_lstm_2TP.py that illustrates how to create a simple LSTM model with TensorFlow 1.x code.

Listing 5.4: dynamic_lstm_2TP.py

```python
import tensorflow as tf
import numpy as np

n_steps = 2   # number of time steps
n_inputs = 3  # number of inputs per time unit
n_neurons = 5 # number of hidden units

X_batch = np.array([
  # t = 0        t = 1
  [[0, 1, 2], [9, 8, 7]], # instance 0
  [[3, 4, 5], [0, 0, 0]], # instance 1
  [[6, 7, 8], [6, 5, 4]], # instance 2
  [[9, 0, 1], [3, 2, 1]], # instance 3
])

seq_length_batch = np.array([2, 1, 2, 2])

X = tf.placeholder(dtype=tf.float32,shape=[None,
    n_steps,n_inputs])
seq_length = tf.placeholder(tf.int32, [None])

basic_cell = tf.nn.rnn_cell.BasicLSTMCell(num_
    units=n_neurons)
outputs, states = tf.nn.dynamic_rnn(basic_cell, X,
    sequence_length=seq_length, dtype=tf.float32)

with tf.Session() as sess:
  sess.run(tf.global_variables_initializer())
  outputs_val, states_val = sess.run([outputs,
    states],
              feed_dict={X:X_batch, seq_
    length:seq_length_batch})

  print("X_batch    shape:", X_batch.shape)
         # (4,2,3)
```

(Continued)

```
print("outputs_val shape:", outputs_val.shape)
      # (4,2,5)
print("states:              ", states_val)
      # LSTMStateTuple(...)

print("outputs_val:",outputs_val)
print("---------------------------\n")
print("states_val: ",states_val)
```

The first half of Listing 5.4 is identical to the first half of Listing 5.3, and the first line of code that is different involves defining `basic_cell` as an LSTM (shown in bold), which is reproduced here:

```
basic_cell = tf.nn.rnn_cell.BasicLSTMCell(num_units=n_
neurons)

outputs, states = tf.nn.dynamic_rnn(basic_cell, X,
sequence_length=seq_length, dtype=tf.float32)
```

Notice that outputs and states in Listing 5.4 are initialized in exactly the same fashion as shown in Listing 5.3. The next portion of code is a `tf.Session()` code block that is the training loop.

Another difference to notice in Listing 5.4: during each computation in the training loop: `states_val` is actually an instance of `LSTMStatesTuple`, whereas `states_val` in Listing 5.3 is a 4x5 tensor. Launch the code in Listing 5.4 and you will see the following output:

```
('X_batch       shape:', (4, 2, 3))
('outputs_val shape:', (4, 2, 5))

('states:             ', LSTMStateTuple(c=array(
  [[-1.0492262 , -0.1059267 , -0.27163735,
  -0.64399946,  0.06018598],
   [-0.7445494 ,  0.00723887, -0.11805946,
  -0.26550752,  0.21816696],
   [-1.4126835 ,  0.05187892, -0.07408151,
  -0.66379607,  0.1348486 ],
   [-0.5987958 ,  0.24536057, -0.16916996,
  -0.8177415 ,  0.39747238]],
```

```
    dtype=float32), h=array(
      [[-7.33636796e-01, -6.07701950e-02,
  -1.40444040e-01,
          -2.65002381e-02, 5.37334010e-04],
        [-4.83454257e-01, 3.39480606e-03,
  -3.36034223e-02,
          -2.59866733e-02, 4.49425131e-02],
        [-7.36429453e-01, 2.63450593e-02,
  -4.42487188e-02,
          -1.05846934e-01, 5.22684120e-03],
        [-3.73311013e-01, 1.35892674e-01,
  -9.72046256e-02,
          -2.79455721e-01, 5.36275432e-02]],
    dtype=float32)))

('outputs_val:', array([
        [[-1.39581457e-01, -8.17378387e-02,
  -8.70967656e-02,
          -3.05497926e-02,  1.16406225e-01],
        [-7.33636796e-01, -6.07701950e-02,
  -1.40444040e-01,
          -2.65002381e-02,  5.37334010e-04]],

        [[-4.83454257e-01,  3.39480606e-03,
  -3.36034223e-02,
          -2.59866733e-02,  4.49425131e-02],
        [ 0.00000000e+00,  0.00000000e+00,
  0.00000000e+00,
          0.00000000e+00,  0.00000000e+00]],

        [[-6.21303201e-01,  4.13885061e-03,
  -6.17417134e-03,
          -8.89408588e-03,  4.83810157e-03],
        [-7.36429453e-01,  2.63450593e-02,
  -4.42487188e-02,
          -1.05846934e-01,  5.22684120e-03]],
```

(Continued)

```
     [[-1.01410240e-01,   4.99857590e-02,
        -9.47358180e-03,
        -3.74739647e-01,   9.64458846e-03],
      [-3.73311013e-01,   1.35892674e-01,
        -9.72046256e-02,
        -2.79455721e-01,   5.36275432e-02]]],
      dtype=float32))
-----------------------------

('states_val: ',  LSTMStateTuple(c=array(
   [[-1.0492262 ,  -0.1059267 ,  -0.27163735,
   -0.64399946,   0.06018598],
    [-0.7445494 ,   0.00723887,  -0.11805946,
   -0.26550752,   0.21816696],
    [-1.4126835 ,   0.05187892,  -0.07408151,
   -0.66379607,   0.1348486 ],
    [-0.5987958 ,   0.24536057,  -0.16916996,
   -0.8177415 ,   0.39747238]],
   dtype=float32), h=array(
     [[-7.33636796e-01,  -6.07701950e-02,
        -1.40444040e-01,
      -2.65002381e-02,   5.37334010e-04],
      [-4.83454257e-01,   3.39480606e-03,
        -3.36034223e-02,
      -2.59866733e-02,   4.49425131e-02],
      [-7.36429453e-01,   2.63450593e-02,
        -4.42487188e-02,
      -1.05846934e-01,   5.22684120e-03],
      [-3.73311013e-01,   1.35892674e-01,
        -9.72046256e-02,
      -2.79455721e-01,   5.36275432e-02]],
      dtype=float32)))
```

There are two things in particular to notice about the output. First, examine the middle portion displayed in bold in the preceding output, and notice that these are the same values that are displayed in the final output block in the output section labeled states_val.

Next, the second code block that is displayed in bold contains two vectors: a non-zero vector followed by a zero vector, which corresponds to the data labeled `instance 1` in Listing 5.4.

What Are GRUs?

A GRU (Gated Recurrent Unit) is an RNN that is a simplified type of LSTM. The key difference between a GRU and an LSTM: a GRU has two gates (reset and update gates) whereas an LSTM has three gates (reset, output and forget gates). The reset gate in a GRU performs the functionality of the input gate and the forget gate of an LSTM.

Keep in mind that GRUs and LSTMs both have the goal of tracking long-term dependencies effectively, and they both address the problem of vanishing gradients and exploding gradients. Navigate to the following link in order to see an example of a GRU:

https://commons.wikimedia.org/wiki/File:Gated_Recurrent_Unit,_base_type.svg

Navigate to the following link in order to see the formulas for a GRU (which are similar to the formulas for an LSTM):

https://en.wikipedia.org/wiki/Gated_recurrent_unit

What Are Autoencoders?

An autoencoder (AE) is a neural network that is similar to an MLP where the output layer is the same as the input layer. The simplest type of AE contains a single hidden layer that has fewer neurons than either the input layer or the output layer. However, there are many different types of AEs in which there are multiple hidden layers, sometimes containing more neurons than the input layer (and sometimes containing fewer neurons).

An AE uses unsupervised learning and back propagation to learn an efficient data encoding. Their purpose is dimensionality reduction: AEs set the input values equal to the inputs and then try to find the identity function. Figure 5.2 displays a simple AE that involves a single hidden layer.

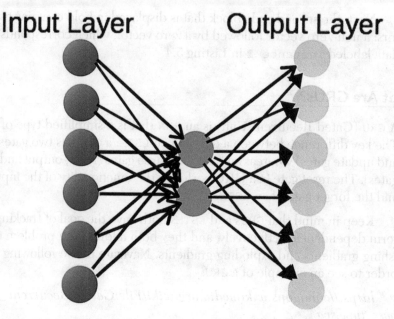

FIGURE 5.2 A Basic Autoencoder.

Image adapted from [Philippe Remy, Source: *http://philipperemy. github.io/anomaly-detection/*

In essence, a basic AE compresses the input to an "intermediate" vector with fewer dimensions than the input data, and then transforms that vector into a tensor with the same shape as the input. Several use cases for AEs are listed below:

- Document retrieval
- Classification
- Anomaly detection
- Adversarial autoencoders
- Image denoising (generating clear images)

An example of using TensorFlow and `Keras` with an autoencoder in order to perform fraud detection is here:

https://www.datascience.com/blog/fraud-detection-with-tensorflow

AEs can also be used for feature extraction because they can yield better results than PCA. Keep in mind that AEs are data-specific, which means that they only work with similar data. However, they differ from image compression (and are mediocre for data compression). For example, an autoencoder trained on faces would work poorly on pictures of trees. In summary, an AE involves:

- "squeezing" the input to a smaller layer

- learning a representation for a set of data

- is done typically for dimensionality reduction (PCA)

- keeping only the middle "compressed" layer

As a high-level example, consider a 10x10 image (100 pixels), and an AE that has 100 neurons (10x10 pixels), a hidden layer with 50 neurons, and an output layer with 100 neurons. Hence, the AE compresses 100 neurons to 50 neurons.

As you saw earlier, there are numerous variations of the basic AE, some of which are listed below:

- LSTM autoencoders

- Denoising autoencoders

- Contractive autoencoders

- Sparse autoencoders

- Stacked autoencoders

- Deep autoencoders

- Linear autoencoders

If you're interested, the following link contains a wide assortment of auto-encoders, including those that are mentioned in this section:

https://www.google.com/search?sa=X&q=Autoencoder&tbm=isch&so urce=univ&ved=2ahUKEwjo-8zRrIniAhUGup4KHVgvC10QiR56BAgME BY&biw=967&bih=672

Perform an online search for code samples and more details regarding AEs and their associated use cases.

Autoencoders and PCA

The optimal solution to an autoencoder is strongly related to principal component analysis (PCA) if the autoencoder involves linear activations or only a single sigmoid hidden layer.

The weights of an autoencoder with a single hidden layer of size p (where p is less than the size of the input) span the same vector subspace as the one spanned by the first p principal components.

The output of the autoencoder is an orthogonal projection onto this subspace. The autoencoder weights are not equal to the principal components, and are generally not orthogonal, yet the principal components may be recovered from them using the singular value decomposition.

What Are Variational Autoencoders?

In very brief terms, a Variational autoencoder is sort of an enhanced regular autoencoder in which the left side acts as an encoder, and the right side acts as a decoder. Both sides have a probability distribution associated with the encoding and decoding process.

In addition, both the encoder and the decoder are actually neural networks. The input for the encoder is a vector x of numeric values, and its output is a hidden representation z that has weights and biases. The decoder has input a (i.e., the output of the encoder), and its output is the parameters of a probability distribution of the data, which also has weights and biases. Note that the probability distributions for the encoder and the decoder are different. If you want to learn more about VAEs, navigate to the Wikipedia page that discusses VAEs in a detailed fashion:

https://en.wikipedia.org/wiki/Autoencoder#Variational_autoencoder_.28VAE.29

Figure 5.3 displays a high-level and simplified VAE that involves a single hidden layer.

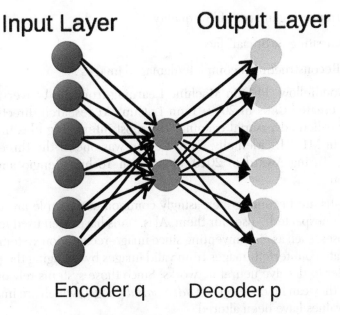

Input Layer

Output Layer

Encoder q

Decoder p

FIGURE 5.3 A Variational Autoencoder.

Another interesting model architecture is a combination of a CNN and a VAE, which you can read about here:

https://towardsdatascience.com/gans-vs-autoencoders-comparison-of-deep-generative-models-985cf15936ea

In the next section, you will learn about GANs and how to combine a VAE with a GAN.

What Are GANs?

A GAN is an acronym for Generative Adversarial Network whose original purpose was to generate synthetic data, typically for augmenting small datasets or unbalanced datasets. One use case pertains to missing persons: supply the available images of those persons to a GAN in order to generate an image of how those people might look today. There are many other use cases for GANs, some of which are listed here:

- Generating art
- Creating fashion styles

- Improving images of low quality

- Creating "artificial" faces

- Reconstructing incomplete/damaged images

Ian Goodfellow (PhD in Machine Learning from the University of Montreal) created GANs in 2014. Yann LeCun (AI research director at Facebook) called adversarial training "the most interesting idea in the last 10 years in ML." Incidentally, Yann LeCun was one of the three recipients of the Turing Award in 2019, along with Yoshua Bengio and Geoffrey Hinton.

GANs are becoming increasingly common and people are finding creative (unexpected?) uses for them. Alas, GANs have been used for nefarious purposes, such as circumventing since image-recognition systems. GANs can generate counterfeit images from valid images by changing the pixel values in order to deceive neural networks. Since those systems rely on pixel patterns, they can be deceived via *adversarial images*, which are images whose pixel values have been altered.

Navigate to the following link in order to see an example of a GAN that distorts the image of a panda: *https://arxiv.org/pdf/1412.6572.pdf*

An article that delves into details of adversarial examples (including the misclassified panda) is here:

https://openai.com/blog/adversarial-example-research/

According to an MIT paper, the modified values that trigger misclassifications exploit precise patterns that the image system associates with specific objects. The researchers noticed that data sets contain two types of correlations: patterns that are correlated with the dataset data, and nongeneralizable patterns in the dataset data. GANs successfully exploit the latter correlations in order to deceive image-recognition systems. Details of the MIT paper are here: *https://gandissect.csail.mit.edu*.

Can Adversarial Attacks Be Stopped?

Unfortunately, there are no long-term solutions to adversarial attacks, and given their nature, it might never be possible to completely defend against them. Although various techniques are being developed to thwart adversarial attacks, their effectiveness tends to be short-lived: new GANs are created that can outwit those techniques. The following article contains more information about adversarial attacks:

https://www.technologyreview.com/s/613170/emtech-digital-dawn-song-adversarial-machine-learning

Interestingly, GANs can have problems in terms of convergence, just like other neural networks. One technique for addressing this problem is called *minibatch discrimination*, details of which are here:

https://www.inference.vc/understanding-minibatch-discrimination-in-gans/

Please note that the preceding link involves Kullback Leibler Divergence and JS Divergence, which are more advanced topics. The preceding blog post also contains a link to the following Jupyter notebook:

https://gist.github.com/fhuszar/a91c7d0672036335c1783d02c3a3dfe5

If you're interested in working with GANs, this GitHub link contains Python and TensorFlow code samples for constructing attacks and defenses:

https://github.com/tensorflow/cleverhans

Creating a GAN

A GAN has two main parts: a *generator* and a *discriminator*. The generator can have a CNN-like architecture for the purpose of generating images, whereas the discriminator can have a CNN-like architecture in order to detect whether or not an image (provided by the generator) is real or fake. By way of analogy, a generator is analogous to a person who makes counterfeit money, and a discriminator is analogous to a law enforcement officer who tries to distinguish between valid currency and counterfeit currency.

The generator (which has previously been initialized) sends fake images to the discriminator (already trained but no longer updateable) for analysis. If the discriminator is highly accurate in terms of detecting real and fake images, then the generator needs to be modified in order to improve the quality of fake images that are produced. The modification to the generator is performed by backward error propagation. On the other hand, if the discriminator performs poorly, then the generator is generating high quality fake images, and therefore the generator does not require significant modification.

Listing 5.5 displays the contents of `keras_create_gan.py` that defines a Python function for creating a GAN.

Listing 5.4: keras_create_gan.py

```python
import tensorflow as tf

def build_generator(img_shape, z_dim):
  model = tf.keras.models.Sequential()
  # Fully connected layer
  model.add(tf.keras.layers.Dense(128, input_dim=z_dim))
  # Leaky ReLU activation
  model.add(tf.keras.layers.
    LeakyReLU(alpha=0.01))
  # Output layer with tanh activation
  model.add(tf.keras.layers.Dense(28 * 28 * 1,
    activation='tanh'))
  # Reshape the Generator output to image dimensions
  model.add(tf.keras.layers.Reshape(img_shape))
  return model

def build_discriminator(img_shape):
  model = tf.keras.models.Sequential()
  # Flatten the input image
  model.add(tf.keras.layers.Flatten(input_
    shape=img_shape))
  # Fully connected layer
  model.add(tf.keras.layers.Dense(128))
  # Leaky ReLU activation
  model.add(tf.keras.layers.
    LeakyReLU(alpha=0.01))
  # Output layer with sigmoid activation
  model.add(tf.keras.layers.Dense(1,
    activation='sigmoid'))
  return model
```

```python
def build_gan(generator, discriminator):
  # ensure that the discriminator is not trainable
  discriminator.trainable = False
  # the GAN connects the generator and descriminator
  gan = tf.keras.models.Sequential()

  # start with the generator:
  gan.add(generator)

  # then add the discriminator:
  gan.add(discriminator)

  # compile gan
  opt = tf.keras.optimizers.Adam(lr=0.0002,
    beta_1=0.5)
  gan.compile(loss='binary_crossentropy',
    optimizer=opt)
  return gan

gen = build_generator(...)
dis = build_discriminator(...)
gan = build_gan(gen, dis)
```

As you can see, the Python function in Listing 5.5 contains three Python methods for build_generator(), build_discriminator(), and build_gan() for creating generator, a discriminator, and a GAN, respectively.

The GAN is initialized with a generator and then a discriminator, both of which are parameters for this function. Notice that the discriminator in the build_gan() method is not trainable, which is ensured with this code snippet:

```python
discriminator.trainable = False
```

Another point to notice is that the preceding Python functions do not create CNN-like architectures. A different way to create a discriminator is shown in the following code block (details are omitted):

```
dis = build_discriminator(...)
gen_model = tf.keras.models.Sequential()
gen_model.add(tf.keras.layers.Dense(...)
gen_model.add(tf.keras.layers.
  LeakyReLU(alpha=0.2))
gen_model.add(tf.keras.layers.Reshape(...)

# code for upsampling
gen_model.add(tf.keras.layers.Conv2DTranspose(...)
gen_model.add(tf.keras.layers.LeakyReLU(...)
...
gen_model.add(tf.keras.layers.Reshape(...)
gen_model.add(tf.keras.layers.LeakyReLU(...)

# output layer
gen_model.add(tf.keras.layers.Conv2D(...))
```

The preceding code block involves the Conv2D() class and the Leaky-ReLU() class (similar to ReLU), but notice there is no max pooling layer. Check online documentation for an explanation of upsampling and the purpose of the TensorFlow/Keras classes LeakyReLU() and Conv2DTranspose().

A High-Level View of GANs

There are numerous types of GANs, such as DCGANs (Deep Convolutional GANs), cGANs (Conditional GANs), and StyleGANs. In general, creating GANs involves the following high-level sequence of steps:

- Step 1) Select a dataset (ex: MNIST or cifar10)
- Step 2) Define and train the Discriminator Model
- Step 3) Define and use the Generator Model
- Step 4) Train the Generator Model
- Step 5) Evaluate GAN Model performance
- Step 6) Use the final Generator Model

Although GANs can be similar to CNNs, there are some important differences in the layers that are used. First, the convolution layer in GANs often has a stride of (2, 2), which is to say that the convolutional filter moves two columns at a time, and then shifts downward two rows at a time. Next, GANs contain a `LeakyReLU` activation function that is slightly different from the `ReLU` activation functions. Third, GANs do not have a max pooling layer.

In addition, GANs also involve the concept of upscaling, which in a sense is like the opposite of downscaling (i.e., max pooling). Perform an online search for more information regarding the details of GANs.

The VAE-GAN Model

Another interesting model is the VAE-GAN model, which is a hybrid of a VAE and a `GAN`, and details about this model are here:

https://towardsdatascience.com/gans-vs-autoencoders-comparison-of-deep-generative-models-985cf15936ea

According to the preceding link, GANs are superior to VAEs, but they are also difficult to work with and require a lot of data and tuning. If you're interested, a `GAN` tutorial (by the same author) is available here:

https://github.com/mrdragonbear/GAN-Tutorial

Summary

In this chapter, you learned about the architecture of an RNN, some tasks that you can solve due to its stateful architecture, followed by a `Keras`-based code sample. Next you saw the architecture of an LSTM, as well as a basic code sample.

In addition, you saw a TensorFlow 1.x code sample for an LSTM cell whose output shows you the path of some of the internal calculations that are performed. In addition, you learned about Variational Autoencoders and some of their use cases.

Finally, you got an introduction to GANs, a high-level description of how to construct them, and also how they are trained.

6

NLP AND REINFORCEMENT LEARNING

This chapter provides a casual introduction to NLP (Natural Language Processing) and Reinforcement Learning (RL). Both topics can easily fill entire books, often involving complex topics, which means that this chapter provides a limited introduction to these topics. If you want to acquire a thorough grasp of BERT (discussed briefly later in the chapter), you need to learn about *attention* and the transformer architecture. Similarly, if you want to acquire a solid understanding of deep reinforcement learning, then you need to understand deep learning architectures. After you finish reading the cursory introduction to NLP and RL in this chapter, you can find additional online information about the facets of NLP or RL that interest you.

The first section discusses NLP, along with some code samples in Keras. This section also discusses NLU (Natural Language Understanding) and NLG (Natural Language Generation).

The second section introduces Reinforcement Learning, along with a description of the types of tasks that are well suited to RL. You will learn about the nchain task and the epsilon-greedy algorithm that can solve problems that you cannot solve using a pure greedy algorithm. In this section you will also learn about the Bellman equation, which is a cornerstone of reinforcement learning.

The third section discusses the TF-Agents toolkit from Google, deep reinforcement learning (deep learning combined with reinforcement learning), and the Google Dopamine toolkit.

Working with NLP (Natural Language Processing)

This section highlights some concepts in NLP, and depending on your background, you might need to perform an online search to learn more about some of the concepts (try Wikipedia). Although the concepts are treated in a very superficial manner, you will know what to pursue in order to further your study of NLP.

NLP is currently the focus of significant interest in the machine learning community. Some of the use cases for NLP are listed here:

- Chatbots
- Search (text and audio)
- Text classification
- Sentiment analysis
- Recommendation systems
- Question answering
- Speech recognition
- NLU (Natural Language Understanding)
- NLG (Natural Language Generation)

You encounter many of these use cases in everyday life: when you visit web pages, or perform an online search for books, or recommendations regarding movies.

NLP Techniques

The earliest approach for solving NLP tasks involved rule-based approaches, which dominated the industry for decades. Examples of techniques using rule-based approaches include Regular Expressions (RegExs) and Context Free Grammars (CFGs). RegExs are sometimes used in order to remove HTML tags from text that has been scraped from a web page or unwanted special characters from a document.

The second approach involved training a machine learning model with some data that is based on some user-defined features. This technique requires a considerable amount of feature engineering (a nontrivial task), and includes analyzing the text to remove undesired and superfluous content (including *stop* words), as well as transforming the words (e.g., converting uppercase to lowercase).

The most recent approach involves deep learning, whereby a neural network learns the features instead of relying on humans to perform feature engineering. One of the key ideas involves mapping words to numbers, which enables us to map sentences to vectors of numbers. After transforming documents to vectors, we can perform a myriad of operations on those vectors. For example, we can use the notion of vector spaces to define vector space models, where the distance between two vectors can be measured by the angle between them (related to cosine similarity). If two vectors are close to each other, then it's likelier that the corresponding sentences are similar in meaning. Their similarity is based on the *distributional hypothesis*, which asserts that words in the same contexts tend to have similar meanings.

A nice article that discusses vector representations of words, along with links to code samples, is here:

https://www.tensorflow.org/tutorials/representation/word2vec

The Transformer Architecture and NLP

In 2017, Google introduced the `Transformer` Neural Network architecture, which is based on a *self-attention* mechanism that is well suited for language understanding.

Google showed that the `Transformer` outperforms earlier benchmarks for both RNNs and CNNs involving the translation of academic English to German as well as English to French. Moreover, the `Transformer` required less computation to train and also improved the training time by as much as an order of magnitude.

The `Transformer` can process the sentence "I arrived at the bank after crossing the river" and correctly determine that the word "bank" refers to the shore of a river and not a financial institution. The `Transformer` makes this determination in a single step by making the association between *bank* and *river*. As another example, the `Transformer` can determine the different meanings of *it* in these two sentences:

"The horse did not cross the street because it was too tired."

"The horse did not cross the street because it was too narrow."

The `Transformer` computes the next representation for a given word by comparing the word to every other word in the sentence, which results in an *attention score* for the words in the sentence. The `Transformer` uses these scores to determine the extent to which other words will contribute to the next representation of a given word.

The result of these comparisons is an attention score for every other word in the sentence. As a result, *river* received a high attention score when computing a new representation for *bank*.

Although `LSTMs` and bidirectional `LSTMs` are heavily utilized in `NLP` tasks, the `Transformer` has gained a lot of traction in the AI community, not only for translation between languages, but also the fact that for some tasks it can outperform both `RNNs` and `CNNs`. The `Transformer` architecture requires much less computation time in order to train a model, which explain why some people believe that the `Transformer` has already begun to supplant `RNNs` and `LSTMs`.

The following link contains a TF 2 code sample of a `Transformer` neural network that you can launch in Google Colaboratory:

https://www.tensorflow.org/alpha/tutorials/text/transformer

Another interesting and recent architecture is called Attention Augmented Convolutional Networks, which is a combination of `CNNs` with self-attention. This combination achieves better accuracy than pure `CNNs`, and you can find more details in this paper: *https://arxiv.org/abs/1904.09925*

Transformer-XL Architecture

The `Transformer-XL` combines a `Transformer` architecture with two techniques called Recurrence Mechanism and Relative Positional Encoding to obtain better results than a `Transformer`. `Transformer-XL` works with word-level and character-level language modeling.

The `Transformer-XL` and `Transformer` both process the first segment of tokens, and the former also keeps the outputs of the hidden layers. Consequently, each hidden layer receives two inputs from the previous hidden layer, and then concatenates them to provide additional information to the neural network.

According to the following article, `Transformer-XL` significantly outperforms `Transformer`, and its dependency is 80% longer than "vanilla" RNNs:

https://hub.packtpub.com/transformer-xl-a-google-architecture-with-80-longer-dependency-than-rnns/

Reformer Architecture

Recently the `Reformer` architecture was released, which uses two techniques to improve the efficiency (i.e., lower memory and faster performance on long sequences) of the `Transformer` architecture. As a result, the `Reformer` architecture also has lower complexity than the `Transformer`. More details regarding the `Reformer` are here:

https://openreview.net/pdf?id=rkgNKkHtvB

Some Reformer-related code is here: *https://pastebin.com/62r5FuEW*

NLP and Deep Learning

The NLP models that use deep learning can comprise CNNs, RNNs, LSTMs, and bidirectional LSTMs. For example, Google released BERT in 2018, which is an extremely powerful framework for NLP. BERT is quite sophisticated and involves bidirectional transformers and so-called attention (discussed briefly later in this chapter).

Deep learning for NLP often yields higher accuracy than other techniques, but keep in mind that sometimes it's not as fast as rule-based and classical machine learning methods. In case you're interested, a code sample that uses TensorFlow and RNNs for text classification is here:

https://www.tensorflow.org/alpha/tutorials/text/text_classification_rnn

A code sample that uses TensorFlow and RNNs for text generation is here:

https://www.tensorflow.org/alpha/tutorials/text/text_generation

Data Preprocessing Tasks in NLP

There are some common preprocessing tasks that are performed on documents, as listed below:

- [1] Lowercasing
- [1] Noise removal
- [2] Normalization
- [3] Text enrichment
- [3] Stopword removal
- [3] Stemming
- [3] Lemmatization

The preceding tasks can be classified as follows:

- [1]: Mandatory tasks
- [2]: Recommended tasks
- [3]: Task dependent

In brief, preprocessing tasks involve at least the removal of redundant words (*a*, *the*, and so forth), removing the endings of words (*running*, *runs*, and *ran* are treated the same as *run*), and converting text from uppercase to lowercase.

Popular NLP Algorithms

Some of the popular NLP algorithms are listed below, and in some cases they are the foundation for more sophisticated NLP toolkits:

- BoW: Bag of Words
- n-grams and skip-grams
- TF-IDF: basic algorithm in extracting keywords
- Word2Vector (Google): O/S project to describe text
- GloVe (Stanford NLP Group)
- LDA: text classification
- CF (collaborative filtering): an algorithm in news recommend system (Google News and Yahoo News)

The topics in the first half of the preceding list are discussed briefly in subsequent sections.

What Is an n-gram?

An *n-gram* is a technique for creating a vocabulary that is based on adjacent words that are grouped together. This technique retains some word positions (unlike BoW). You need to specify the value of "n" that in turn specifies the size of the group.

The idea is simple: for each word in a sentence, construct a vocabulary term that contains the n words on the left side of the given word and n words that are on the right side of the given word. As a simple example, "This is a sentence" has the following 2-grams:

```
(this, is), (is, a), (a, sentence)
```

As another example, we can use the same sentence "This is a sentence" to determine its 3-grams:

```
(this, is, a), (is, a, sentence)
```

The notion of n-grams is surprisingly powerful, and it's used heavily in popular open source toolkits such as ELMo and BERT when they pretrain their models.

What Is a skip-gram?

Given a word in a sentence, a *skip gram* creates a vocabulary term by constructing a list that contains the n words on both sides of a given word, followed by the word itself. For example, consider the following sentence:

```
the quick brown fox jumped over the lazy dog
```

A skip-gram of size 1 yields the following vocabulary terms:

```
([the,brown],    quick),    ([quick,fox],    brown),
([brown,jumped], fox),...
```

A skip-gram of size 2 yields the following vocabulary terms:

```
([the,quick,fox,jumped],                        brown),
([quick,brown,jumped,over], fox), ([brown,fox,over,the],
jumped),...
```

More details regarding skip-grams are discussed here:

https://www.tensorflow.org/tutorials/representation/word2vec#the_skip-gram_model

What Is BoW?

BoW (Bag of Words) assigns a numeric value to each word in a sentence and treats those words as a set (or bag). Hence, BoW does not keep track of adjacent words, so it's a very simple algorithm.

Listing 6.1 displays the contents of the Python script `bow_to_vector.py` that illustrates how to use the BoW algorithm.

Listing 6.1: bow_to_vector.py

```
VOCAB = ['dog', 'cheese', 'cat', 'mouse']
TEXT1 = 'the mouse ate the cheese'
TEXT2 = 'the horse ate the hay'

def to_bow(text):
 words = text.split(" ")
 return [1 if w in words else 0 for w in VOCAB]

print("VOCAB: ",VOCAB)
print("TEXT1:",TEXT1)
print("BOW1: ",to_bow(TEXT1)) # [0, 1, 0, 1]
print("")

print("TEXT2:",TEXT2)
print("BOW2: ",to_bow(TEXT2)) # [0, 0, 0, 0]
```

Listing 6.6 initializes a list VOCAB and two text strings TEXT1 and TEXT2. The next portion of Listing 6.6 defines the Python function to_bow() that returns an array containing 0s and 1s: if a word in the current sentence appears in the vocabulary, then a 1 is returned (otherwise a 0 is returned). The last portion of Listing 6.6 invokes the Python function with two different sentences. The output from launching the code in Listing 6.6 is here:

```
('VOCAB: ', ['dog', 'cheese', 'cat', 'mouse'])
('TEXT1:', 'the mouse ate the cheese')
('BOW1: ', [0, 1, 0, 1])

('TEXT2:', 'the horse ate the hay')
('BOW2: ', [0, 0, 0, 0])
fitting model...
```

What Is Term Frequency?

Term frequency is the number of times that a word appears in a document, which can vary among different documents. Consider the following simple example that consists of two "documents" Doc1 and Doc2:

```
Doc1 = "This is a short sentence"

Doc2 = "yet another short sentence"
```

The term frequency for the word *is* and the word *short* is given below:

```
tf(is) = 1/5 for doc1
tf(is) = 0 for doc2
tf(short) = 1/5 for doc1
tf(short) = 1/4 for doc2
```

The preceding values will be used in the calculation of `tf-idf` that is explained in a later section.

What Is Inverse Document Frequency (idf)?

Given a set of N documents and given a word in a document, let's define `dc` and `idf` of each word as follows:

```
dc = # of documents containing a given word
idf = log(N/dc)
```

Now let's use the same two documents Doc1 and Doc2 from a previous section:

```
Doc1 = "This is a short sentence"
Doc2 = "yet another short sentence"
```

The calculations of the `idf` value for the word *is* and the word *short* are shown here:

```
idf(is) = log(2/1) = log(2)
idf(short) = log(2/2) = 0
```

The following link provides more detailed information about inverse document frequency: *https://en.wikipedia.org/wiki/Tf–idf#Example_of_tf–idf*.

What Is tf-idf?

The term `tf-idf` is an abbreviation for Term Frequency, Inverse Document Frequency, and it's the product of the `tf` value and the `idf` value of a word, as shown here:

```
tf-idf = tf * idf
```

A high frequency word has a higher `tf` value but a lower `idf` value. In general, "rare" words are more relevant than "popular" ones, so they help to extract *relevance*. For example, suppose you have a collection of ten documents (real documents, not the toy documents we used earlier). The word *the* occurs frequently in English sentences, but it does not provide any indication of the topics in any of the documents. On the other hand, if you determine that the word *universe* appears multiple times in a single document, this information can provide some indication of the theme of that document, and with the help of NLP techniques, assist in determining the topic (or topics) in that document.

What Are Word Embeddings?

An *embedding* is a fixed-length vector to encode and represent an entity (document, sentence, word, graph). Each word is represented by a real-valued vector, which can result in hundreds of dimensions. Furthermore, such an encoding can result in sparse vectors: one example is one-hot encoding, where one position has the value 1 and all other positions have the value 0.

Three popular word embedding algorithms are Word2vec, GloVe, and FastText. Keep in mind that these three algorithms involve unsupervised approaches. They are also based on the distributional hypothesis: words in the same contexts tend to have similar meanings: *https://aclweb.org/aclwiki/Distributional_Hypothesis*.

A good article regarding Word2Vec in TensorFlow is here:

https://towardsdatascience.com/learn-word2vec-by-implementing-it-in-tensorflow-45641adaf2ac

This article is useful if you want to see Word2Vec with FastText in gensim:

https://towardsdatascience.com/word-embedding-with-word2vec-and-fasttext-a209c1d3e12c

Another good article, and this one pertains to the skip-gram model:

https://towardsdatascience.com/word2vec-skip-gram-model-part-1-in-tuition-78614e4d6e0b

A useful article that describes how FastText works under the hood:

https://towardsdatascience.com/fasttext-under-the-hood-11efc57b2b3

Along with the preceding popular algorithms there are also some popular embedding models, some of which are listed below:

- Baseline Averaged Sentence Embeddings
- Doc2Vec
- Neural-Net Language Models
- Skip-Thought Vectors
- Quick-Thought Vectors
- InferSent
- Universal Sentence Encoder

Perform an online search for more information about the preceding embedding models.

ELMo, ULMFit, OpenAI, BERT, and ERNIE 2.0

During 2018 there were some significant advances in NLP-related research, resulting in the following toolkits and frameworks:

- `ELMo:` released in 02/2018
- `ULMFit:` released in 05/2018
- `OpenAI:` released in 06/2018
- `BERT:` released in 10/2018
- `MT-DNN:` released in 01/2019
- `ERNIE 2.0:` released in 08/2019

ELMo is an acronym for Embeddings from Language Models, which provides Deep Contextualized Word Representations and state-of-the-art contextual word vectors, resulting in noticeable improvements in word embeddings.

Jeremy Howard and Sebastian Ruder created ULMFit (Universal Language Model Fine-tuning), which is a transfer learning method that can be applied to any task in NLP. ULMFit significantly outperforms the state-of-the-art on six text classification tasks, reducing the error by 18–24% on the majority of datasets.

Furthermore, with only 100 labeled examples, it matches the performance of training from scratch on 100x more data. ULMFit is downloadable from GitHub:

https://github.com/jannenev/ulmfit-language-model

OpenAI developed GPT-2 (a successor to GPT), which is a model that was trained to predict the next word in 40GB of Internet text. OpenAI chose not to release the trained model due to concerns regarding malicious applications of their technology.

GPT-2 is a large transformer-based language model with 1.5 billion parameters, trained on a dataset of 8 million web pages (curated by humans), with an emphasis on diversity of content. GPT-2 is trained to predict the next word, given all the previous words within some text. The diversity of the dataset causes this goal to contain naturally occurring demonstrations of many tasks across diverse domains. GPT-2 is a direct scale-up of GPT, with more than 10X the parameters and trained on more than 10X the amount of data.

BERT is an acronym for Bidirectional Encoder Representations from Transformers. BERT can pass this simple English test (i.e., BERT can determine the correct choice among multiple choices):

```
On stage, a woman takes a seat at the piano. She:

a) sits on a bench as her sister plays with the doll.

b) smiles with someone as the music plays.

c) is in the crowd, watching the dancers.

d) nervously sets her fingers on the keys.
```

Details of BERT and this English test are here:

https://www.lyrn.ai/2018/11/07/explained-bert-state-of-the-art-language-model-for-nlp/

The BERT (TensorFlow) source code is available here on GitHub:

https://github.com/google-research/bert
https://github.com/hanxiao/bert-as-service

Another interesting development is MT-DNN from Microsoft, which asserts that MT-DNN can outperform Google BERT:

https://medium.com/syncedreview/microsofts-new-mt-dnn-outperforms-google-bert-b5fa15b1a03e

A Jupyter notebook with BERT is available, and you need the following in order to run the notebook in Google Colaboratory:

- A GCP (Google Compute Engine) account
- A GCS (Google Cloud Storage) bucket

Here is the link to the notebook in Google Colaboratory:

https://colab.research.google.com/github/tensorflow/tpu/blob/master/tools/colab/bert_finetuning_with_cloud_tpus.ipynb

In March 2019, Baidu open sourced ERNIE 1.0 (Enhanced Representation through kNowledge IntEgration) that (according to Baidu) outperformed BERT in tasks involving Chinese language understanding. In August, 2019 Baidu open sourced ERNIE 2.0, which is downloadable here:

https://github.com/PaddlePaddle/ERNIE/

An article with additional information about ERNIE 2.0 (including its architecture) is here:

https://hub.packtpub.com/baidu-open-sources-ernie-2-0-a-continual-pre-training-nlp-model-that-outperforms-bert-and-xlnet-on-16-nlp-tasks/

What Is Translatotron?

Translatotron is an End-to-End Speech-to-Speech Translation Model (from Google) whose output retains the original speaker's voice; moreover, it's trained with less data.

Speech-to-speech translation systems have been developed over the past several decades with the goal of helping people who speak different languages to communicate with each other. Such systems have three parts:

- Automatic speech recognition to transcribe the source speech as text
- Machine translation to translate the transcribed text into the target language
- Text-to-speech synthesis (TTS) to generate speech in the target language from the translated text

The preceding approach has been successful in commercial products (including Google Translate). However, Translatatron does not require separate stages, resulting in the following advantages:

- Faster inference speed

- Avoiding compounding errors between recognition and translation

- Easier to retain the voice of the original speaker after translation

- Better handling of untranslated words (names and proper nouns)

This concludes the portion of this chapter that pertains to NLP. Another area of great interest in the AI community is Reinforcement Learning, which is introduced later in this chapter.

Deep Learning and NLP

In Chapter 4, you learned about CNNs and how they are well suited for image classification tasks. You might be surprised to discover that CNNs also work with NLP tasks. However, you must first map each word in a dictionary (which can be a subset of the words in English or some other language) to numeric values and then construct a vector of numeric values from the words in a sentence. A document can be transformed into a set of numeric vectors (involving various techniques that are not discussed here) in order to create a dataset that's suitable for input to a CNN.

Another option involves the use of RNNs and LSTMs instead of CNNs for NLP-related tasks. By contrast, a bidirectional transformer is the basis for in BERT (Bidirectional Encoder Representations from Transformers). The Google AI team developed BERT (open sourced in 2018) and it's considered a breakthrough in its ability to solve NLP problems. The source code is here: *https://github.com/google-research/bert*

NLU versus NLG

NLU is an acronym for Natural Language Understanding. NLU pertains to machine reading comprehension, and it's considered a difficult problem. At the same time, NLU is relevant to machine translation, question answering, and text categorization (among others). NLU attempts to discern the meaning of fragmented sentences and run-on sentences, after which some type of action can be performed (e.g., respond to voice queries).

NLG is an acronym for Natural Language Generation, which involves generating documents. The Markov chain (discussed later in this chapter) was one of the first algorithms for natural language generation. Another technique involves RNNs (discussed in Chapter 5) that can retain some history of previous words, and the probability of the next word in a sequence is calculated. Recall that RNNs suffer from limited memory, which limits the length of the sentences that can be generated. A third technique involves LSTMs, which can maintain state for a long period of time and also avoid the exploding gradient problem.

Recently (circa 2017) Google introduced the transformer architecture, which involves a stack of encoders for processing inputs and a set of decoders to produce generated sentences. A transformer-based architecture is more efficient than an LSTM because a transformer requires a small and fixed number of steps in order to apply the so-called self-attention mechanism in order to simulate the relationship among all the words in a sentence.

In fact, the transformer differs from previous models in one important way: it uses the representation of all words in context without compressing all the information into a single fixed-length representation. This technique enables a transformer to handle longer sentences without high computational costs.

The transformer architecture is the foundation for the GPT-2 language model (from OpenAI). The model learns to predict the next word in a sentence by focusing on words that were previously seen in the model and related to predicting the next word. In 2018, Google released the BERT architecture for NLP, which is based on transformers with a two-way encoder representation.

What Is Reinforcement Learning (RL)?

Reinforcement Learning is a subset of machine learning that attempts to find the maximum reward for a so-called agent that interacts with an environment. RL is suitable for solving tasks that involve deferred rewards, especially when those rewards are greater than intermediate rewards.

In fact, RL can handle tasks that involve a combination of negative, zero, and positive rewards. For example, if you decide to leave your job in order to attend school on a full-time basis, you are spending money (a negative reward) with the belief that your investment of time and money will lead to a higher-paying position (a positive reward) that outweighs the cost of school and lost earnings.

One thing that might surprise you is that Reinforcement Learning agents are susceptible to GANs. Chapter 5 contains a section devoted to GANs, and you can find additional details (along with related links) in this article:

https://openai.com/blog/adversarial-example-research/

Reinforcement Learning Applications

There are many RL applications, some of which are listed here:

- Game theory
- Control theory
- Operations research
- Information theory
- Simulation-based optimization
- Multiagent systems
- Swarm intelligence
- Statistics and genetic algorithms
- Resources management in computer clusters
- Traffic light control (congestion problems)
- Robotics operations
- Autonomous cars/helicopters
- Web System Configuration/web-page indexing
- Personalized recommendations
- Bidding and advertising

- Robot-legged locomotion
- Marketing strategy selection
- Factory control

RL refers to goal-oriented algorithms for reaching a complex goal, such as winning games that involve multiple moves (e.g., chess or Go). RL algorithms are penalized for incorrect decisions and rewarded for correct decisions: this reward mechanism is reinforcement.

NLP and Reinforcement Learning

More recently Reinforcement Learning with NLP has become a successful area of research. One technique for NLP-related tasks involves RNN-based encoder-decoder models that have achieved good results for short input and output sequences. Another technique involves a neural network, supervised word prediction, and Reinforcement Learning. This particular combination avoids exposure bias, which can occur in models that use only supervised learning. More details are here: *https://arxiv.org/pdf/1705.04304.pdf*

Yet another interesting technique involves Deep Reinforcement Learning (i.e., DL combined with RL) with NLP. In case you don't already know, DRL has achieved success in various areas, such as Atari games, defeating Lee Sedol (the world champion Go player), and robotics. In addition, DRL is also applicable to NLP-related tasks, which involves the key challenge of designing of a suitable model. Perform an online search for more information about solving NLP-related tasks with RL and DRL.

Values, Policies, and Models in RL

There are three main approaches in Reinforcement Learning. *Value-based* RL estimates the optimal value function $Q(s,a)$, which is the maximum value achievable under any policy. *Policy-based* RL searches directly for the optimal policy π, which is the policy achieving maximum future reward. *Model-based* RL builds a model of the environment and plans (by lookahead) using the model.

In addition to the preceding approaches to RL (value functions, policies, and models), you will need to learn the following RL concepts:

- MDPs (Markov Decision Processes)
- A policy (a sequence of actions)
- The state/value function
- The action/value function
- Bellman equation (for calculating rewards)

The RL material in this chapter only addresses the following list of topics (after which you can learn the concepts in the previous list):

- NFAs (Non-Deterministic Finite Automata)
- Markov Chains
- MDPs (Markov Decision Processes)
- Epsilon-Greedy Algorithm
- Bellman Equation

Another key point: *almost all RL problems can be formulated as Markov Decision Processes*, which in turn are based on Markov Chains. Let's take a look at NFAs and Markov Chains and then we can define Markov Decision Processes.

From NFAs to MDPs

Let's start with the two-minute summary. The underlying structure for an MDP is an NFA (nondeterministic finite automata), which is studied in great detail in an automata theory course (as part of a computer science degree). An NFA is a collection of states and transitions, each of which has equal probability. An NFA also has a start state and one or more end states.

Now add probabilities to transitions in an NFA, in such a way that the sum of the probabilities of the outgoing transitions of any state equals one. The result is a Markov Chain. A Markov Decision Process is a Markov Chain with several additional properties.

The following subsections expand the two-minute summary by providing additional explanatory details.

What Are NFAs?

An NFA is a Non Deterministic Finite Automata, which is a generalization of a DFA (Deterministic Finite Automata). Figure 6.1 displays an example of a NFA.

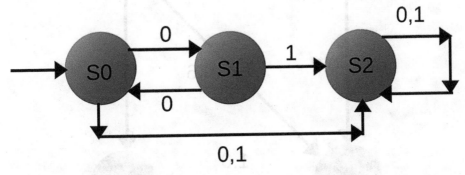

FIGURE 6.1 An Example of an NFA.

Image adapted from [Source: *https://math.stackexchange.com/questions/1240601/what-is-the-easiest-way-to-determine-the-accepted-language-of-a-deterministic-fi?rq=1*]

An NFA enables you to define multiple transitions from a given state to other states. By way of analogy, consider the location of many (most?) gas stations. Usually they are located at an intersection of two streets, which means there are at least two entrances to the gas station. After you make your purchase, you can exit from the same entrance or from the second entrance. In some cases, you might even be able to exit from one location and return to the gas station from the other entrance: this would be comparable to a loop transition of a state in a state machine.

The next step involves adding probabilities to NFAs in order to create a Markov Chain, which is described in more detail in the next section.

What Are Markov Chains?

Markov Chains are NFAs with an additional constraint: the sum of the probabilities of the outgoing edges of every state equals one. Figure 6.2 displays a Markov Chain.

Markov Chain

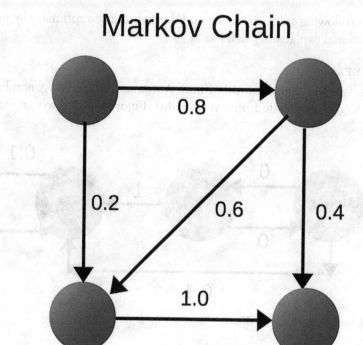

FIGURE 6.2 An Example of a Markov Chain.

Image adapted from [Source: *https://en.wikipedia.org/wiki/Markov_chain*]

As you can see in Figure 6.2, a Markov Chain is an NFA because a state can have multiple transitions. The constraint involving probabilities ensures that we can perform statistical sampling in MDPs that are described in the next section.

Markov Decision Processes (MDPs)

In high-level terms, a Markov Decision Process is a method that samples from a complex distribution to infer its properties. More specifically, MDPs are an extension of Markov chains, which involves the addition of actions (allowing choice) and rewards (giving motivation). Conversely, if only one action exists for each state (e.g. "wait") and all rewards are the same (e.g. "zero"), an MDP reduces to a Markov chain. Figure 6.3 displays an example of an MDP.

Markov Decision Process

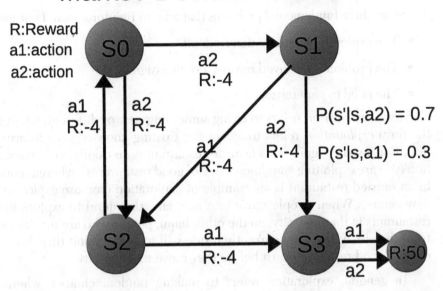

FIGURE 6.3 An Example of an MDP.

Thus, an MDP consists of a set of states and actions, as well as the rules for transitioning from one state to another. One episode of this process (e.g., a single "game") produces a finite sequence of states, actions, and rewards. A key property of MDPs: history does not affect future decisions. In other words, the process of selecting the next state is independent of everything that happened before reaching the current state.

MDPs are nondeterministic search problems that are solved via dynamic programming and RL, where outcomes are partly random and partly under control. As you learned earlier in this section, almost all RL problems can be formulated as MDPs; consequently, RL can solve tasks that cannot be solved by greedy algorithms. However, the epsilon-greedy algorithm is a clever algorithm that *can* solve such tasks. In addition, the Bellman Equation enables us to compute rewards for states. Both are discussed in subsequent sections.

The Epsilon-Greedy Algorithm

There are three fundamental problems that arise in Reinforcement Learning:

- The exploration-exploitation tradeoff
- The problem of delayed reward (credit assignment)
- The need to generalize

The term *exploration* refers to trying something new or different, whereas the term *exploitation* refers to leveraging existing knowledge or information. For instance, going to a favorite restaurant is an example of exploitation (you are exploiting your knowledge of good restaurants), whereas going to an untried restaurant is an example of exploration (you are exploring a new venue). When people move to a new city, they tend to explore new restaurants in that new city; on the other hand, people who are moving out from the city where they currently reside will tend to exploit their knowledge of good restaurants just before they move to a new city.

In general, exploration refers to making random choices, whereas exploitation refers to using a greedy algorithm. The epsilon-greedy algorithm is an example of exploration and exploitation, where the *epsilon* portion of the algorithm refers to making random selections, and *exploitation* involves a greedy algorithm.

An example of a simple task that can be solved via the epsilon-greedy algorithm is Open AI Gym's NChain environment, as shown in Figure 6.4.

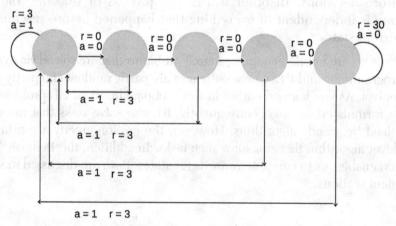

FIGURE 6.4 The Open AI Gym's NChain Environment.

Image adapted from [*http://ceit.aut.ac.ir/~shiry/lecture/machine-learning/papers/BRL-2000.pdf*]

Each state in Figure 6.4 has two actions, and each action has an associated reward. For each state, its forward action has reward 0, whereas its backward action has reward 3. Since a greedy algorithm will always select the larger reward at any state, this means that the backward action is always selected. Hence, we can never move toward the final state 4 that has a reward of 10. Indeed, we can never leave state 0 (the initial state) if we adhere to the greedy algorithm.

Here is the key question: how do we go from the initial state 0 to the final state, which contains a large reward? *We need a modified or hybrid algorithm in order to go through intermediate low-reward states that lead to the high reward state.*

The hybrid algorithm is simple to describe: adhere to the greedy algorithm about 90% of the time and randomly select a state for the remaining 10% of the time. This technique is simple, elegant, and effective, and it's called the *epsilon-greedy* algorithm (there are additional details required for a complete implementation).

Incidentally, a Python-based solution for OpenAI's NChain task is here:

https://github.com/openai/gym/blob/master/gym/envs/toy_text/nchain.py

Another central concept in Reinforcement Learning involves the Bellman Equation, which is the topic of the next section.

The Bellman Equation

The Bellman equations are named after Richard Bellman, who derived these equations that are ubiquitous in Reinforcement Learning. There are several Bellman equations, including one for the state value function and one for the action value function. Figure 6.5 displays the Bellman equation for the state value function.

$$V^{\pi}(s) = E_{\pi}\left[\sum_{k=0}^{\infty} \gamma^k r_{t+k+1} \middle| s_t = s\right]$$

FIGURE 6.5 The Bellman Equation.

As you can see in Figure 6.5, the value of a given state depends on the discounted value of future states. The following analogy might help you understand the purpose of the discounted value called *gamma* in this equation. Suppose that you have USD 100 that you invest at a 5% annual interest rate. After one year you will have USD 105 (=100 + 5%*100 = 100*(1+0.05)), after two years you will have USD 110.25 (=100*(1+0.05)*(1+0.05)), and so forth.

Conversely, if you have a future value of USD 100 (with a 5% annual investment rate) that is two years in the future, what is its present value? The answer involves dividing 100 by powers of (1+0.05). Specifically, the present value of USD 100 from two years in the future equals 100/ [(1+0.05)*(1+0.05)].

In analogous fashion, the Bellman equation enables us to calculate the current value of a state by calculating the discounted reward of subsequent states. The discount factor is called *gamma*, and it's often a value between 0.9 and 0.99. In the preceding example involving USD 100, the value of gamma is 0.9523.

Other Important Concepts in RL

After you have studied the basic concepts in RL, you can delve into the topics that are listed below:

- Policy Gradient (rules for "best" actions)
- Q-value
- Monte Carlo
- Dynamic programming
- Temporal Difference (TD)
- Q-learning
- Deep Q Network

The preceding topics are explained in online articles (suggestion: use Wikipedia as a starting point for RL concepts), and they will be much more relevant after you grasp the introductory concepts in RL that are discussed in earlier sections. Be prepared to spend some time learning these topics because some of them are quite challenging in nature.

RL Toolkits and Frameworks

There are many toolkits and libraries for Reinforcement Learning, typically based on Python, Keras, Torch, or Java. Some of them are listed here:

- OpenAI gym: A toolkit for developing and comparing reinforcement learning algorithms

- OpenAI universe: A software platform for measuring and training an AI's general intelligence across the world's supply of games, websites and other applications

- DeepMind Lab: A customizable 3D platform for agent-based AI research

- rllab: A framework for developing and evaluating reinforcement learning algorithms, fully compatible with OpenAI Gym

- TensorForce: Practical deep reinforcement learning on TensorFlow with Gitter support and OpenAI Gym/Universe/DeepMind Lab integration

- tf-TRFL: A library built on top of TensorFlow that exposes several useful building blocks for implementing RL agents

- OpenAI lab: An experimentation system for RL using OpenAI Gym, Tensorflow, and Keras

- MAgent: A platform for Many-agent Reinforcement Learning

- Intel Coach: A Python reinforcement learning research framework containing implementation of many state-of-the-art algorithms

As you can see from the preceding list, there is a considerable variety of available RL toolkits, and visit their homepages to determine which ones have the features that meet your specific requirements.

TF-Agents

Google created the TF-Agents library for RL in TensorFlow. Google TF-Agents is open source and downloadable from Github:

https://github.com/tensorflow/agents

The core elements of RL algorithms are implemented as *agents*. An agent encompasses two main responsibilities: defining a *policy* to interact with the *environment*, and how to learn/train that policy from collected experience. TF-Agents implements the following algorithms:

- DQN: Human level control through deep reinforcement learning (Mnih et al., 2015)

- DDQN: Deep Reinforcement Learning with Double Q-learning (Hasselt et al., 2015)

- DDPG: Continuous control with deep reinforcement learning (Lillicrap et al., 2015)

- TD3: Addressing Function Approximation Error in Actor-Critic Methods (Fujimoto et al., 2018)

- REINFORCE: Simple Statistical Gradient-Following Algorithms for Connectionist Reinforcement Learning (Williams, 1992)

- PPO: Proximal Policy Optimization Algorithms (Schulman et al., 2017)

- SAC: Soft Actor Critic (Haarnoja et al., 2018)

Before you can use TF-Agents, first install the nightly build version of TF-Agents with this command (`pip` or `pip3`):

```
# the --upgrade flag ensures you'll get the latest
  version
pip install --user --upgrade tf-nightly
pip install --user --upgrade tf-agents-nightly #
  requires tf-nightly
```

There are end-to-end examples training agents under each agent directory, an example of which is here for DQN:

```
tf_agents/agents/dqn/examples/v1/train_eval_gym.py
```

Keep in mind that TF-Agents is in prerelease status and therefore under active development, which means that interfaces may change at any time.

What Is Deep Reinforcement Learning (DRL)?

Deep Reinforcement Learning is a surprisingly effective combination of deep learning and RL that has shown remarkable results in a variety of tasks. For example, DRL has won game competitions such as Go (Alpha Go versus world champion Lee Sedol) and even prevailed in the complexity of StarCraft (AlphaStar of DeepMind) and Dota.

With the release of ELMo and BERT in 2018 (discussed earlier in this chapter), DRL made significant advances in NLP with these toolkits, surpassing previous benchmarks in NLP.

Google released the Dopamine toolkit for DRL, which is downloadable here from GitHub: *https://github.com/google/dopamine.*

The keras-rl toolkit supports state-of-the-art Deep RL algorithms in Keras, which are also designed for compatibility with OpenAI (discussed earlier in this Appendix). This toolkit includes the following:

- Deep Q Learning (DQN)

- Double DQN

- Deep Deterministic Policy Gradient (DDPG)

- Continuous DQN (CDQN or NAF)

- Cross-Entropy Method (CEM)

- Dueling network DQN (Dueling DQN)

- Deep SARSA

- Asynchronous Advantage Actor-Critic (A3C)

- Proximal Policy Optimization Algorithms (PPO)

Please keep in mind that the details of the algorithms in the preceding list require a decent understanding of Reinforcement Learning. The keras-rl toolkit is downloadable here from GitHub: *https://github.com/keras-rl/keras-rl*

Summary

This chapter introduced you to NLP, along with some code samples in Keras, as well as NLU (Natural Language Understanding) and NLG (Natural Language Generation). In addition, you learned about some basic concepts in NLP, such as n-grams, BoW, tf-idf, and word embeddings.

Then you got an introduction to Reinforcement Learning, along with a description of the types of tasks that are well-suited to RL. You learned about the nchain task and the epsilon-greedy algorithm that can solve problems that you cannot solve using a pure greedy algorithm. You also learned about the Bellman equation, which is a cornerstone of reinforcement learning.

Next, you were exposed to the TF-Agents toolkit from Google, deep reinforcement learning (deep learning combined with reinforcement learning), and the Google Dopamine toolkit.

Congratulations! You have reached the end of this book, which has covered many machine learning concepts. You also learned about `Keras`, as well as linear regression, logistic regression, and deep learning. You are now in a good position to delve further into machine learning algorithms or proceed with deep learning, and good luck in your journey!

INTRODUCTION TO KERAS

This appendix introduces you to Keras, along with code samples that illustrate how to define basic neural networks as well as and deep neural networks with various datasets with as MNIST and Cifar10.

The first part of this appendix briefly discusses some of the important namespaces (such as tf.keras.layers) and their contents, as well as a simple Keras-based model.

The second section contains an example of performing linear regression with Keras and a simple CSV file. You will also see a Keras-based MLP neural network that is trained on the MNIST dataset.

The third section contains a simple example of training a neural network with the cifar10 dataset. This code sample is similar to training a neural network on the MNIST dataset, and requires a very small code change.

The final section contains two examples of Keras-based models that perform *early stopping*, which is convenient when the model exhibits minimal improvement (that is specified by you) during the training process.

What Is Keras?

If you are already comfortable with Keras, you can skim this section to learn about the new namespaces and what they contain, and then proceed to the next section that contains details for creating a Keras-based model.

If you are new to `Keras`, you might be wondering why this section is included in this appendix. First, `Keras` is well integrated into TF 2, and it's in the `tf.keras` namespace. Second, `Keras` is well suited for defining models to solve a myriad of tasks, such as linear regression and logistic regression, as well as deep learning tasks involving CNNs, RNNs, and LSTMs that are discussed in the Appendix.

The next several subsections contain lists of bullet items for various `Keras`-related namespaces, and they will be very familiar if you have worked with TF 1.x. If you are new to TF 2, you'll see examples of some of the classes in subsequent code samples.

Working with `Keras` Namespaces in TF 2

TF 2 provides the `tf.keras` namespace, which in turn contains the following namespaces:

- tf.keras.layers
- tf.keras.models
- tf.keras.optimizers
- tf.keras.utils
- tf.keras.regularizers

The preceding namespaces contain various layers in `Keras` models, different types of `Keras` models, optimizers (Adam et al.), utility classes, and regularizers (such as L1 and L2), respectively.

Currently there are three ways to create `Keras`-based models:

- The Sequential API
- The Functional API
- The Model API

The `Keras`-based code samples in this book use primarily the Sequential API (it's the most intuitive and straightforward). The Sequential API enables you to specify a list of layers, most of which are available in the `tf.keras.layers` namespace (discussed later).

The `Keras`-based models that use the functional API involve specifying layers that are passed as function-like elements in a pipeline-like fashion. Although the functional API provides some additional flexibility, you will probably use the Sequential API to define Keras-based models if you are a TF 2 beginner.

The model-based API provides the greatest flexibility, and it involves defining a Python class that encapsulates the semantics of your Keras model. This class is a subclass of the tf.model.Model class, and you must implement the two methods __init__ and call in order to define a Keras model in this subclass.

Perform an online search for more details regarding the Functional API and the Model API.

Working with the tf.keras.layers Namespace

The most common (and also the simplest) Keras-based model is the Sequential() class that is in the tf.keras.models namespace. This model is comprised of various layers that belong to the tf.keras.layers namespace, as shown here:

- tf.keras.layers.Conv2D()
- tf.keras.layers.MaxPooling2D()
- tf.keras.layers.Flatten()
- tf.keras.layers.Dense()
- tf.keras.layers.Dropout()
- tf.keras.layers.BatchNormalization()
- tf.keras.layers.embedding()
- tf.keras.layers.RNN()
- tf.keras.layers.LSTM()
- tf.keras.layers.Bidirectional (ex: BERT)

The Conv2D() and MaxPooling2D() classes are used in Keras-based models for CNNs, which are discussed in Chapter 5. Generally speaking, the next six classes in the preceding list can appear in models for CNNs as well as models for machine learning. The RNN() class is for simple RNNS and the LSTM class is for LSTM-based models. The Bidirectional() class is a bidirectional LSTM that you will often see in models for solving NLP (Natural Language Processing) tasks. Two very important NLP frameworks that use bidirectional LSTMs were released as open source (on GitHub) in 2018: ELMo from Facebook and BERT from Google.

Working with the tf.keras.activations Namespace

Machine learning and deep learning models require activation functions. For Keras-based models, the activation functions are in the `tf.keras.activations` namespace, some of which are listed here:

- `tf.keras.activations.relu`
- `tf.keras.activations.selu`
- `tf.keras.activations.linear`
- `tf.keras.activations.elu`
- `tf.keras.activations.sigmoid`
- `tf.keras.activations.softmax`
- `tf.keras.activations.softplus`
- `tf.keras.activations.tanh`
- `Others …`

The ReLU/SELU/ELU functions are closely related, and they often appear in ANNs (Artificial Neural Networks) and CNNs. Before the `relu()` function became popular, the `sigmoid()` and `tanh()` functions were used in ANNs and CNNs. However, they are still important and they are used in various gates in GRUs and LSTMs. The `softmax()` function is typically used in the pair of layers consisting of the rightmost hidden layer and the output layer.

Working with the keras.tf.datasets Namespace

For your convenience, TF 2 provides a set of built-in datasets in the `tf.keras.datasets` namespace, some of which are listed here:

- `tf.keras.datasets.boston_housing`
- `tf.keras.datasets.cifar10`
- `tf.keras.datasets.cifar100`
- `tf.keras.datasets.fashion_mnist`
- `tf.keras.datasets.imdb`

- `tf.keras.datasets.mnist`

- `tf.keras.datasets.reuters`

The preceding datasets are popular for training models with small datasets. The `mnist` dataset and `fashion_mnist` dataset are both popular when training CNNs, whereas the `boston_housing` dataset is popular for linear regression. The `Titanic` dataset is also popular for linear regression, but it's not currently supported as a default dataset in the `tf.keras.datas-ets` namespace.

Working with the `tf.keras.experimental` Namespace

The `contrib` namespace in TF 1.x has been deprecated in TF 2, and its successor is the `tf.keras.experimental` namespace, which contains the following classes (among others):

- `tf.keras.experimental.CosineDecay`

- `tf.keras.experimental.CosineDecayRestarts`

- `tf.keras.experimental.LinearCosineDecay`

- `tf.keras.experimental.NoisyLinearCosineDecay`

- `tf.keras.experimental.PeepholeLSTMCell`

If you are a beginner, you probably won't use any of the classes in the preceding list. Although the `PeepholeLSTMCell` class is a variation of the LSTM class, there are limited use cases for this class.

Working with Other `tf.keras` Namespaces

TF 2 provides a number of other namespaces that contain useful classes, some of which are listed here:

- `tf.keras.callbacks`   (early stopping)

- `tf.keras.optimizers`   (Adam et al)

- `tf.keras.regularizers`   (L1 and L2)

- `tf.keras.utils`   (`to_categorical`)

The `tf.keras.callbacks` namespace contains a class that you can use for *early stopping*, which is to say that it's possible to terminate the training process if there is insufficient reduction in the cost function in two successive iterations.

The `tf.keras.optimizers` namespace contains the various optimizers that are available for working in conjunction with cost functions, which includes the popular `Adam` optimizer.

The `tf.keras.regularizers` namespace contains two popular regularizers: the L1 regularizer (also called `LASSO` in machine learning) and the L2 regularizer (also called the `Ridge` regularizer in machine learning). L1 is for MAE (Mean Absolute Error) and L2 is for MSE (Mean Squared Error). Both regularizers act as "penalty" terms that are added to the chosen cost function in order to reduce the influence of features in a machine learning model. Note that `LASSO` can drive values to zero, with the result that features are actually eliminated from a model, and hence is related to something called *feature selection* in machine learning.

The `tf.keras.utils` namespace contains an assortment of functions, including the `to_categorical()` function for converting a class vector into a binary class.

Although there are other namespaces in TF 2, the classes listed in all the preceding subsections will probably suffice for the majority of your tasks if you are a beginner in TF 2 and machine learning.

TF 2 `Keras` versus "Standalone" `Keras`

The original `Keras` is actually a specification, with various backend frameworks such as TensorFlow, Theano, and CNTK. Currently `Keras` standalone does not support TF 2, whereas the implementation of `Keras` in `tf.keras` has been optimized for performance.

`Keras` standalone will live in perpetuity in the `keras.io` package, which is discussed in detail at the `Keras` website: `keras.io`.

Now that you have a high-level view of the TF 2 namespaces for `Keras` and the classes that they contain, let's find out how to create a `Keras`-based model, which is the subject of the next section.

Creating a `Keras`-based Model

The following list of steps describe the high-level sequence involved in creating, training, and testing a `Keras` model:

- Step 1: Determine a model architecture (the number of hidden layers, various activation functions, and so forth)

- Step 2: Invoke the compile() method
- Step 3: Invoke the fit() method to train the model
- Step 4: Invoke the evaluate() method to evaluate the trained model
- Step 5: Invoke the predict() method to make predictions

Step 1 involves determining the values of a number of hyperparameters, including:

- The number of hidden layers
- The number of neurons in each hidden layer
- The initial values of the weights of edges
- The cost function
- The optimizer
- The learning rate
- The dropout rate
- The activation function(s)

Steps 2 through 4 involve the training data, whereas step 5 involves the test data, which are included in the following more detailed sequence of steps for the preceding list:

- Specify a dataset (if necessary, convert data to numeric data)
- Split the dataset into training data and test data (usually 80/20 split)
- Define the `Keras` model (such as the `tf.keras.models.Sequential()` **API**)
- Compile the `Keras` model (the `compile()` **API**)
- Train (fit) the `Keras` model (the `fit()` **API**)
- Make a prediction (the `prediction()` **API**)

Note that the preceding bullet items skip some steps that are part of a real `Keras` model, such as evaluating the `Keras` model on the test data, as well as dealing with issues such as overfitting.

The first bullet item states that you need a dataset, which can be as simple as a CSV file with 100 rows of data and just 3 columns (or even smaller).

In general, a dataset is substantially larger: it can be a file with 1,000,000 rows of data and 10,000 columns in each row. We'll look at a concrete dataset in a subsequent section.

Next, a Keras model is in the `tf.keras.models` namespace, and the simplest (and also very common) Keras model is `tf.keras.models.Sequential`. In general, a Keras model contains layers that are in the `tf.keras.layers` namespace, such as `tf.keras.Dense` (which means that two adjacent layers are completely connected).

The activation functions that are referenced in Keras layers are in the `tf.nn` namespace, such as the `tf.nn.ReLU` for the ReLU activation function.

Here's a code block of the Keras model that's described in the preceding paragraphs (which covers the first four bullet points):

```
import tensorflow as tf
model = tf.keras.models.Sequential([
  tf.keras.layers.Dense(512, activation=tf.
    nn.relu),
])
```

We have three more bullet items to discuss, starting with the compilation step. Keras provides a `compile()` API for this step, an example of which is here:

```
model.compile(optimizer='adam',
              loss='sparse_categorical_crossentropy',
              metrics=['accuracy'])
```

Next we need to specify a training step, and Keras provides the `fit()` API (as you can see, it's not called `train()`), an example of which is here:

```
model.fit(x_train, y_train, epochs=5)
```

The final step is the prediction that is performed via the `predict()` API, an example of which is here:

```
pred = model.predict(x)
```

Keep in mind that the `evaluate()` method is used for evaluating an trained model, and the output of this method is accuracy or loss. On the other hand, the `predict()` method makes predictions from the input data.

Listing A.1 displays the contents of `tf2_basic_keras.py` that combines the code blocks in the preceding steps into a single code sample.

Listing A.1: tf2_basic_keras.py

```
import tensorflow as tf

# NOTE: we need the train data and test data

model = tf.keras.models.Sequential([
  tf.keras.layers.Dense(1, activation=tf.
    nn.relu),
])

model.compile(optimizer='adam',
              loss='sparse_categorical_crossentropy',
              metrics=['accuracy'])

model.fit(x_train, y_train, epochs=5)
model.evaluate(x_test, y_test)
```

Listing A.1 contains no new code, and we've essentially glossed over some of the terms such as the optimizer (an algorithm that is used in conjunction with a loss function), the loss (the type of loss function) and the metrics (how to evaluate the efficacy of a model).

The explanations for these details cannot be condensed into a few paragraphs (alas), but the good news is that you can find a plethora of detailed online blog posts that discuss these terms.

Keras and Linear Regression

This section contains a simple example of creating a Keras-based model in order to solve a task involving linear regression: given a positive number representing kilograms of pasta, predict its corresponding price. Listing A.2 displays the contents of `pasta.csv` and Listing A.3 displays the contents of `keras_pasta.py` that performs this task.

Listing A.2: pasta.csv

```
weight,price
5,30
10,45
15,70
20,80
25,105
30,120
35,130
40,140
50,150
```

Listing A.3: keras_pasta.py

```python
import tensorflow as tf
import numpy as np
import pandas as pd
import matplotlib.pyplot as plt

# price of pasta per kilogram
df = pd.read_csv("pasta.csv")

weight = df['weight']
price  = df['price']

model = tf.keras.models.Sequential([
    tf.keras.layers.Dense(units=1,input_shape=[1])
])

# MSE loss function and Adam optimizer
model.compile(loss='mean_squared_error',
            optimizer=tf.keras.optimizers.Adam(0.1))

# train the model
history = model.fit(weight, price, epochs=100,
    verbose=False)

# graph the # of epochs versus the loss
plt.xlabel('Number of Epochs')
plt.ylabel("Loss Values")
```

```
plt.plot(history.history['loss'])
plt.show()
print("Cost for 11kg:",model.predict([11.0]))
  print("Cost for 45kg:",model.predict([45.0]))
```

Listing A.3 initializes the `Pandas Dataframe df` with the contents of the CSV file `pasta.csv`, and then initializes the variables `weight` and `cost` with the first and second columns, respectively, of `df`.

The next portion of Listing A.3 defines a `Keras`-based model that consists of a single `Dense` layer. This model is compiled and trained, and then a graph is displayed that shows the *number of epochs* on the horizontal axis and the corresponding value of the loss function for the vertical axis. Launch the code in Listing A.3 and you will see the following output:

```
Cost for 11kg:  [[41.727108]]

Cost for 45kg:  [[159.02121]]
```

Figure A.1 displays a graph of epochs versus loss during the training process.

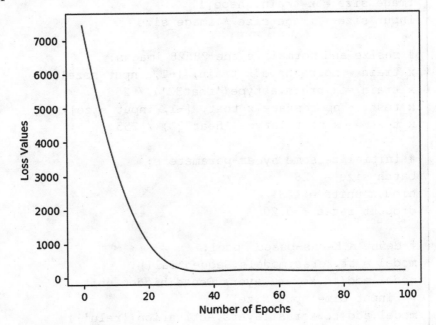

FIGURE A.1 A Graph of Epochs versus Loss.

Keras, MLPs, and MNIST

This section contains a simple example of creating a `Keras`-based MLP neural network that will be trained with the MNIST dataset. Listing A.4 displays the contents of `keras_mlp_mnist.py` that performs this task.

Listing A.4: keras_mlp_mnist.py

```
import tensorflow as tf
import numpy as np

# instantiate mnist and load data:
mnist = tf.keras.datasets.mnist
(x_train, y_train), (x_test, y_test) = mnist.load_data()

# one-hot encoding for all labels to create 1x10
# vectors that are compared with the final layer:
y_train = tf.keras.utils.to_categorical(y_train)
y_test  = tf.keras.utils.to_categorical(y_test)

image_size = x_train.shape[1]
input_size = image_size * image_size

# resize and normalize the 28x28 images:
x_train = np.reshape(x_train, [-1, input_size])
x_train = x_train.astype('float32') / 255
x_test  = np.reshape(x_test, [-1, input_size])
x_test  = x_test.astype('float32') / 255

# initialize some hyper-parameters:
batch_size = 128
hidden_units = 128
dropout_ratea = 0.20

# define a Keras-based model:
model = tf.keras.models.Sequential()
model.add(tf.keras.layers.Dense(hidden_units,
    input_dim=input_size))
model.add(tf.keras.layers.Activation('relu'))
```

```
model.add(tf.keras.layers.Dropout(dropout_rate))
model.add(tf.keras.layers.Dense(hidden_units))
model.add(tf.keras.layers.Activation('relu'))
model.add(tf.keras.layers.Dense(10))
model.add(tf.keras.layers.Activation('softmax'))

model.summary()

model.compile(loss='categorical_crossentropy',
              optimizer='adam',
              metrics=['accuracy'])

# train the network on the training data:
model.fit(x_train, y_train, epochs=10, batch_
    size=batch_size)

# calculate and then display the accuracy:
loss, acc = model.evaluate(x_test, y_test, batch_
    size=batch_size)
print("\nTest accuracy: %.1f%%" % (100.0 * acc))
```

Listing A.4 contains the usual `import` statements and then initializes the variable `mnist` as a reference to the MNIST dataset. The next portion of Listing A.4 contains some typical code that populates the training dataset and the test dataset and converts the labels to numeric values via the technique known as *one-hot* encoding.

Next, several hyperparameters are initialized, and a `Keras`-based model is defined that specifies three `Dense` layers and the `relu` activation function. This model is compiled and trained, and the accuracy on the test dataset is computed and then displayed. Launch the code in Listing A.4 and you will see the following output:

Model: "sequential"

Layer (type)	Output Shape Shape	Param #
dense (Dense)	(None, 256)	200960
activation (Activation)	(None, 256)	0

dropout (Dropout)	(None, 256)	0
dense_1 (Dense)	(None, 256)	65792
activation_1 (Activation)	(None, 256)	0
dropout_1 (Dropout)	(None, 256)	0
dense_2 (Dense)	(None, 10)	2570
activation_2 (Activation)	(None, 10)	0

```
Total params: 269,322
Trainable params: 269,322
Non-trainable params: 0


Train on 60000 samples
Epoch 1/10
60000/60000 [==================================] - 4s
    74us/sample - loss: 0.4281 - accuracy: 0.8683
Epoch 2/10
60000/60000 [==================================] - 4s
    66us/sample - loss: 0.1967 - accuracy: 0.9417
Epoch 3/10
60000/60000 [==================================] - 4s
    63us/sample - loss: 0.1507 - accuracy: 0.9547
Epoch 4/10
60000/60000 [==================================] - 4s
    63us/sample - loss: 0.1298 - accuracy: 0.9600
Epoch 5/10
60000/60000 [==================================] - 4s
    60us/sample - loss: 0.1141 - accuracy: 0.9651
Epoch 6/10
60000/60000 [==================================] - 4s
    66us/sample - loss: 0.1037 - accuracy: 0.9677
Epoch 7/10
60000/60000 [==================================] - 4s
    61us/sample - loss: 0.0940 - accuracy: 0.9702
Epoch 8/10
60000/60000 [==================================] - 4s
    61us/sample - loss: 0.0897 - accuracy: 0.9718
```

```
Epoch 9/10
60000/60000 [==============================] - 4s
    62us/sample - loss: 0.0830 - accuracy: 0.9747
Epoch 10/10
60000/60000 [==============================] - 4s
    64us/sample - loss: 0.0805 - accuracy: 0.9748
10000/10000 [==============================] - 0s
    39us/sample - loss: 0.0654 - accuracy: 0.9797

Test accuracy: 98.0%
```

Keras, CNNs, and cifar10

This section contains a simple example of training a neural network with the cifar10 dataset. This code sample is similar to training a neural network on the MNIST dataset and requires a very small code change.

Keep in mind that images in MNIST have dimensions 28x28, whereas images in cifar10 have dimensions 32x32. Always ensure that images have the same dimensions in a dataset, otherwise the results can be unpredictable.

Note: make sure that the images in your dataset have the same dimensions

Listing A.5 displays the contents of keras_cnn_cifar10.py that trains a CNN with the cifar10 dataset.

Listing A.5: keras_cnn_cifar10.py

```
import tensorflow as tf

batch_size = 32
num_classes = 10
epochs = 100
num_predictions = 20

cifar10 = tf.keras.datasets.cifar10

# The data, split between train and test sets:
(x_train, y_train), (x_test, y_test) = cifar10.
    load_data()
```

(Continued)

```
print('x_train shape:', x_train.shape)
print(x_train.shape[0], 'train samples')
print(x_test.shape[0], 'test samples')

# Convert class vectors to binary class matrices
y_train = tf.keras.utils.to_categorical(y_train,
    num_classes)
y_test = tf.keras.utils.to_categorical(y_test,
    num_classes)

model = tf.keras.models.Sequential()
model.add(tf.keras.layers.Conv2D(32, (3, 3),
    padding='same',
                input_shape=x_train.shape[1:]))
model.add(tf.keras.layers.Activation('relu'))
model.add(tf.keras.layers.Conv2D(32, (3, 3)))
model.add(tf.keras.layers.Activation('relu'))
model.add(tf.keras.layers.MaxPooling2D(pool_
    size=(2, 2)))
model.add(tf.keras.layers.Dropout(0.25))

# you can also duplicate the preceding code block here

model.add(tf.keras.layers.Flatten())
model.add(tf.keras.layers.Dense(512))
model.add(tf.keras.layers.Activation('relu'))
model.add(tf.keras.layers.Dropout(0.5))
model.add(tf.keras.layers.Dense(num_classes))
model.add(tf.keras.layers.Activation('softmax'))

# use RMSprop optimizer to train the model
model.compile(loss='categorical_crossentropy',
            optimizer=opt,
            metrics=['accuracy'])

x_train = x_train.astype('float32')
x_test = x_test.astype('float32')
x_train /= 255
```

```
x_test /= 255

model.fit(x_train, y_train,
        batch_size=batch_size,
        epochs=epochs,
        validation_data=(x_test, y_test),
        shuffle=True)

# evaluate and display results from test data
scores = model.evaluate(x_test, y_test,
    verbose=1)
print('Test loss:', scores[0])
print('Test accuracy:', scores[1])
```

Listing A.5 contains the usual `import` statement and then initializes the variable `cifar10` as a reference to the `cifar10` dataset. The next section of code is similar to the contents of Listing A.4: the main difference is that this `Keras`-based model defines a CNN instead of an MLP. Hence, the first layer is a convolutional layer, as shown here:

```
model.add(tf.keras.layers.Conv2D(32, (3, 3),
    padding='same',
                input_shape=x_train.shape[1:]))
```

Note that a vanilla CNN involves a convolutional layer (which is the purpose of the preceding code snippet), followed by the ReLU activation function, and a max pooling layer, both of which are displayed in Listing A.5. In addition, the final layer of the `Keras` model is the `softmax` activation function, which converts the 10 numeric values in the *fully connected* layer to a set of 10 non-negative numbers between 0 and 1, whose sum equals 1 (this gives us a probability distribution).

This model is compiled and trained, and then evaluated on the test dataset. The last portion of Listing A.5 displays the value of the test-related loss and accuracy, both of which are calculated during the preceding evaluation step. Launch the code in Listing A.5 and you will see the following output (note that the code was stopped after partially completing the second epoch):

```
x_train shape: (50000, 32, 32, 3)
50000 train samples
10000 test samples
```

```
Epoch 1/100
50000/50000 [==============================] -
    285s 6ms/sample - loss: 1.7187 - accuracy:
    0.3802 - val_loss: 1.4294 - val_accuracy:
    0.4926
Epoch 2/100
 1888/50000 [>.............................] -
    ETA: 4:39 - loss: 1.4722 - accuracy: 0.4635
```

Resizing Images in Keras

Listing A.6 displays the contents of keras_resize_image.py that illustrates how to resize an image in Keras.

Listing A.6: keras_resize_image.py

```python
import tensorflow as tf
import numpy as np
import imageio
import matplotlib.pyplot as plt

# use any image that has 3 channels
inp = tf.keras.layers.Input(shape=(None, None, 3))
out = tf.keras.layers.Lambda(lambda image:
    tf.image.resize(image, (128, 128)))(inp)

model = tf.keras.Model(inputs=inp, outputs=out)
model.summary()

# read the contents of a PNG or JPG
X = imageio.imread('sample3.png')

out = model.predict(X[np.newaxis, ...])

fig, axes = plt.subplots(nrows=1, ncols=2)
axes[0].imshow(X)
axes[1].imshow(np.int8(out[0,...]))

plt.show()
```

Listing A.6 contains the usual `import` statements and then initializes the variable `inp` so that it can accommodate a color image, followed by the variable `out` that is the result of resizing `inp` so that it has dimensions 28x23. Next, `inp` and `out` are specified as the values of `inputs` and `outputs`, respectively, for the `Keras` model, as shown in this code snippet:

```
model = tf.keras.Model(inputs=inp, outputs=out)
```

Next, the variable X is initialized as a reference to the result of reading the contents of the image `sample3.png`. The remainder of Listing A.6 involves displaying two images: the original image and the resized image. Launch the code in Listing A.6 and you will see a graph of an image and its resized image as shown in Figure A.2.

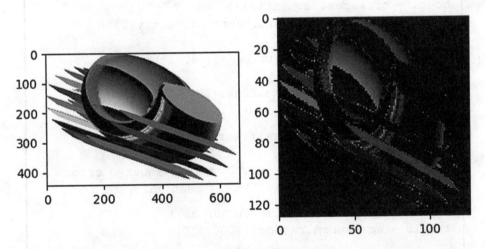

FIGURE A.2 A Graph of an Image and its Resized Image.

`Keras` **and Early Stopping (1)**

After specifying the training set and the test set from a dataset, you also decide on the number of training epochs. A value that's too large can lead to overfitting, whereas a value that's too small can lead to underfitting. Moreover, model improvement can diminish and subsequent training iterations become redundant.

Early stopping is a technique that allows you to specify a large value for the number of epochs, and yet the training will stop if the model performance improvement drops below a threshold value.

There are several ways that you can specify early stopping, and they involve the concept of a *callback function*. Listing A.7 displays the contents of `tf2_keras_callback.py` that performs early stopping via a callback mechanism.

Listing A.7: tf2_keras_callback.py

```
import tensorflow as tf
import numpy as np

model = tf.keras.Sequential()
model.add(tf.keras.layers.Dense(64, activation
        ='relu'))
model.add(tf.keras.layers.Dense(64, activation
        ='relu'))
model.add(tf.keras.layers.Dense(10, activation
        ='softmax'))

model.compile(optimizer=tf.keras.optimizers.
  Adam(0.01),
          loss='mse',           # mean squared error
          metrics=['mae'])      # mean absolute error
data   = np.random.random((1000, 32))
labels = np.random.random((1000, 10))

val_data   = np.random.random((100, 32))
val_labels = np.random.random((100, 10))

callbacks = [
  # stop training if "val_loss" stops improving
   for over 2 epochs
  tf.keras.callbacks.EarlyStopping(patience=2,
   monitor='val_loss'),
  # write TensorBoard logs to the ./logs directory
```

```
    tf.keras.callbacks.TensorBoard(log_dir='./logs')
]

model.fit(data, labels, batch_size=32, epochs=50,
    callbacks=callbacks,
        validation_data=(val_data, val_labels))

model.evaluate(data, labels, batch_size=32)
```

Listing A.7 defines a `Keras`-based model with three hidden layers and then compiles the model. The next portion of Listing A.7 uses the `np.random.random` function in order to initialize the variables `data`, `labels`, `val_data`, and `val_labels`.

The interesting code involves the definition of the `callbacks` variable that specifies `tf.keras.callbacks.EarlyStopping` class with a value of 2 for `patience`, which means that the model will stop training if there is an insufficient reduction in the value of `val_loss`. The `callbacks` variable includes the `tf.keras.callbacks.TensorBoard` class to specify the logs subdirectory as the location for the TensorBoard files.

Next, the `model.fit()` method is invoked with a value of 50 for `epochs` (shown in bold), followed by the `model.evaluate()` method. Launch the code in Listing A.7 and you will see the following output:

```
Epoch 1/50
1000/1000 [==============================] - 0s
    354us/sample - loss: 0.2452 - mae: 0.4127 - val_
    loss: 0.2517 - val_mae: 0.4205
Epoch 2/50
1000/1000 [==============================] - 0s
    63us/sample - loss: 0.2447 - mae: 0.4125 - val_
    loss: 0.2515 - val_mae: 0.4204
Epoch 3/50
1000/1000 [==============================] - 0s
    63us/sample - loss: 0.2445 - mae: 0.4124 - val_
    loss: 0.2520 - val_mae: 0.4209
```

```
Epoch 4/50
1000/1000 [==============================] - 0s
   68us/sample - loss: 0.2444 - mae: 0.4123 - val_
   loss: 0.2519 - val_mae: 0.4205
1000/1000 [==============================] - 0s
   37us/sample - loss: 0.2437 - mae: 0.4119
(1000, 10)
```

Notice that the code stopped training after four epochs, even though 50 epochs are specified in the code.

Keras and Early Stopping (2)

The previous section contains a code sample with minimalistic functionality with respect to the use of callback functions in Keras. However, you can also define a custom class that provides finer-grained functionality that uses a callback mechanism.

Listing A.8 displays the contents of tf2_keras_callback2.py that performs early stopping via a callback mechanism (the new code is shown in bold).

Listing A.8: tf2_keras_callback2.py

```
import tensorflow as tf
import numpy as np

model = tf.keras.Sequential()
model.add(tf.keras.layers.Dense(64, activation
      ='relu'))
model.add(tf.keras.layers.Dense(64, activation
      ='relu'))
model.add(tf.keras.layers.Dense(10, activation
      ='softmax'))

model.compile(optimizer=tf.keras.optimizers.
   Adam(0.01),
```

```
          loss='mse',          # mean squared error
          metrics=['mae'])     # mean absolute error

data    = np.random.random((1000, 32))
labels  = np.random.random((1000, 10))

val_data   = np.random.random((100, 32))
val_labels = np.random.random((100, 10))

class MyCallback(tf.keras.callbacks.Callback):
  def on_train_begin(self, logs={}):
    print("on_train_begin")

  def on_train_end(self, logs={}):
    print("on_train_begin")
    return

  def on_epoch_begin(self, epoch, logs={}):
    print("on_train_begin")
    return

  def on_epoch_end(self, epoch, logs={}):
    print("on_epoch_end")
    return

  def on_batch_begin(self, batch, logs={}):
    print("on_batch_begin")
    return

  def on_batch_end(self, batch, logs={}):
    print("on_batch_end")
    return

callbacks = [MyCallback()]

model.fit(data, labels, batch_size=32, epochs=50,
          callbacks=callbacks,
          validation_data=(val_data, val_labels))

model.evaluate(data, labels, batch_size=32)
```

The new code in Listing A.8 differs from Listing A.7 is limited to the code block that is displayed in bold. This new code defines a custom Python class with several methods, each of which is invoked during the appropriate point during the `Keras` lifecycle execution. The six methods consist of three pairs of methods for the start event and end event associated with training, epochs, and batches, as listed here:

- `def on_train_begin()`
- `def on_train_end()`
- `def on_epoch_begin()`
- `def on_epoch_end()`
- `def on_batch_begin()`
- `def on_batch_end()`

The preceding methods contain just a `print()` statement in Listing A.8, and you can insert any code you wish in any of these methods. Launch the code in Listing A.8 and you will see the following output:

```
on_train_begin
on_train_begin
Epoch 1/50
on_batch_begin
on_batch_end
  32/1000 [..............................] - ETA:
  4s - loss: 0.2489 - mae: 0.4170on_batch_begin
on_batch_end
on_batch_begin on_batch_end
// details omitted for brevity
on_batch_begin
on_batch_end
on_batch_begin
on_batch_end
 992/1000 [==============================>.] - ETA: 0s
  - loss: 0.2468 - mae: 0.4138on_batch_begin
on_batch_end
on_epoch_end
1000/1000 [==============================] - 0s
  335us/sample - loss: 0.2466 - mae: 0.4136 - val_
  loss: 0.2445 - val_mae: 0.4126
```

```
on_train_begin
Epoch 2/50
on_batch_begin
on_batch_end
  32/1000 [...........................] - ETA: 0s
    - loss: 0.2465 - mae: 0.4133on_batch_begin
on_batch_end
on_batch_begin
on_batch_end
// details omitted for brevity
on_batch_end
on_epoch_end
1000/1000 [==============================] - 0s
    51us/sample - loss: 0.2328 - mae: 0.4084 - val_
    loss: 0.2579 - val_mae: 0.4241
on_train_begin
  32/1000 [...........................] - ETA: 0s
    - loss: 0.2295 - mae: 0.4030
1000/1000 [==============================] - 0s
    22us/sample - loss: 0.2313 - mae: 0.4077
(1000, 10)
```

Keras **and Metrics**

Many `Keras`-based models only specify *accuracy* as the metric for evaluating a trained model, as shown here:

```
model.compile(optimizer='adam',
              loss='sparse_categorical_crossentropy',
              metrics=['accuracy'])
```

However, there are many other built-in metrics available, each of which is encapsulated in a `Keras` class in the `tf.keras.metrics` namespace. A list of many such metrics are displayed in the following list:

- class Accuracy: how often predictions matches labels
- class BinaryAccuracy: how often predictions matches labels
- class CategoricalAccuracy: how often predictions matches labels

- class FalseNegatives: the number of false negatives
- class FalsePositives: the number of false positives
- class Mean: the (weighted) mean of the given values
- class Precision: the precision of the predictions wrt the labels
- class Recall: the recall of the predictions wrt the labels
- class TrueNegatives: the number of true negatives
- class TruePositives: the number of true positives

Earlier in this chapter you learned about the *confusion matrix* that provides numeric values for TP, TN, FP, and FN; each of these values has a corresponding Keras class TruePositive, TrueNegative, FalsePositive, and FalseNegative, respectively. Perform an online search for code samples that use the metrics in the preceding list.

Saving and Restoring Keras Models

Listing A.9 displays the contents of tf2_keras_save_model.py that creates, trains, and saves a Keras-based model, then creates a new model that is populated with the data from the saved model.

Listing A.8: tf2_keras_save_model.py

```
import tensorflow as tf
import os

def create_model():
  model = tf.keras.models.Sequential([
    tf.keras.layers.Flatten(input_shape=(28, 28)),
    tf.keras.layers.Dense(512, activation=tf.
  nn.relu),
    tf.keras.layers.Dropout(0.2),
    tf.keras.layers.Dense(10, activation=tf.
  nn.softmax)
  ])

  model.compile(optimizer=tf.keras.optimizers.
  Adam(),
```

```
                loss=tf.keras.losses.sparse_
    categorical_crossentropy,
                metrics=['accuracy'])

  return model
# Create a basic model instance
model = create_model()
model.summary()

checkpoint_path = "checkpoint/cp.ckpt"
checkpoint_dir = os.path.dirname(checkpoint_path)

# Create checkpoint callback
cp_callback = tf.keras.callbacks.
    ModelCheckpoint(checkpoint_path,
save_weights_only=True, verbose=1)

# => model #1: create the first model
model = create_model()

mnist = tf.keras.datasets.mnist
(X_train, y_train),(X_test, y_test) = mnist.load_
    data()

X_train, X_test = X_train / 255.0, X_test / 255.0
print("X_train.shape:",X_train.shape)

model.fit(X_train, y_train,  epochs = 2,
        validation_data = (X_test,y_test),
        callbacks = [cp_callback])  # pass
    callback to training
# => model #2: create a new model and load saved
    model
model = create_model()
loss, acc = model.evaluate(X_test, y_test)
print("Untrained model, accuracy: {:5.2f}%".
    format(100*acc))

model.load_weights(checkpoint_path)
loss,acc = model.evaluate(X_test, y_test)
print("Restored model, accuracy: {:5.2f}%".
    format(100*acc))
```

Listing A.8 starts with the create_model() Python function that creates and compiles a Keras-based model. The next portion of Listing A.8 defines the location of the file that will be saved as well as the checkpoint callback, as shown here:

```
checkpoint_path = "checkpoint/cp.ckpt"
checkpoint_dir = os.path.dirname(checkpoint_path)

# Create checkpoint callback
cp_callback = tf.keras.callbacks.
   ModelCheckpoint(checkpoint_path,
save_weights_only=True, verbose=1)
```

The next portion of Listing A.8 trains the current model using the MNIST dataset, and also specifies cp_callback so that the model can be saved.

The final code block in Listing A.8 creates a new Keras-based model by invoking the Python method create_model() again, evaluating this new model on the test-related data, and displaying the value of the accuracy. Next, the model is loaded with the saved model weights via the load_weights() API. The relevant code block is reproduced here:

```
model = create_model()
loss, acc = model.evaluate(X_test, y_test)
print("Untrained model, accuracy: {:5.2f}%".
   format(100*acc))


model.load_weights(checkpoint_path)
loss,acc = model.evaluate(X_test, y_test)
print("Restored model, accuracy: {:5.2f}%".
   format(100*acc))
```

Now launch the code in Listing A.8 and you will see the following output:

```
on_train_begin
Model: "sequential"
```

Layer (type)	Output Shape	Param #
flatten (Flatten)	(None, 784)	0
dense (Dense)	(None, 512)	401920
dropout (Dropout)	(None, 512)	0
dense_1 (Dense)	(None, 10)	5130

```
Total params: 407,050
Trainable params: 407,050
Non-trainable params: 0

Train on 60000 samples, validate on 10000 samples
Epoch 1/2
59840/60000 [=============================>.] - ETA:
    0s - loss: 0.2173 - accuracy: 0.9351
Epoch 00001: saving model to checkpoint/cp.ckpt
60000/60000 [==============================] - 10s
    168us/sample - loss: 0.2170 - accuracy: 0.9352 -
    val_loss: 0.0980 - val_accuracy: 0.9696
Epoch 2/2
59936/60000 [=============================>.] - ETA:
    0s - loss: 0.0960 - accuracy: 0.9707
Epoch 00002: saving model to checkpoint/cp.ckpt
60000/60000 [==============================] - 10s
    174us/sample - loss: 0.0959 - accuracy: 0.9707 -
    val_loss: 0.0735 - val_accuracy: 0.9761
10000/10000 [==============================] - 1s
    86us/sample - loss: 2.3986 - accuracy: 0.0777
Untrained model, accuracy:  7.77%
10000/10000 [==============================] - 1s
    67us/sample - loss: 0.0735 - accuracy: 0.9761
Restored model, accuracy: 97.61%
```

The directory where you launched this code sample contains a new subdirectory called checkpoint whose contents are shown here:

```
-rw-r--r--  1 owner  staff     1222 Aug 17 14:34
    cp.ckpt.index
-rw-r--r--  1 owner  staff  4886716 Aug 17 14:34
    cp.ckpt.data-00000-of-00001
-rw-r--r--  1 owner  staff       71 Aug 17 14:34
    checkpoint
```

Summary

This appendix introduced you to some of the features of `Keras` and an assortment of `Keras`-based code samples involving basic neural networks with the MNIST and Cifar10 datasets. You learned about some of the important namespaces (such as `tf.keras.layers`) and their contents.

Next, you saw an example of performing linear regression with `Keras` and a simple CSV file. Then you learned how to create a `Keras`-based MLP neural network that is trained on the MNIST dataset.

In addition, you saw examples of `Keras`-based models that perform *early stopping*, which is convenient when the model exhibits minimal improvement (that is specified by you) during the training process.

B

INTRODUCTION TO TF 2

Welcome to TensorFlow 2! This appendix introduces you to various features of TensorFlow 2 (abbreviated as TF 2), as well as some of the TF 2 tools and projects that are covered under the TF 2 umbrella. You will see TF 2 code samples that illustrate new TF 2 features (such as `tf.GradientTape` and the `@tf.function` decorator), plus an assortment of code samples that illustrate how to write code the TF 2 way.

Despite the simplicity of many topics in this appendix, they provide you with a foundation for TF 2. This appendix prepares you for complex code, which delves into frequently used TF 2 APIs that you will encounter in other chapters of this book.

Keep in mind that the TensorFlow 1.x releases are considered legacy code after the production release of TF 2. Google will provide only security-related updates for TF 1.x (i.e., no new code development), and support TensorFlow 1.x for at least another year beyond the initial production release of TF 2. For your convenience, TensorFlow provides a conversion script to facilitate the automatic conversion of TensorFlow 1.x code to TF 2 code in many cases (details provided later in this chapter).

As you saw in the preface, this appendix contains several sections regarding TF 1.x, all of which are placed near the end of this chapter. If you do not have TF 1.x code, obviously these sections are optional (and they are labeled as such).

The first part of this appendix briefly discusses some TF 2 features and some of the tools that are included under the TF 2 umbrella. The second section of this appendix shows you how to write TF 2 code involving TF constants and TF variables.

The third section digresses a bit: you will learn about the new TF 2 Python function decorator `@tf.function` that is used in many code samples in this chapter. Although this decorator is not always required, it's important to become comfortable with this feature, and there are some nonintuitive caveats regarding its use that are discussed in this section.

The fourth section of this appendix shows you how to perform typical arithmetic operations in TF 2, how to use some of the built-in TF 2 functions, and how to calculate trigonometric values. If you need to perform scientific calculations, see the code samples that pertain to the type of precision that you can achieve with floating point numbers in TF 2. This section also shows you how to use `for` loops and how to calculate exponential values.

The fifth section contains TF 2 code samples involving arrays, such as creating an identity matrix, a constant matrix, a random uniform matrix, and a truncated normal matrix, along with an explanation about the difference between a truncated matrix and a random matrix. This section also shows you how to multiply second-order tensors in TF 2 and how to convert Python arrays to second-order tensors in TF 2. The sixth section contains code samples that illustrate how to use some of the new features of TF 2, such as `tf.GradientTape`.

Although the TF 2 code samples in this book use Python 3.x, it's possible to modify the code samples in order to run under Python 2.7. Also make note of the following convention in this book (and only this book): TF 1.x files have a "tf_" prefix and TF 2 files have a "tf2_" prefix.

With all that in mind, the next section discusses a few details of TF 2, its architecture, and some of its features.

What Is TF 2?

TF 2 is an open source framework from Google that is the newest version of TensorFlow. The TF 2 framework is a modern framework that's well suited for machine learning and deep learning, and it's available through an Apache license. Interestingly, TensorFlow surprised many people, perhaps even members of the TF team, in terms of the creativity and plethora of use cases for TF in areas such as art, music, and medicine. For a variety of reasons, the TensorFlow team created TF 2 with the goal of consolidating the TF APIs, eliminating duplication of APIs, enabling rapid prototyping, and making debugging an easier experience.

There is good news if you are a fan of `Keras`: improvements in TF 2 are partially due to the adoption of `Keras` as part of the core functionality of TF 2. In fact, TF 2 extends and optimizes `Keras` so that it can take advantage of all the advanced features in TF 2.

If you work primarily with deep learning models (CNNs, RNNs, LSTMs, and so forth), you'll probably use some of the classes in the `tf.keras` namespace, which is the implementation of `Keras` in TF 2. Moreover, `tf.keras.layers` provides several standard layers for neural networks. As you'll see later, there are several ways to define `Keras`-based models, via the `tf.keras.Sequential` class, a functional style definition, and via a subclassing technique. Alternatively, you can still use lower-level operations and automatic differentiation if you wish to do so.

Furthermore, TF 2 removes duplicate functionality, provides a more intuitive syntax across APIs, as well as compatibility throughout the TF 2 ecosystem. TF 2 even provides a backward compatibility module called `tf.compat.v1` (which does not include `tf.contrib`), and a conversion script `tf_upgrade_v2` to help users migrate from TF 1.x to TF 2.

Another significant change in TF 2 is eager execution as the default mode (not deferred execution), with new features such as the `@tf.function` decorator and TF 2 privacy-related features. Here is a condensed list of some TF 2 features and related technologies:

- Support for `tf.keras`: a specification for high-level code for ML and DL
- Tensorflow.js v1.0: TF in modern browsers
- TensorFlow Federated: an open source framework for ML and decentralized data
- Ragged Tensors: nested variable-length ("uneven") lists
- TensorFlow Probability: probabilistic models combined with deep learning
- Tensor2Tensor: a library of DL models and datasets

TF 2 also supports a variety of programming languages and hardware platforms, including:

- Support for Python, Java, C++
- Desktop, server, mobile device (TF Lite)
- CPU/GPU/TPU support
- Linux and Mac OS X support
- VM for Windows

Navigate to the TF 2 home page, where you will find links to many resources for TF 2: *https://www.tensorflow.org*

TF 2 Use Cases

TF 2 is designed to solve tasks that arise in a plethora of use cases, some of which are listed here:

- Image recognition
- Computer vision
- Voice/sound recognition
- Time series analysis
- Language detection
- Language translation
- Text-based processing
- Handwriting recognition

The preceding list of use cases can be solved in TF 1.x as well as TF 2, and in the latter case, the code tends to be simpler and cleaner compared to their TF 1.x counterpart.

TF 2 Architecture: The Short Version

TF 2 is written in C++ and supports operations involving primitive values and tensors (discussed later). The default execution mode for TF 1.x is *deferred execution* whereas TF 2 uses *eager execution* (think *immediate mode*). Although TF 1.4 introduced eager execution, the vast majority of TF 1.x code samples that you will find online use deferred execution.

TF 2 supports arithmetic operations on tensors (i.e., multidimensional arrays with enhancements) as well as conditional logic, "for" loops, and "while" loops. Although it's possible to switch between eager execution mode and deferred mode in TF 2, all the code samples in this book use eager execution mode.

Data visualization is handled via TensorBoard (discussed in Chapter 2) that is included as part of TF 2. As you will see in the code samples in this book, TF 2 APIs are available in Python and can therefore be embedded in Python scripts.

So, enough already with the high-level introduction: let's learn how to install TF 2, which is the topic of the next section.

TF 2 Installation

Install TensorFlow by issuing the following command from the command line:

```
pip install tensorflow==2.0.0-beta1
```

When a production release of TF 2 is available, you can issue the following command from the command line (which will be the most current version of TF 2):

```
pip install --upgrade tensorflow
```

If you want to install a specific version (let's say version 1.13.1) of TensorFlow, type the following command:

```
pip install --upgrade tensorflow==1.13.1
```

You can also downgrade the installed version of TensorFlow. For example, if you have installed version 1.13.1 and you want to install version 1.10, specify the value 1.10 in the preceding code snippet. TensorFlow will uninstall your current version and install the version that you specified (i.e., 1.10).

As a sanity check, create a Python script with the following three lines of code to determine the version number of TF that is installed on your machine:

```
import tensorflow as tf

print("TF Version:",tf.__version__)

print("eager execution:",tf.executing_eagerly())
```

Launch the preceding code and you ought to see something similar to the following output:

```
TF version: 2.0.0-beta1
eager execution: True
```

As a simple example of TF 2 code, place this code snippet in a text file:

```
import tensorflow as tf
print("1 + 2 + 3 + 4 =", tf.reduce_sum([1, 2, 3, 4]))
```

Launch the preceding code from the command line and you should see the following output:

```
1 + 2 + 3 + 4 = tf.Tensor(10, shape=(), dtype=int32)
```

TF 2 and the Python REPL

In case you aren't already familiar with the Python REPL (read-eval-print-loop), it's accessible by opening a command shell and then typing the following command:

```
python
```

As a simple illustration, access TF 2-related functionality in the REPL by importing the TF 2 library as follows:

```
>>> import tensorflow as tf
```

Now check the version of TF 2 that is installed on your machine with this command:

```
>>> print('TF version:',tf.__version__)
```

The output of the preceding code snippet is shown here (the number that you see depends on which version of TF 2 that you installed):

```
TF version: 2.0.0-beta1
```

Although the REPL is useful for short code blocks, the TF 2 code samples in this book are Python scripts that you can launch with the Python executable.

Other TF 2-based Toolkits

In addition to providing support for TF 2-based code on multiple devices, TF 2 provides the following toolkits:

- TensorBoard for visualization (included as part of TensorFlow)
- TensorFlow Serving (hosting on a server)

- TensorFlow Hub
- TensorFlow Lite (for mobile applications)
- Tensorflow.js (for Web pages and NodeJS)

TensorBoard is a graph visualization tool that runs in a browser. Launch TensorBoard from the command line as follows: open a command shell and type the following command to access a saved TF graph in the subdirectory /tmp/abc (or a directory of your choice):

```
tensorboard -logdir /tmp/abc
```

Note that there are two consecutive dashes ("-") that precede the logdir parameter in the preceding command. Now launch a browser session and navigate to this URL: localhost:6006

After a few moments you will see a visualization of the TF 2 graph that was created in your code and then saved in the directory /tmp/abc.

TensorFlow Serving is a cloud-based flexible, high-performance serving system for ML models that is designed for production environments. TensorFlow Serving makes it easy to deploy new algorithms and experiments, while keeping the same server architecture and APIs. More information is here: *https://www.TF 2.org/serving/*

TensorFlow Lite was specifically created for mobile development (both Android and iOS). Please keep in mind that TensorFlow Lite supersedes TF 2 Mobile, which was an earlier SDK for developing mobile applications. TensorFlow Lite (which also exists for TF 1.x) supports on-device ML inference with low latency and a small binary size. Moreover, TensorFlow Lite supports hardware acceleration with the Android Neural Networks API. More information about TensorFlow Lite is here:

https://www.tensorflow.org/lite/

A more recent addition is tensorflow.js that provides JavaScript APIs to access TensorFlow in a Web page. The tensorflow.js toolkit was previously called deeplearning.js. You can also use tensorflow.js with NodeJS. More information about tensorflow.js is here: *https://js.tensorflow.org*.

TF 2 Eager Execution

TF 2 eager execution mode makes TF 2 code much easier to write compared to TF 1.x code (which used deferred execution mode). You might be surprised to discover that TF introduced eager execution as an alternative to deferred execution in version 1.4.1, but this feature was vastly underutilized. With TF 1.x code, TensorFlow creates a dataflow graph that consists of 1) a set of `tf.Operation` objects that represent units of computation, and 2) `tf.Tensor` objects that represent the units of data that flow between operations.

On the other hand, TF 2 evaluates operations immediately without instantiating a Session object or a creating a graph. Operations return concrete values instead of creating a computational graph. TF 2 eager execution is based on Python control flow instead of graph control flow. Arithmetic operations are simpler and intuitive, as you will see in code samples later in this chapter. Moreover, TF 2 eager execution mode simplifies the debugging process. However, keep in mind that there isn't a 1:1 relationship between a graph and eager execution.

TF 2 Tensors, Data Types, and Primitive Types

In simplified terms, a TF 2 tensor is an n-dimensional array that is similar to a `NumPy` `ndarray`. A TF 2 tensor is defined by its dimensionality, as illustrated here:

```
scalar number:          a zeroth-order tensor
vector:                 a first-order tensor
matrix:                 a second-order tensor
3-dimensional array:    a 3rd order tensor
```

The next section discusses some of the data types that are available in TF 2, followed by a section that discusses TF 2 primitive types.

TF 2 Data Types

TF 2 supports the following data types (similar to the supported data types in TensorFlow 1.x):

- tf.float32
- tf.float64

- `tf.int8`

- `tf.int16`

- `tf.int32`

- `tf.int64`

- `tf.uint8`

- `tf.string`

- `tf.bool`

The data types in the preceding list are self-explanatory: two floating point types, four integer types, one unsigned integer type, one string type, and one Boolean type. As you can see, there is a 32-bit and a 64-bit floating point type, and integer types that range from 8-bit through 64-bit.

TF 2 Primitive Types

TF 2 supports `tf.constant()` and `tf.Variable()` as primitive types. Notice the capital V in `tf.Variable()`: this indicates a TF 2 class (which is not the case for lowercase initial letter such as `tf.constant()`).

A TF 2 *constant* is an immutable value, and a simple example is shown here:

```
aconst = tf.constant(3.0)
```

A TF 2 *variable* is a trainable value in a TF 2 graph. For example, the slope m and y-intercept b of a best-fitting line for a dataset consisting of points in the Euclidean plane are two examples of trainable values. Some examples of TF variables are shown here:

```
b = tf.Variable(3, name="b")
x = tf.Variable(2, name="x")
z = tf.Variable(5*x, name="z")

W = tf.Variable(20)
lm = tf.Variable(W*x + b, name="lm")
```

Notice that b, x, and z are defined as TF variables. In addition, b and x are initialized with numeric values, whereas the value of the variable z is an expression that depends on the value of x (which equals 2).

Constants in TF 2

Here is a short list of some properties of TF 2 constants:

- They are initialized during their definition
- They are cannot change its value ("immutable")
- They are can specify its name (optional)
- Their type is required (ex: tf.float32)
- They are not modified during training

Listing B.1 displays the contents of `tf2_constants1.py` that illustrates how to assign and print the values of some TF 2 constants.

Listing B.1: tf2_constants1.py

```
import tensorflow as tf

scalar = tf.constant(10)
vector = tf.constant([1,2,3,4,5])
matrix = tf.constant([[1,2,3],[4,5,6]])
cube   = tf.consta
   nt([[[1],[2],[3]],[[4],[5],[6]],[[7],[8],[9]]])

print(scalar.get_shape())
print(vector.get_shape())
print(matrix.get_shape())
print(cube.get_shape())
```

Listing B.1 contains four `tf.constant()` statements that define TF 2 tensors of dimension 0, 1, 2, and 3, respectively. The second part of Listing B.1 contains four `print()` statements that display the shape of the four TF 2 constants that are defined in the first section of Listing B.1. The output from Listing B.1 is here:

```
()
(5,)
(2, 3)
(3, 3, 1)
```

Listing B.2 displays the contents of `tf2_constants2.py` that illustrates how to assign values to TF 2 constants and then print those values.

Listing B.2: tf2_constants2.py

```
import tensorflow as tf
x = tf.constant(5,name="x")
y = tf.constant(8,name="y")

@tf.function
def calc_prod(x, y):
  z = 2*x + 3*y
  return z

result = calc_prod(x, y)
print('result =',result)
```

Listing B.2 defines a *decorated* (shown in bold) Python function `calc_prod()` with TF 2 code that would otherwise be included in a TF 1.x `tf.Session()` code block. Specifically, z would be included in a `sess.run()` statement, along with a `feed_dict` that provides values for x and y. Fortunately, a decorated Python function in TF 2 makes the code look like normal Python code.

Variables in TF 2

TF 2.0 eliminates global collections and their associated APIs, such as `tf.get_variable`, `tf.variable_scope`, and `tf.initializers. global_variables`. Whenever you need a `tf.Variable` in TF 2, construct and initialize it directly, as shown here:

```
tf.Variable(tf.random.normal([2, 4])
```

Listing B.3 displays the contents of `tf2_variables.py` that illustrates how to compute values involving TF constants and variables in a `with` code block.

Listing B.3: tf2_variables.py

```
import tensorflow as tf

v = tf.Variable([[1., 2., 3.], [4., 5., 6.]])
print("v.value():", v.value())
print("")
print("v.numpy():", v.numpy())
print("")

v.assign(2 * v)
v[0, 1].assign(42)
v[1].assign([7., 8., 9.])
print("v:",v)
print("")

try:
  v [1] = [7., 8., 9.]
except TypeError as ex:
  print(ex)
```

Listing B.3 defines a TF 2 variable v and prints its value. The next portion of Listing B.3 updates the value of v and prints its new value. The last portion of Listing B.3 contains a `try/except` block that attempts to update the value of v[1]. The output from Listing B.3 is here:

```
v.value(): tf.Tensor(
[[1. 2. 3.]
 [4. 5. 6.]], shape=(2, 3), dtype=float32)

v.numpy(): [[1. 2. 3.]
 [4. 5. 6.]]

v: <tf.Variable 'Variable:0' shape=(2, 3)
   dtype=float32, numpy=
array([[ 2., 42.,  6.],
       [ 7.,  8.,  9.]], dtype=float32)>

'ResourceVariable' object does not support item
   assignment
```

This concludes the quick tour involving TF 2 code that contains various combinations of TF constants and TF variables. The next few sections delve into more details regarding the TF primitive types that you saw in the preceding sections.

The `tf.rank()` API

The *rank* of a TF 2 tensor is the dimensionality of the tensor, whereas the *shape* of a tensor is the number of elements in each dimension. Listing B.4 displays the contents of `tf2_rank.py` that illustrates how to find the rank of TF 2 tensors.

Listing B.4: tf2_rank.py

```
import tensorflow as tf # tf2_rank.py

A = tf.constant(3.0)
B = tf.fill([2,3], 5.0)
C = tf.constant([3.0, 4.0])

@tf.function
def show_rank(x):
    return tf.rank(x)

print('A:',show_rank(A))
print('B:',show_rank(B))
print('C:',show_rank(C))
```

Listing B.4 contains familiar code for defining the TF constant A, followed by the TF tensor B, which is a 2x3 tensor in which every element has the value 5. The TF tensor C is a 1x2 tensor with the values 3.0 and 4.0.

The next code block defines the decorated Python function show_ rank() that returns the rank of its input variable. The final section invokes show_rank() with A and then with B. The output from Listing B.4 is here:

```
A: tf.Tensor(0, shape=(), dtype=int32)
B: tf.Tensor(2, shape=(), dtype=int32)
C: tf.Tensor(1, shape=(), dtype=int32)
```

The `tf.shape()` API

The *shape* of a TF 2 tensor is the number of elements in each dimension of a given tensor.

Listing B.5 displays the contents of `tf2_getshape.py` that illustrates how to find the shape of TF 2 tensors.

Listing B.5: tf2_getshape.py

```
import tensorflow as tf

a = tf.constant(3.0)
print("a shape:",a.get_shape())

b = tf.fill([2,3], 5.0)
print("b shape:",b.get_shape())

c = tf.constant([[1.0,2.0,3.0], [4.0,5.0,6.0]])
print("c shape:",c.get_shape())
```

Listing B.5 contains the definition of the TF constant a whose value is 3.0. Next, the TF variable b is initialized as a 1x2 vector with the value `[[2,3], 5.0]`, followed by the constant c whose value is `[[1.0,2.0,3.0],[4.0,5.0,6.0]]`. The thrree `print()` statements display the values of a, b, and c. The output from Listing B.5 is here:

```
a shape: ()
b shape: (2, 3)
c shape: (2, 3)
```

Shapes that specify a 0-D Tensor (scalar) are numbers (9, -5, 2.34, and so forth), [], and (). As another example, Listing B.6 displays the contents of `tf2_shapes.py` that contains an assortment of tensors and their shapes.

Listing B.6: tf2_shapes.py

```
import tensorflow as tf

list_0 = []
tuple_0 = ()
print("list_0:",list_0)
print("tuple_0:",tuple_0)
```

```
list_1 = [3]
tuple_1 = (3)
print("list_1:",list_1)
print("tuple_1:",tuple_1)

list_2 = [3, 7]
tuple_2 = (3, 7)
print("list_2:",list_2)
print("tuple_2:",tuple_2)

any_list1 = [None]
any_tuple1 = (None)
print("any_list1:",any_list1)
print("any_tuple1:",any_tuple1)

any_list2 = [7,None]
any_list3 = [7,None,None]
print("any_list2:",any_list2)
print("any_list3:",any_list3)
```

Listing B.6 contains simple lists and tuples of various dimensions in order to illustrate the difference between these two types. The output from Listing B.6 is probably what you would expect, and it's shown here:

```
list_0: []
tuple_0: ()
list_1: [3]
tuple_1: 3
list_2: [3, 7]
tuple_2: (3, 7)
any_list1: [None]
any_tuple1: None
any_list2: [7, None]
any_list3: [7, None, None]
```

Variables in TF 2 (Revisited)

TF 2 variables can be updated during backward error propagation. TF 2 variables can also be saved and then restored at a later point in time. The following list contains some properties of TF 2 variables:

- The initial value is optional
- They must be initialized before graph execution

- They are updated during training
- They are constantly recomputed
- They hold values for weights and biases
- They have an in-memory buffer (saved/restored from disk)

Here are some simple examples of TF 2 variables:

```
b = tf.Variable(3, name='b')
x = tf.Variable(2, name='x')
z = tf.Variable(5*x, name="z")

W = tf.Variable(20)
lm = tf.Variable(W*x + b, name="lm")
```

Notice that the variables `b`, `x`, and `W` specify constant values, whereas the variables `z` and `lm` specify expressions that are defined in terms of other variables. If you are familiar with linear regression, you undoubtedly noticed that the variable `lm` ("linear model") defines a line in the Euclidean plane. Other properties of TF 2 variables are listed below:

- They have a tensor that's updateable via operations
- They exist outside the context of `session.run`
- They are like a regular variable
- They hold the learned model parameters
- Their variables can be shared (or non-trainable)
- They are used for storing/maintaining state
- They internally store a persistent tensor
- You can read/modify the values of the tensor
- Multiple workers see the same values for `tf.Variables`
- They are the best way to represent shared, persistent state manipulated by your program

TF 2 also provides the method `tf.assign()` in order to modify values of TF 2 variables; be sure to read the relevant code sample later in this chapter so that you learn how to use this API correctly.

TF 2 Variables vs Tensors

Keep in mind the following distinction between TF variables and TF tensors:

TF *variables* represent your model's trainable parameters (ex: weights and biases of a neural network), whereas TF *tensors* represents the data fed into your model and the intermediate representations of that data as it passes through your model.

In the next section, you will learn about the `@tf.function` decorator for Python functions and how it can improve performance.

What Is `@tf.function` in TF 2?

TF 2 introduced the `@tf.function` decorator for Python functions that defines a graph and performs session execution: it's sort of a successor to `tf.Session()` in TF 1.x. Since graphs can still be useful, `@tf.function` transparently converts Python functions into functions that are backed by graphs. This decorator also converts tensor-dependent Python control flow into TF control flow and adds control dependencies to order read and write operations to TF 2 state. Remember that `@tf.function` works best with TF 2 operations instead of `NumPy` operations or Python primitives.

In general, you won't need to decorate functions with @tf.function; use it to decorate high-level computations, such as one step of training, or the forward pass of a model.

Although TF 2 eager execution mode facilitates a more intuitive user interface, this ease-of-use can be at the expense of decreased performance. Fortunately, the `@tf.function` decorator is a technique for generating graphs in TF 2 code that execute more quickly than eager execution mode.

The performance benefit depends on the type of operations that are performed: matrix multiplication does not benefit from the use of `@tf.function`, whereas optimizing a deep neural network can benefit from `@tf.function`.

How Does `@tf.function` Work?

Whenever you decorate a Python function with `@tf.function`, TF 2 automatically builds the function in graph mode. If a Python function that is decorated with `@tf.function` invokes other Python functions that are not decorated with `@tf.function`, then the code in those nondecorated Python functions will also be included in the generated graph.

Another point to keep in mind is that a `tf.Variable` in eager mode is actually a plain Python object: this object is destroyed when it's out of scope. On the other hand, a `tf.Variable` object defines a persistent object if the function is decorated via `@tf.function`. In this scenario, eager mode is disabled and the `tf.Variable` object defines a node in a persistent TF 2 graph. Consequently, a function that works in eager mode without annotation can fail when it is decorated with `@tf.function`.

A Caveat About `@tf.function` in TF 2

If constants are defined *before* the definition of a decorated Python function, you can print their values inside the function using the Python `print()` function. On the other hand, if constants are defined *inside* the definition of a decorated Python function, you can print their values inside the function using the TF 2 `tf.print()` function. Consider this code block:

```
import tensorflow as tf

a = tf.add(4, 2)

@tf.function
def compute_values():
  print(a) # 6

compute_values()

# output:
# tf.Tensor(6, shape=(), dtype=int32)
```

As you can see, the correct result is displayed (shown in bold). However, if you define constants *inside* a decorated Python function, the output contains types and attributes but *not* the execution of the addition operation. Consider the following code block:

```
import tensorflow as tf

@tf.function
def compute_values():
```

```
 a = tf.add(4, 2)
 print(a)

compute_values()

# output:
# Tensor("Add:0", shape=(), dtype=int32)
```

The zero in the preceding output is part of the tensor name and not an outputted value. Specifically, Add:0 is output zero of the tf.add() operation. Any additional invocation of compute_values() prints nothing. If you want actual results, one solution is to return a value from the function, as shown here:

```
import tensorflow as tf

@tf.function
def compute_values():
  a = tf.add(4, 2)
  return a

 result = compute_values()
 print("result:", result)
```

The output from the preceding code block is here:

```
result: tf.Tensor(6, shape=(), dtype=int32)
```

A second solution involves the TF tf.print() function instead of the Python print() function, as shown in bold in this code block:

```
@tf.function
def compute_values():
  a = tf.add(4, 2)
  tf.print(a)
```

A third solution is to cast the numeric values to Tensors if they do not affect the shape of the generated graph, as shown here:

```
import tensorflow as tf

@tf.function
def compute_values():
  a = tf.add(tf.constant(4), tf.constant(2))
```

```
 return a
result = compute_values()
print("result:", result)
```

The `tf.print()` Function and Standard Error

There is one more detail to remember: the Python `print()` function sends output to something called *standard output* that is associated with a file descriptor whose value is 1; on the other hand, `tf.print()` sends output to *standard error* that is associated with a file descriptor whose value is 2. In programming languages such as C, only errors are sent to standard error, so keep in mind that the behavior of `tf.print()` differs from the convention regarding standard out and standard error. The following code snippets illustrate this difference:

```
python3 file_with_print.py     1>print_output
python3 file_with_tf.print.py 2>tf.print_output
```

If your Python file contains both `print()` and `tf.print()` you can capture the output as follows:

```
python3 both_prints.py 1>print_output 2>tf.print_output
```

However, keep in mind that the preceding code snippet might also redirect *real* error messages to the file `tf.print_output`.

Working with `@tf.function` in TF 2

The preceding section explained how the output will differ depending on whether you use the Python `print()` function versus the `tf.print()` function in TF 2 code, where the latter function also sends output to standard error instead of standard output.

This section contains several examples of the `@tf.function` decorator in TF 2 to show you some nuances in behavior that depend on where you define constants and whether you use the `tf.print()` function or the Python `print()` function. Also keep in mind the comments in the previous section regarding `@tf.function`, as well as the fact that you don't need to use `@tf.function` in all your Python functions.

An Example Without `@tf.function`

Listing B.7 displays the contents of `tf2_simple_function.py` that illustrates how to define a Python function with TF 2 code.

Listing B.7: tf2_simple_function.py

```
import tensorflow as tf

def func():
  a = tf.constant([[10,10],[11.,1.]])
  b = tf.constant([[1.,0.],[0.,1.]])
  c = tf.matmul(a, b)
  return c

print(func().numpy())
```

The code in Listing B.7 is straightforward: a Python function `func()` defines two TF 2 constants, computes their product, and returns that value.

Since TF 2 works in eager mode by default, the Python function `func()` is treated as a normal function. Launch the code and you will see the following output:

```
[[20. 30.]
 [22. 3.]]
```

An Example With `@tf.function`

Listing B.8 displays the contents of `tf2_at_function.py` that illustrates how to define a decorated Python function with TF code.

Listing B.8: tf2_at_function.py

```
import tensorflow as tf

@tf.function
def func():
  a = tf.constant([[10,10],[11.,1.]])
  b = tf.constant([[1.,0.],[0.,1.]])
  c = tf.matmul(a, b)
  return c

print(func().numpy())
```

Listing B.8 defines a decorated Python function: the rest of the code is identical to Listing B.7. However, because of the `@tf.function` annotation, the Python `func()` function is wrapped in a `tensorflow.python.eager.def_function.Function` object. The Python function is assigned to the `.python_function` property of the object.

When `func()` is invoked, the graph construction begins. Only the Python code is executed, and the behavior of the function is traced so that TF 2 can collect the required data to construct the graph. The output is shown here:

```
[[20. 30.]
 [22.  3.]]
```

Overloading Functions with `@tf.function`

If you have worked with programming languages such as Java and C++, you are already familiar with the concept of overloading a function. If this term is new to you, the idea is simple: an overloaded function is a function that can be invoked with different data types. For example, you can define an overloaded *add* function that can add two numbers as well as add (i.e., concatenate) two strings.

If you're curious, overloaded functions in various programming languages are implemented via *name mangling*, which means that the signature (the parameters and their data types for the function) are appended to the function name in order to generate a unique function name. This happens under the hood, which means that you don't need to worry about the implementation details.

Listing B.9 displays the contents of `tf2_overload.py` that illustrates how to define a decorated Python function that can be invoked with different data types.

Listing B.9: tf2_overload.py

```
import tensorflow as tf

@tf.function
def add(a):
  return a + a
```

```
print("Add 1:            ", add(1))
print("Add 2.3:          ", add(2.3))
print("Add string tensor:", add(tf.
    constant("abc")))

c = add.get_concrete_function(tf.
    TensorSpec(shape=None, dtype=tf.string))
c(a=tf.constant("a"))
```

Listing B.9 defines a decorated Python function add() is preceded by a @tf.function decorator. This function can be invoked by passing an integer, a decimal value, or a TF 2 tensor and the correct result is calculated. Launch the code and you will see the following output:

```
Add 1:             tf.Tensor(2, shape=(), dtype=int32)
Add 2.3:           tf.Tensor(4.6, shape=(), dtype=float32)
Add string tensor: tf.Tensor(b'abcabc', shape=(),
                   dtype=string)
c: <tensorflow.python.eager.function.
   ConcreteFunction object at 0x1209576a0>
```

What Is AutoGraph in TF 2?

AutoGraph refers to the conversion from Python code to its graph representation, which is a significant new feature in TF 2. In fact, AutoGraph is automatically applied to functions that are decorated with @tf.function; this decorator creates callable graphs from Python functions.

AutoGraph transforms a subset of Python syntax into its portable, high-performance and language agnostic graph representation, thereby bridging the gap between TF 1.x and TF 2.0. In fact, AutoGraph allows you to inspect its auto-generated code with this code snippet. For example, if you define a Python function called my_product(), you can inspect its auto-generated code with this snippet:

```
print(tf.autograph.to_code(my_product))
```

In particular, the Python for/while construct in implemented in TF 2 via tf.while_loop (break and continue are also supported). The Python if construct is implemented in TF 2 via `tf.cond`. The "for _ in dataset" is implemented in TF 2 via `dataset.reduce`.

`AutoGraph` also has some rules for converting loops. A `for` loop is converted if the iterable in the loop is a Tensor, and a `while` loop is converted if the `while` condition depends on a Tensor. If a loop is converted, it will be dynamically unrolled with `tf.while_loop`, as well as the special case of a `for x in tf.data.Dataset` (the latter is transformed into `tf.data.Dataset.reduce`). If a loop is not converted, it will be statically unrolled.

`AutoGraph` supports control flow that is nested arbitrarily deep, so you can implement many types of ML programs. Check the online documentation for more information regarding `AutoGraph`.

Arithmetic Operations in TF 2

Listing B.10 displays the contents of `tf2_arithmetic.py` that illustrates how to perform arithmetic operations in a TF 2.

Listing B.10: tf2_arithmetic.py

```
import tensorflow as tf

@tf.function # replace print() with tf.print()
def compute_values():
  a = tf.add(4, 2)
  b = tf.subtract(8, 6)
  c = tf.multiply(a, 3)
  d = tf.math.divide(a, 6)

  print(a) # 6
  print(b) # 2
  print(c) # 18
  print(d) # 1

compute_values()
```

Listing B.10 defines the decorated Python function `compute_values()` with simple code for computing the sum, difference, product, and quotient of two numbers via the `tf.add()`, `tf.subtract()`, `tf.multiply()`, and the `tf.math.divide()` APIs, respectively. The four `print()` statements display the values of a, b, c, and d. The output from Listing B.10 is here:

```
tf.Tensor(6,   shape=(), dtype=int32)
tf.Tensor(2,   shape=(), dtype=int32)
tf.Tensor(18,  shape=(), dtype=int32)
tf.Tensor(1.0, shape=(), dtype=float64)
```

Caveats for Arithmetic Operations in TF 2

As you can probably surmise, you can also perform arithmetic operations involves TF 2 constants and variables. Listing B.11 displays the contents of `tf2_const_var.py` that illustrates how to perform arithmetic operations involving a TF 2 constant and a variable.

Listing B.11: tf2_const_var.py

```
import tensorflow as tf

v1 = tf.Variable([4.0, 4.0])
c1 = tf.constant([1.0, 2.0])

diff = tf.subtract(v1,c1)
print("diff:",diff)
```

Listing B.11 computes the difference of the TF variable v1 and the TF constant c1, and the output is shown here:

```
diff: tf.Tensor([3. 2.], shape=(2,), dtype=float32)
```

However, if you update the value of v1 and then print the value of `diff`, it will *not* change. You must reset the value of `diff`, just as you would in other imperative programming languages.

Listing B.12 displays the contents of `tf2_const_var2.py` that illustrates how to perform arithmetic operations involving a TF 2 constant and a variable.

Listing B.12: tf2_const_var2.py

```
import tensorflow as tf

v1 = tf.Variable([4.0, 4.0])
c1 = tf.constant([1.0, 2.0])

diff = tf.subtract(v1,c1)
print("diff1:",diff.numpy())

# diff is NOT updated:
v1.assign([10.0, 20.0])
print("diff2:",diff.numpy())

# diff is updated correctly:
diff = tf.subtract(v1,c1)
print("diff3:",diff.numpy())
```

Listing B.12 recomputes the value of `diff` in the final portion of Listing B.11, after which it has the correct value. The output is shown here:

```
diff1: [3. 2.]
diff2: [3. 2.]
diff3: [9. 18.]
```

TF 2 and Built-in Functions

Listing B.13 displays the contents of `tf2_math_ops.py` that illustrates how to perform additional arithmetic operations in a TF graph.

Listing B.13: tf2_math_ops.py

```
import tensorflow as tf

PI = 3.141592

@tf.function # replace print() with tf.print()
def math_values():
  print(tf.math.divide(12,8))
```

```
print(tf.math.floordiv(20.0,8.0))
print(tf.sin(PI))
print(tf.cos(PI))
print(tf.math.divide(tf.sin(PI/4.),
  tf.cos(PI/4.)))

math_values()
```

Listing B.13 contains a hard-coded approximation for PI, followed by the decorated Python function math_values() with five print() statements that display various arithmetic results. Note, in particular, the third output value is a very small number (the correct value is zero). The output from Listing B.13 is here:

```
1.5
tf.Tensor(2.0,            shape=(), dtype=float32)
tf.Tensor(6.2783295e-07, shape=(), dtype=float32)
tf.Tensor(-1.0,           shape=(), dtype=float32)
tf.Tensor(0.99999964,     shape=(), dtype=float32)
```

Listing B.14 displays the contents of tf2_math-ops_pi.py that illustrates how to perform arithmetic operations in TF 2.

Listing B.14: tf2_math_ops_pi.py

```
import tensorflow as tf
import math as m

PI = tf.constant(m.pi)

@tf.function # replace print() with tf.print()
def math_values():
  print(tf.math.divide(12,8))
  print(tf.math.floordiv(20.0,8.0))
  print(tf.sin(PI))
  print(tf.cos(PI))
  print(tf.math.divide(tf.sin(PI/4.),
    tf.cos(PI/4.)))

math_values()
```

Listing B.14 is almost identical to the code in Listing B.13: the only difference is that Listing B.14 specifies a hard-coded value for PI, whereas Listing B.14 assigns m.pi to the value of PI. As a result, the approximated value is one decimal place closer to the correct value of zero. The output from Listing B.14 is here, and notice how the output format differs from Listing B.13 due to the Python print() function:

```
1.5
tf.Tensor(2.0,          shape=(), dtype=float32)
tf.Tensor(-8.742278e-08,  shape=(), dtype=float32)
tf.Tensor(-1.0,         shape=(), dtype=float32)
tf.Tensor(1.0,          shape=(), dtype=float32)
```

Calculating Trigonometric Values in TF 2

Listing B.15 displays the contents of tf2_trig_values.py that illustrates how to compute values involving trigonometric functions in TF 2.

Listing B.15: tf2_trig_values.py

```
import tensorflow as tf
import math as m

PI = tf.constant(m.pi)

a = tf.cos(PI/3.)
b = tf.sin(PI/3.)
c = 1.0/a # sec(60)
d = 1.0/tf.tan(PI/3.) # cot(60)

@tf.function # this decorator is okay
def math_values():
  print("a:",a)
  print("b:",b)
  print("c:",c)
  print("d:",d)

math_values()
```

Listing B.14 is straightforward: there are several of the same TF 2 APIs that you saw in Listing B.13. In addition, Listing B.14 contains the tf.tan() API, which computes the tangent of a number (in radians). The output from Listing B.14 is here:

```
a: tf.Tensor(0.49999997, shape=(), dtype=float32)
b: tf.Tensor(0.86602545, shape=(), dtype=float32)
c: tf.Tensor(2.0000002,  shape=(), dtype=float32)
d: tf.Tensor(0.57735026, shape=(), dtype=float32)
```

Calculating Exponential Values in TF 2

Listing B.15 displays the contents of tf2_exp_values.py that illustrates how to compute values involving additional trigonometric functions in TF 2.

Listing B.15: tf2_exp_values.py

```
import tensorflow as tf

a  = tf.exp(1.0)
b  = tf.exp(-2.0)
s1 = tf.sigmoid(2.0)
s2 = 1.0/(1.0 + b)
t2 = tf.tanh(2.0)

@tf.function # this decorator is okay
def math_values():
  print('a: ', a)
  print('b: ', b)
  print('s1:', s1)
  print('s2:', s2)
  print('t2:', t2)

math_values()
```

Listing B.15 starts with the TF 2 APIs tf.exp(), tf.sigmoid(), and tf.tanh() that compute the exponential value of a number, the sigmoid value of a number, and the hyperbolic tangent of a number, respectively. The output from Listing B.15 is here:

```
a:  tf.Tensor(2.7182817,  shape=(), dtype=float32)
b:  tf.Tensor(0.13533528, shape=(), dtype=float32)
```

```
s1: tf.Tensor(0.880797,    shape=(), dtype=float32)
s2: tf.Tensor(0.880797,    shape=(), dtype=float32)
t2: tf.Tensor(0.9640276,   shape=(), dtype=float32)
```

Working with Strings in TF 2

Listing B.16 displays the contents of tf2_strings.py that illustrates how to work with strings in TF 2.

Listing B.16: tf2_strings.py

```
import tensorflow as tf
x1 = tf.constant("café")
print("x1:",x1)
tf.strings.length(x1)
print("")

len1 = tf.strings.length(x1, unit="UTF8_CHAR")
len2 = tf.strings.unicode_decode(x1, "UTF8")

print("len1:",len1.numpy())
print("len2:",len2.numpy())
print("")

# String arrays
x2 = tf.constant(["Café", "Coffee", "caffè",
    "咖啡"])
print("x2:",x2)
print("")

len3 = tf.strings.length(x2, unit="UTF8_CHAR")
print("len2:",len3.numpy())
print("")

r = tf.strings.unicode_decode(x2, "UTF8")
print("r:",r)
```

Listing B.16 defines the TF 2 constant x1 as a string that contains an accent mark. The first print() statement displays the first three characters of x1, followed by a pair of hexadecimal values that represent the accented *e* character. The second and third print() statements display the number of characters in x1, followed by the UTF8 sequence for the string x1.

The next portion of Listing B.16 defines the TF 2 constant x2 as a first-order TF 2 tensor that contains four strings. The next `print()` statement displays the contents of x2, using UTF8 values for characters that contain accent marks.

The final portion of Listing B.16 defines r as the Unicode values for the characters in the string x2. The output from Listing B.14 is here:

```
x1: tf.Tensor(b'caf\xc3\xa9', shape=(),
    dtype=string)

len1: 4
len2: [ 99  97 102 233]

x2: tf.Tensor([b'Caf\xc3\xa9' b'Coffee' b'caff\xc3\
    xa8' b'\xe5\x92\x96\xe5\x95\xa1'], shape=(4,),
    dtype=string)

len2: [4 6 5 2]

r: <tf.RaggedTensor [[67, 97, 102, 233], [67, 111,
    102, 102, 101, 101], [99, 97, 102, 102, 232],
    [21654, 21857]]>
```

Chapter 2 contains a complete code sample with more examples of a `RaggedTensor` in TF 2.

Working with Tensors and Operations in TF 2

Listing B.17 displays the contents of `tf2_tensors_operations.py` that illustrates how to use various operators with tensors in TF 2.

Listing B.17: tf2_tensors_operations.py

```
import tensorflow as tf

x = tf.constant([[1., 2., 3.], [4., 5., 6.]])

print("x:", x)
print("")
print("x.shape:", x.shape)
print("")
print("x.dtype:", x.dtype)
```
(Continued)

```
print("")
print("x[:, 1:]:", x[:, 1:])
print("")
print("x[..., 1, tf.newaxis]:", x[..., 1,
    tf.newaxis])
print("")
print("x + 10:", x + 10)
print("")
print("tf.square(x):", tf.square(x))
print("")
print("x @ tf.transpose(x):", x @ tf.transpose(x))

m1 = tf.constant([[1., 2., 4.], [3., 6., 12.]])
print("m1:               ", m1 + 50)
print("m1 + 50:          ", m1 + 50)
print("m1 * 2:           ", m1 * 2)
print("tf.square(m1):    ", tf.square(m1))
```

Listing B.17 defines the TF tensor x that contains a 2x3 array of real numbers. The bulk of the code in Listing B.17 illustrates how to display properties of x by invoking x.shape and x.dtype, as well as the TF function tf.square(x). The output from Listing B.17 is here:

```
x: tf.Tensor(
[[1. 2. 3.]
 [4. 5. 6.]], shape=(2, 3), dtype=float32)

x.shape: (2, 3)

x.dtype: <dtype: 'float32'>

x[:, 1:]: tf.Tensor(
[[2. 3.]
 [5. 6.]], shape=(2, 2), dtype=float32)

x[..., 1, tf.newaxis]: tf.Tensor(
[[2.]
 [5.]], shape=(2, 1), dtype=float32)

x + 10: tf.Tensor(
[[11. 12. 13.]
 [14. 15. 16.]], shape=(2, 3), dtype=float32)
```

```
tf.square(x): tf.Tensor(
[[ 1.  4.  9.]
 [16. 25. 36.]], shape=(2, 3), dtype=float32)

x @ tf.transpose(x): tf.Tensor(
[[14. 32.]
 [32. 77.]], shape=(2, 2), dtype=float32)

m1:             tf.Tensor(
[[51. 52. 54.]
 [53. 56. 62.]], shape=(2, 3), dtype=float32)

m1 + 50:        tf.Tensor(
[[51. 52. 54.]
 [53. 56. 62.]], shape=(2, 3), dtype=float32)

m1 * 2:         tf.Tensor(
[[ 2.  4.  8.]
 [ 6. 12. 24.]], shape=(2, 3), dtype=float32)

tf.square(m1):   tf.Tensor(
[[ 1.   4.  16.]
 [ 9.  36. 144.]], shape=(2, 3), dtype=float32)
```

Second-Order Tensors in TF 2 (1)

Listing B.18 displays the contents of tf2_elem2.py that illustrates how to
define a second-order TF tensor and access elements in that tensor.

Listing B.18: tf2_elem2.py

```
import tensorflow as tf
arr2 = tf.constant([[1,2],[2,3]])

@tf.function
def compute_values():
  print('arr2: ',arr2)
  print('[0]: ',arr2[0])
  print('[1]: ',arr2[1])

compute_values()
```

Listing B.18 contains the TF constant `arr1` that is initialized with the value `[[1,2],[2,3]]`. The three `print()` statements display the value of `arr1`, the value of the element whose index is 1, and the value of the element whose index is `[1,1]`. The output from Listing B.18 is here:

```
arr2:   tf.Tensor(
[[1 2]
 [2 3]], shape=(2, 2), dtype=int32)
[0]:   tf.Tensor([1 2], shape=(2,), dtype=int32)
[1]:   tf.Tensor([2 3], shape=(2,), dtype=int32)
```

2nd Order Tensors in TF 2 (2)

Listing B.19 displays the contents of `tf2_elem3.py` that illustrates how to define a second-order TF 2 tensor and access elements in that tensor.

Listing B.19: tf2_elem3.py

```
import tensorflow as tf

arr3 = tf.constant([[[1,2],[2,3]],[[3,4],[5,6]]])

@tf.function # replace print() with tf.print()
def compute_values():
  print('arr3:   ',arr3)
  print('[1]:    ',arr3[1])
  print('[1,1]:  ',arr3[1,1])
  print('[1,1,0]:',arr3[1,1,0])

compute_values()
```

Listing B.19 contains the TF constant `arr3` that is initialized with the value `[[[1,2],[2,3]],[[3,4],[5,6]]]`. The four `print()` statements display the value of `arr3`, the value of the element whose index is 1, the value of the element whose index is `[1,1]`, and the value of the element whose index is `[1,1,0]`. The output from Listing B.19 (adjusted slightly for display purposes) is here:

```
arr3:   tf.Tensor(
[[[1 2]
  [2 3]]

 [[3 4]
```

```
     [5 6]]], shape=(2, 2, 2), dtype=int32)
[1]:    tf.Tensor(
[[3 4]
 [5 6]], shape=(2, 2), dtype=int32)
[1,1]:   tf.Tensor([5 6], shape=(2,), dtype=int32)
[1,1,0]: tf.Tensor(5, shape=(), dtype=int32)
```

Multiplying Two Second-Order Tensors in TF 2

Listing B.20 displays the contents of tf2_mult.py that illustrates how to multiply second-order tensors in TF 2.

Listing B.20: tf2_mult.py

```
import tensorflow as tf

m1 = tf.constant([[3., 3.]])        # 1x2
m2 = tf.constant([[2.],[2.]])       # 2x1
p1 = tf.matmul(m1, m2)              # 1x1

@tf.function
def compute_values():
  print('m1:',m1)
  print('m2:',m2)
  print('p1:',p1)

compute_values()
```

Listing B.20 contains two TF constant m1 and m2 that are initialized with the value [[3., 3.]] and [[2.],[2.]]. Due to the nested square brackets, m1 has shape 1x2, whereas m2 has shape 2x1. Hence, the product of m1 and m2 has shape (1, 1).

The three print() statements display the value of m1, m2, and p1. The output from Listing B.20 is here:

```
m1: tf.Tensor([[3. 3.]], shape=(1, 2), dtype=float32)
m2: tf.Tensor(
[[2.]
 [2.]], shape=(2, 1), dtype=float32)
p1: tf.Tensor([[12.]], shape=(1, 1), dtype=float32)
```

Convert Python Arrays to TF Tensors

Listing B.21 displays the contents of tf2_convert_tensors.py that illustrates how to convert a Python array to a TF 2 tensor.

Listing B.21: tf2_convert_tensors.py

```
import tensorflow as tf
import numpy as np

x1 = np.array([[1.,2.],[3.,4.]])
x2 = tf.convert_to_tensor(value=x1, dtype=tf.
    float32)

print ('x1:',x1)
print ('x2:',x2)
```

Listing B.21 is straightforward, starting with an import statement for TensorFlow and one for NumPy. Next, the x_data variable is a NumPy array, and x is a TF tensor that is the result of converting x_data to a TF tensor. The output from Listing B.21 is here:

```
x1: [[1. 2.]
 [3. 4.]]
x2: tf.Tensor(
[[1. 2.]
 [3. 4.]], shape=(2, 2), dtype=float32)
```

Conflicting Types in TF 2

Listing B.22 displays the contents of tf2_conflict_types.py that illustrates what happens when you try to combine incompatible tensors in TF 2.

Listing B.22: tf2_conflict_types.py

```
import tensorflow as tf

try:
  tf.constant(1) + tf.constant(1.0)
except tf.errors.InvalidArgumentError as ex:
  print(ex)
```

```
try:
  tf.constant(1.0, dtype=tf.float64) +
    tf.constant(1.0)
except tf.errors.InvalidArgumentError as ex:
  print(ex)
```

Listing B.22 contains two `try/except` blocks. The first block adds two constants 1 and 1.0, which are compatible. The second block attempts to add the value 1.0 that's declared as a `tf.float64` with 1.0, which are not compatible tensors. The output from Listing B.22 is here:

```
cannot compute Add as input #1(zero-based) was expected
to be a int32 tensor but is a float tensor [Op:Add] name: add/

cannot compute Add as input #1(zero-based) was expected to
be a double tensor but is a float tensor [Op:Add] name: add/
```

Differentiation and `tf.GradientTape` in TF 2

Automatic differentiation (i.e., calculating derivatives) is useful for implementing ML algorithms such as back propagation for training various types of NNs (Neural Networks). During eager execution, the TF 2 context manager `tf.GradientTape` traces operations for computing gradients. This context manager provides a `watch()` method for specifying a tensor that will be differentiated (in the mathematical sense of the word).

The `tf.GradientTape` context manager records all forward-pass operations on a "tape." Next, it computes the gradient by playing the tape backward, and then discards the tape after a single gradient computation. Thus, a `tf.GradientTape` can only compute one gradient: subsequent invocations throw a runtime error. Keep in mind that the `tf.GradientTape` context manager only exists in eager mode.

Why do we need the `tf.GradientTape` context manager? Consider deferred execution mode, where we have a graph in which we know how nodes are connected. The gradient computation of a function is performed in two steps: 1) backtracking from the output to the input of the graph, and 2) computing the gradient to obtain the result.

By contrast, in eager execution the only way to compute the gradient of a function using automatic differentiation is to construct a graph. After constructing the graph of the operations executed within the tf.GradientTape context manager on some watchable element (such as a variable), we can instruct the tape to compute the required gradient. If you want a more detailed explanation, the tf.GradientTape documentation page contains an example that explains how and why tapes are needed.

The default behavior for tf.GradientTape is to play once and then discard. However, it's possible to specify a persistent tape, which means that the values are persisted and therefore the tape can be played multiple times. The next section contains several examples of tf.GradientTape, including an example of a persistent tape.

Examples of tf.GradientTape

Listing B.23 displays the contents of tf2_gradient_tape1.py that illustrates how to invoke tf.GradientTape in TF 2. This example is one of the simplest examples of using tf.GradientTape in TF 2.

Listing B.23: tf2_gradient_tape1.py

```
import tensorflow as tf
w = tf.Variable([[1.0]])

with tf.GradientTape() as tape:
  loss = w * w

grad = tape.gradient(loss, w)
print("grad:",grad)
```

Listing B.23 defines the variable w, followed by a with statement that initializes the variable loss with expression w*w. Next, the variable grad is initialized with the derivative that is returned by the tape, and then evaluated with the current value of w.

As a reminder, if we define the function z = w*w, then the first derivative of z is the term 2*w, and when this term is evaluated with the value of 1.0 for w, the result is 2.0. Launch the code in Listing B.23 and you will see the following output:

```
grad: tf.Tensor([[2.]], shape=(1, 1), dtype=float32)
```

Using the `watch()` Method of `tf.GradientTape`

Listing B.24 displays the contents of `tf2_gradient_tape2.py` that also illustrates the use of `tf.GradientTape` with the `watch()` method in TF 2.

Listing B.24: tf2_gradient_tape2.py

```python
import tensorflow as tf

x = tf.constant(3.0)

with tf.GradientTape() as g:
  g.watch(x)
  y = 4 * x * x

dy_dx = g.gradient(y, x)
```

Listing B.24 contains a similar `with` statement as Listing B.23, but this time a `watch()` method is also invoked to watch the tensor x. As you saw in the previous section, if we define the function `y = 4*x*x`, then the first derivative of y is the term `8*x`; when the latter term is evaluated with the value `3.0`, the result is 24.0.

Launch the code in Listing B.24 and you will see the following output:

```
dy_dx: tf.Tensor(24.0, shape=(), dtype=float32)
```

Using Nested Loops with `tf.GradientTape`

Listing B.25 displays the contents of `tf2_gradient_tape3.py` that also illustrates how to define nested loops with `tf.GradientTape` in order to calculate the first and the second derivative of a tensor in TF 2.

Listing B.25: tf2_gradient_tape3.py

```python
import tensorflow as tf

x = tf.constant(4.0)
with tf.GradientTape() as t1:
  with tf.GradientTape() as t2:
    t1.watch(x)
    t2.watch(x)
    z = x * x * x
  dz_dx = t2.gradient(z, x)
d2z_dx2 = t1.gradient(dz_dx, x)
```

(Continued)

```
print("First  dz_dx:  ",dz_dx)
print("Second d2z_dx2:",d2z_dx2)
x = tf.Variable(4.0)
with tf.GradientTape() as t1:
  with tf.GradientTape() as t2:
    z = x * x * x
  dz_dx = t2.gradient(z, x)
d2z_dx2 = t1.gradient(dz_dx, x)

print("First  dz_dx:  ",dz_dx)
print("Second d2z_dx2:",d2z_dx2)
```

The first portion of Listing B.25 contains a nested loop, where the outer loop calculates the first derivative and the inner loop calculates the second derivative of the term x*x*x when x equals 4. The second portion of Listing B.25 contains another nested loop that produces the same output with slightly different syntax.

In case you're a bit rusty regarding derivatives, the next code block shows you a function z, its first derivative z', and its second derivative z'':

```
z   = x*x*x
z'  = 3*x*x
z'' = 6*x
```

When we evaluate z, z', and z'' with the value 4.0 for x, the result is 64.0, 48.0, and 24.0, respectively. Launch the code in Listing B.25 and you will see the following output:

```
First  dz_dx:   tf.Tensor(48.0, shape=(), dtype=float32)
Second d2z_dx2: tf.Tensor(24.0, shape=(), dtype=float32)
First  dz_dx:   tf.Tensor(48.0, shape=(), dtype=float32)
Second d2z_dx2: tf.Tensor(24.0, shape=(), dtype=float32)
```

Other Tensors with tf.GradientTape

Listing B.26 displays the contents of tf2_gradient_tape4.py that illustrates how to use tf.GradientTape in order to calculate the first derivative of an expression that depends on a 2x2 tensor in TF 2.

Listing B.26: tf2_gradient_tape4.py

```python
import tensorflow as tf

x = tf.ones((3, 3))

with tf.GradientTape() as t:
  t.watch(x)
  y = tf.reduce_sum(x)
  print("y:",y)
  z = tf.multiply(y, y)
  print("z:",z)
  z = tf.multiply(z, y)
  print("z:",z)

# the derivative of z with respect to y
dz_dy = t.gradient(z, y)
print("dz_dy:",dz_dy)
```

In Listing B.26, y equals the sum of the elements in the 3x3 tensor x, which is 9.

Next, z is assigned the term y*y and then multiplied again by y, so the final expression for z (and its derivative) is here:

```
z  = y*y*y
z' = 3*y*y
```

When z' is evaluated with the value 9 for y, the result is 3*9*9, which equals 243. Launch the code in Listing B.26 and you will see the following output (slightly reformatted for readability):

```
y: tf.Tensor(9.0,      shape=(), dtype=float32)
z: tf.Tensor(81.0,     shape=(), dtype=float32)
z: tf.Tensor(729.0,    shape=(), dtype=float32)
dz_dy: tf.Tensor(243.0,  shape=(), dtype=float32)
```

A Persistent Gradient Tape

Listing B.27 displays the contents of tf2_gradient_tape5.py that illustrates how to define a persistent gradient tape in order to with tf.GradientTape in order to calculate the first derivative of a tensor in TF 2.

Listing B.27: tf2_gradient_tape5.py

```
import tensorflow as tf

x = tf.ones((3, 3))

with tf.GradientTape(persistent=True) as t:
  t.watch(x)
  y = tf.reduce_sum(x)
  print("y:",y)
  w = tf.multiply(y, y)
  print("w:",w)
  z = tf.multiply(y, y)
  print("z:",z)
  z = tf.multiply(z, y)
  print("z:",z)

# the derivative of z with respect to y
dz_dy = t.gradient(z, y)
print("dz_dy:",dz_dy)
dw_dy = t.gradient(w, y)
print("dw_dy:",dw_dy)
```

Listing B.27 is almost the same as Listing B.26: the new sections are displayed in bold. Note that w is the term y*y and therefore the first derivative w' is 2*y. Hence, the values for w and w' are 81 and 18, respectively, when they are evaluated with the value 9.0. Launch the code in Listing B.27 and you will see the following output (slightly reformatted for readability), where the new output is shown in bold:

```
y: tf.Tensor(9.0,       shape=(), dtype=float32)
w: tf.Tensor(81.0,      shape=(), dtype=float32)
z: tf.Tensor(81.0,      shape=(), dtype=float32)
z: tf.Tensor(729.0,     shape=(), dtype=float32)
dz_dy: tf.Tensor(243.0, shape=(), dtype=float32)
dw_dy: tf.Tensor(18.0,  shape=(), dtype=float32)
```

Google Colaboratory

Depending on the hardware, GPU-based TF 2 code is typically at least fifteen times faster than CPU-based TF 2 code. However, the cost of a good GPU can be a significant factor. Although NVIDIA provides GPUs, those consumer-based GPUs are not optimized for multi-GPU support (which *is* supported by TF 2).

Fortunately, Google Colaboratory is an affordable alternative that provides free GPU and TPU support, and also runs as a `Jupyter` notebook environment. In addition, Google Colaboratory executes your code in the cloud and involves zero configuration, and it's available here:

https://colab.research.google.com/notebooks/welcome.ipynb

This `Jupyter` notebook is suitable for training simple models and testing ideas quickly. Google Colaboratory makes it easy to upload local files, install software in `Jupyter` notebooks, and even connect Google Colaboratory to a `Jupyter` runtime on your local machine.

Some of the supported features of Colaboratory include TF 2 execution with GPUs, visualization using Matplotlib, and the ability to save a copy of your Google Colaboratory notebook to Github by using `File > Save a copy to GitHub`.

Moreover, you can load any .ipynb on GitHub by just adding the path to the URL `colab.research.google.com/github/` (see the Colaboratory website for details).

Google Colaboratory has support for other technologies such as HTML and SVG, enabling you to render SVG-based graphics in notebooks that are in Google Colaboratory. One point to keep in mind: any software that you install in a Google Colaboratory notebook is only available on a per-session basis: if you log out and log in again, you need to perform the same installation steps that you performed during your earlier Google Colaboratory session.

As mentioned earlier, there is one other *very* nice feature of Google Colaboratory: you can execute code on a GPU for up to twelve hours per day for free. This free GPU support is extremely useful for people who don't have a suitable GPU on their local machine (which is probably the majority of users), and now they launch TF 2 code to train neural networks in less than twenty or thirty minutes that would otherwise require multiple hours of CPU-based execution time.

In case you're interested, you can launch Tensorboard inside a Google Colaboratory notebook with the following command (replace the specified directory with your own location):

```
%tensorboard --logdir /logs/images
```

Keep in mind the following details about Google Colaboratory. First, whenever you connect to a server in Google Colaboratory, you start what's known as a *session*. You can execute the code in a session with a GPU or a TPU, and you can execute your code without any time limit for your session. However, if you select the GPU option for your session, *only the first twelve hours of GPU execution time are free*. Any additional GPU time during that same session incurs a small charge (see the website for those details).

The other point to keep in mind is that any software that you install in a Jupyter notebook during a given session will *not* be saved when you exit that session. For example, the following code snippet installs TFLearn in a Jupyter notebook:

```
!pip install tflearn
```

When you exit the current session and at some point later you start a new session, you need to install TFLearn again, as well as any other software (such as Github repositories) that you also installed in any previous session.

Incidentally, you can also run TF 2 code and TensorBoard in Google Colaboratory, with support for CPUs and GPUs (and support for TPUs will be available later). Navigate to this link for more information:

https://www.tensorflow.org/tensorboard/r2/tensorboard_in_notebooks

Other Cloud Platforms

GCP (Google Cloud Platform) is a cloud-based service that enables you to train TF 2 code in the cloud. GCP provides deep learning DL images (similar in concept to Amazon AMIs) that are available here:

https://cloud.google.com/deep-learning-vm/docs

The preceding link provides documentation and a link to DL images based on different technologies, including TF 2 and PyTorch, with GPU and CPU versions of those images. Along with support for multiple versions of Python, you can work in a browser session or from the command line.

GCP SDK

Install GCloud SDK on a Mac-based laptop by downloading the software at this link: *https://cloud.google.com/sdk/docs/quickstart-macos*

You will also receive USD 300 worth of credit (over one year) if you have never used Google cloud.

Summary

This chapter introduced you to TF 2, a very brief view of its architecture, and some of the tools that are part of the TF 2 family. Then you learned how to write basic Python scripts containing TF 2 code with TF constants and variables. You also learned how to perform arithmetic operations and some built-in TF functions.

Next, you learned how to calculate trigonometric values, how to use for loops, and how to calculate exponential values. You also saw how to perform various operations on second-order TF 2 tensors. In addition, you saw code samples that illustrate how to use some of the new features of TF 2, such as the `@tf.function` decorator and `tf.GradientTape`.

Then you got an introduction to Google Colaboratory, which is a cloud-based environment for machine learning and deep learning. This environment is based on Jupyter notebooks, with support for Python and various other languages. Google Colaboratory also provides up to twelve hours of free GPU use on a daily basis, which is a very nice feature.

INTRODUCTION TO PANDAS

This appendix starts with an introduction to the `Pandas` package for Python that provides a rich and powerful set of APIs for managing datasets. These APIs are very useful for machine learning and deep learning tasks that involve dynamically slicing and dicing subsets of datasets.

The first part of this appendix briefly describes `Pandas` and some of its useful features. This section contains code samples that illustrate some nice features of `DataFrames` and a brief discussion of series, which are two of the main features of `Pandas`. The second part of this appendix discusses various types of `DataFrames` that you can create, such as numeric and Boolean `DataFrames`. In addition, you will see examples of creating `DataFrames` with `NumPy` functions and random numbers.

The second section of this appendix shows you how to manipulate the contents of `DataFrames` with various operations. In particular, you will also see code samples that illustrate how to create `Pandas DataFrames` from CSV files, Excel spreadsheets, and data that is retrieved from a URL. The third section of this appendix gives you an overview of important data cleaning tasks that you can perform with `Pandas` APIs.

The final section of this appendix introduces you to `Jupyter`, which is a Python-based application for displaying and executing Python code in a browser. You will also learn about the Google Colaboratory environment, which is fully online and supports `Jupyter` notebooks and provides 12 hours of daily `GPU` usage for free.

After you have completed this appendix, glance through the following blog post that discusses an initiative for parallelizing `Pandas`, as well as a chart containing the most frequently used `Pandas` APIs in Kaggle competitions:

https://rise.cs.berkeley.edu/blog/pandas_on_ray_early_lessons

What Is Pandas?

`Pandas` is a Python package that is compatible with other Python packages, such as `NumPy`, `Matplotlib`, and so forth. Install `Pandas` by opening a command shell and invoking this command for Python 2.x:

```
pip install pandas
```

Launch this command to install `Pandas` for Python 3.x:

```
pip3 install pandas
```

In many ways the `Pandas` package has the semantics of a spreadsheet, and it also works with `xls`, `xml`, `html`, `csv` file types. `Pandas` provides a data type called a `DataFrame` (similar to a Python dictionary) with extremely powerful functionality, which is discussed in the next section.

`Pandas DataFrames` support a variety of input types, such as `ndar-rays`, `lists`, `dicts`, or `Series`. `Pandas` also provides another data type called `Pandas Series` (not discussed in this appendix), this data structure provides another mechanism for managing data (search online for more details).

Pandas Dataframes

In simplified terms, a `Pandas DataFrame` is a two-dimensional data structure, and it's convenient to think of the data structure in terms of rows and columns. `DataFrames` can be labeled (rows as well as columns), and the columns can contain different data types.

By way of analogy, it might be useful to think of a `DataFrame` as the counterpart to a spreadsheet, which makes it a very useful data type in `Pandas` related Python scripts. The source of the dataset can be a data file, database tables, web service, and so forth. `Pandas DataFrame` features include:

- Data Frame Methods
- Data Frame Statistics

- Grouping, Pivoting, and Reshaping
- Dealing with Missing Data
- Joining Data Frames

Dataframes and Data Cleaning Tasks

The specific tasks that you need to perform depend on the structure and contents of a dataset. In general, you will perform a workflow with the following steps (not necessarily always in this order), all of which can be performed with a `Pandas DataFrame`:

- Read data into a dataframe
- Display top of dataframe
- Display column data types
- Display non-missing values
- Replace NA with a value
- Iterate through the columns
- Statistics for each column
- Find Missing Values
- Total missing values
- Percentage of missing values
- Sort table values
- Print summary information
- Columns with > 50% missing
- Rename columns.

A Labeled Pandas Dataframe

Listing C.1 displays the contents of `pandas_labeled_df.py` that illustrates how to define a `Pandas DataFrame` whose rows and columns are labeled.

Listing C.1: pandas_labeled_df.py

```
import numpy
import pandas

myarray = numpy.array([[10,30,20],
        [50,40,60], [1000,2000,3000]])

rownames = ['apples', 'oranges', 'beer']
colnames = ['January', 'February', 'March']
mydf = Pandas.DataFrame(myarray, index=rownames,
        columns=colnames)

print(mydf)
print(mydf.describe())
```

Listing C.1 contains two `import` statements followed by the variable `myarray`, which is a 3x3 `NumPy` array of numbers. The variables `rownames` and `colnames` provide names for the rows and columns, respectively, of the data in `myarray`. Next, the variable `mydf` is initialized as a `Pandas DataFrame` with the specified datasource (i.e., `myarray`).

You might be surprised to see that the first portion of the output below requires a single `print` statement (which simply displays the contents of `mydf`). The second portion of the output is generated by invoking the `describe()` method that is available for any `NumPy DataFrame`. The `describe()` method is very useful: you will see various statistical quantities, such as the mean, standard deviation minimum, and maximum performed column-wise (not row-wise), along with values for the 25th, 50th, and 75th percentiles. The output of Listing C.1 is here:

```
         January  February  March
apples        10        30     20
oranges       50        40     60
beer        1000      2000   3000

         January     February      March
count   3.000000     3.000000    3.000000
mean  353.333333   690.000000 1026.666667
std   560.386771  1134.504297 1709.073823
min    10.000000    30.000000   20.000000
25%    30.000000    35.000000   40.000000
50%    50.000000    40.000000   60.000000
75%   525.000000  1020.000000 1530.000000
max  1000.000000  2000.000000 3000.000000
```

Pandas Numeric `DataFrames`

Listing C.2 displays the contents of `pandas_numeric_df.py` that illustrates how to define a `Pandas DataFrame` whose rows and columns are numbers (but the column labels are characters).

Listing C.2: pandas_numeric_df.py>

```
import pandas as pd

df1 = pd.DataFrame(np.random.randn(10, 4),columns
      =['A','B','C','D'])
df2 = pd.DataFrame(np.random.randn(7, 3), columns
      =['A','B','C'])
df3 = df1 + df2
```

The essence of Listing C.2 involves initializing the `DataFrames` `df1` and `df2`, and then defining the `DataFrame` `df3` as the sum of `df1` and `df2`. The output from Listing C.2 is here:

```
         A        B        C      D
0   0.0457  -0.0141   1.3809  NaN
1  -0.9554  -1.5010   0.0372  NaN
2  -0.6627   1.5348  -0.8597  NaN
3  -2.4529   1.2373  -0.1337  NaN
4   1.4145   1.9517  -2.3204  NaN
5  -0.4949  -1.6497  -1.0846  NaN
6  -1.0476  -0.7486  -0.8055  NaN
7     NaN      NaN      NaN  NaN
8     NaN      NaN      NaN  NaN
9     NaN      NaN      NaN  NaN
```

Keep in mind that the default behavior for operations involving a `DataFrame` and `Series` is to align the `Series` index on the `DataFrame` columns; this results in a row-wise output. Here is a simple illustration:

```
names = pd.Series(['SF', 'San Jose', 'Sacramento'])
sizes = pd.Series([852469, 1015785, 485199])

df = pd.DataFrame({ 'Cities': names, 'Size': sizes })
```

```
df = pd.DataFrame({ 'City name': names,'sizes':
    sizes })

print(df)
```
The output of the preceding code block is here:

```
   City name      sizes
0         SF     852469
1   San Jose    1015785
2  Sacramento    485199
```

Pandas Boolean DataFrames

Pandas supports Boolean operations on DataFrames, such as the logical or, the logical and, and the logical negation of a pair of DataFrames. Listing C.3 displays the contents of pandas_boolean_df.py that illustrates how to define a Pandas DataFrame whose rows and columns are Boolean values.

Listing C.3: pandas_boolean_df.py

```
import pandas as pd

df1 = pd.DataFrame({'a' : [1, 0, 1], 'b' : [0, 1, 1] },
    dtype=bool)
df2 = pd.DataFrame({'a' : [0, 1, 1], 'b' : [1, 1, 0] },
    dtype=bool)

print("df1 & df2:")
print(df1 & df2)

print("df1 | df2:")
print(df1 | df2)

print("df1 ^ df2:")
print(df1 ^ df2)
```

Listing C.3 initializes the DataFrames df1 and df2, and then computes df1 & df2, df1 | df2, df1 ^ df2, which represent the logical AND, the logical OR, and the logical negation, respectively, of df1 and df2. The output from launching the code in Listing C.3 is here:

```
df1 & df2:
       a      b
0  False  False
1  False   True
2   True  False
df1 | df2:
       a      b
0   True   True
1   True   True
2   True   True
df1 ^ df2:
       a      b
0   True   True
1   True  False
2  False   True
```

Transposing a Pandas Dataframe

The T attribute (as well as the transpose function) enables you to generate the transpose of a Pandas DataFrame, similar to a NumPy ndarray.

For example, the following code snippet defines a Pandas dataFrame df1 and then displays the transpose of df1:

```
df1 = pd.DataFrame({'a' : [1, 0, 1], 'b' : [0, 1, 1] },
       dtype=int)
print("df1.T:")
print(df1.T)
```

The output is here:

```
df1.T:
   0  1  2
a  1  0  1
b  0  1  1
```

The following code snippet defines Pandas dataFrames df1 and df2 and then displays their sum:

```
df1 = pd.DataFrame({'a' : [1, 0, 1], 'b' : [0, 1, 1] },
       dtype=int)
```

```
df2 = pd.DataFrame({'a' : [3, 3, 3], 'b' : [5, 5, 5] },
        dtype=int)
print("df1 + df2:")
print(df1 + df2)
```

The output is here:

```
df1 + df2:
    a  b
0   4  5
1   3  6
2   4  6
```

Pandas Dataframes and Random Numbers

Listing C.4 displays the contents of pandas_random_df.py that illustrates how to create a Pandas DataFrame with random numbers.

Listing C.4: pandas_random_df.py

```
import pandas as pd
import numpy as np

df = pd.DataFrame(np.random.randint(1, 5, size=(5, 2)),
    columns=['a','b'])
df = df.append(df.agg(['sum', 'mean']))

print("Contents of dataframe:")
print(df)
```

Listing C.4 defines the Pandas DataFrame df that consists of five rows and two columns of random integers between 1 and 5. Notice that the columns of df are labeled *a* and *b*. In addition, the next code snippet appends two rows consisting of the sum and the mean of the numbers in both columns. The output of Listing C.4 is here:

```
      a     b
0     1.0   2.0
1     1.0   1.0
2     4.0   3.0
3     3.0   1.0
4     1.0   2.0
sum   10.0  9.0
mean  2.0   1.8
```

Combining Pandas `DataFrames` (1)

Listing C.5 displays the contents of `pandas_combine_df.py` that illustrates how to combine Pandas DataFrames.

Listing C.5: pandas_combine_df.py

```
import pandas as pd
import numpy as np

df = pd.DataFrame({'foo1' : np.random.randn(5),
                   'foo2' : np.random.randn(5)})

print("contents of df:")
print(df)

print("contents of foo1:")
print(df.foo1)

print("contents of foo2:")
print(df.foo2)
```

Listing C.5 defines the Pandas DataFrame df that consists of five rows and two columns (labeled "foo1" and "foo2") of random real numbers between 0 and 5. The next portion of Listing C.5 displays the contents of df and foo1. The output of Listing C.5 is here:

```
contents of df:
       foo1      foo2
0  0.274680 -0.848669
1 -0.399771 -0.814679
2  0.454443 -0.363392
3  0.473753  0.550849
4 -0.211783 -0.015014

contents of foo1:
0   0.256773
1   1.204322
2   1.040515
3  -0.518414
4   0.634141
```

```
Name: foo1, dtype: float64
contents of foo2:
0   -2.506550
1   -0.896516
2   -0.222923
3    0.934574
4    0.527033
Name: foo2, dtype: float64
```

Combining Pandas DataFrames (2)

Pandas supports the "concat" method in DataFrames in order to concatenate DataFrames. Listing C.6 displays the contents of concat_frames.py that illustrates how to combine two Pandas DataFrames.

Listing C.6: concat_frames.py

```
import pandas as pd

can_weather = pd.DataFrame({
    "city": ["Vancouver","Toronto","Montreal"],
    "temperature": [72,65,50],
    "humidity": [40, 20, 25]
})

us_weather = pd.DataFrame({
    "city": ["SF","Chicago","LA"],
    "temperature": [60,40,85],
    "humidity": [30, 15, 55]
})

df = pd.concat([can_weather, us_weather])
print(df)
```

The first line in Listing C.6 is an import statement, followed by the definition of the Pandas dataframes can_weather and us_weather that contain weather-related information for cities in Canada and the USA, respectively. The Pandas dataframe df is the concatenation of `can_weather` and `us_weather`. The output from Listing C.6 is here:

```
0       Vancouver          40              72
1       Toronto            20              65
2       Montreal           25              50
0       SF                 30              60
1       Chicago            15              40
2       LA                 55              85
```

Data Manipulation with Pandas Dataframes (1)

As a simple example, suppose that we have a two-person company that keeps track of income and expenses on a quarterly basis, and we want to calculate the profit/loss for each quarter and the overall profit/loss.

Listing C.7 displays the contents of `pandas_quarterly_df1.py` that illustrates how to define a `Pandas DataFrame` consisting of income-related values.

Listing C.7: pandas_quarterly_df1.py

```
import pandas as pd

summary = {
    'Quarter': ['Q1', 'Q2', 'Q3', 'Q4'],
    'Cost':    [23500, 34000, 57000, 32000],
    'Revenue': [40000, 40000, 40000, 40000]
}

df = pd.DataFrame(summary)

print("Entire Dataset:\n",df)
print("Quarter:\n",df.Quarter)
print("Cost:\n",df.Cost)
print("Revenue:\n",df.Revenue)
```

Listing C.7 defines the variable `summary` that contains hard-coded quarterly information about cost and revenue for our two-person company. In general, these hard-coded values would be replaced by data from another source (such as a CSV file), so think of this code sample as a simple way to illustrate some of the functionality that is available in `Pandas DataFrames`.

The variable df is a Pandas DataFrame based on the data in the sum-mary variable. The three print statements display the quarters, the cost per quarter, and the revenue per quarter.

The output from Listing C.7 is here:

```
Entire Dataset:
        Cost       Quarter     Revenue
0       23500        Q1         40000
1       34000        Q2         60000
2       57000        Q3         50000
3                    Q4         30000
Quarter:
0       Q1
1       Q2
2       Q3
3       Q4
Name: Quarter, dtype: object
Cost:
0       23500
1       34000
2       57000
3       32000
Name: Cost, dtype: int64
Revenue:
0       40000
1       60000
2       50000
3       30000
Name: Revenue, dtype: int64
```

Data Manipulation with Pandas DataFrames (2)

In this section, let's suppose that we have a two-person company that keeps track of income and expenses on a quarterly basis, and we want to calculate the profit/loss for each quarter and the overall profit/loss.

Listing C.8 displays the contents of pandas_quarterly_df1.py that illustrates how to define a Pandas DataFrame consisting of income-related values.

Listing C.8: pandas_quarterly_df2.py

```python
import pandas as pd
summary = {
    'Quarter':    ['Q1', 'Q2', 'Q3', 'Q4'],
    'Cost':       [-23500, -34000, -57000, -32000],
    'Revenue':    [40000, 40000, 40000, 40000]
}
df = pd.DataFrame(summary)
print("First Dataset:\n",df)

df['Total'] = df.sum(axis=1)
print("Second Dataset:\n",df)
```

Listing C.8 defines the variable `summary` that contains quarterly information about cost and revenue for our two-person company. The variable `df` is a `Pandas DataFrame` based on the data in the `summary` variable. The three `print` statements display the quarters, the cost per quarter, and the revenue per quarter.

The output from Listing C.8 is here:

```
First Dataset:
     Cost     Quarter      Revenue
0  -23500       Q1          40000
1  -34000       Q2          60000
2  -57000       Q3          50000
3  -32000       Q4          30000
Second Dataset:
     Cost     Quarter      Revenue      Total
0  -23500       Q1          40000       16500
1  -34000       Q2          60000       26000
2  -57000       Q3          50000       -7000
3  -32000       Q4          30000       -2000
```

Data Manipulation with Pandas Dataframes (3)

Let's start with the same assumption as the previous section: we have a two-person company that keeps track of income and expenses on a quarterly basis, and we want to calculate the profit/loss for each quarter and the overall profit/loss. In addition, we want to compute column totals and row totals.

Listing C.9 displays the contents of `pandas_quarterly_df1.py` that illustrates how to define a `Pandas DataFrame` consisting of income-related values.

Listing C.9: pandas_quarterly_df3.py

```
import pandas as pd

summary = {
    'Quarter': ['Q1', 'Q2', 'Q3', 'Q4'],
    'Cost':    [-23500, -34000, -57000, -32000],
    'Revenue': [40000, 40000, 40000, 40000]
}

df = pd.DataFrame(summary)
print("First Dataset:\n",df)

df['Total'] = df.sum(axis=1)
df.loc['Sum'] = df.sum()
print("Second Dataset:\n",df)


# or df.loc['avg'] / 3
#df.loc['avg'] = df[:3].mean()
#print("Third Dataset:\n",df)
```

Listing C.9 defines the variable `summary` that contains quarterly information about cost and revenue for our two-person company. The variable `df` is a `Pandas DataFrame` based on the data in the `summary` variable. The three `print` statements display the quarters, the cost per quarter, and the revenue per quarter. The output from Listing C.9 is here:

```
First Dataset:
     Cost    Quarter    Revenue
0   -23500    Q1         40000
1   -34000    Q2         60000
2   -57000    Q3         50000
3   -32000    Q4         30000
```

```
Second Dataset:
      Cost    Quarter      Revenue      Total
0   -23500      Q1         40000        16500
1   -34000      Q2         60000        26000
2   -57000      Q3         50000        -7000
3   -32000      Q4         30000        -2000

Sum -146500  Q1Q2Q3Q4     180000       33500
```

Pandas DataFrames and CSV Files

The code samples in several earlier sections contain hard-coded data inside the Python scripts. However, it's also very common to read data from a CSV file. You can use the Python CSV.reader() function, the NumPy load-txt() function, or the Pandas function read_csv() function (shown in this section) to read the contents of CSV files.

Listing C.10 displays the contents of the CSV file weather_data.csv and Listing C.11 displays the contents of weather_data.py that illustrates how to read a CSV file, initialize a Pandas DataFrame with the contents of that CSV file, and display various subsets of the data in the Pandas DataFrames.

Listing C.10: weather_data.csv

```
day,temperature,windspeed,event
7/1/2018,42,16,Rain
7/2/2018,45,3,Sunny
7/3/2018,78,12,Snow
7/4/2018,74,9,Snow
7/5/2018,42,24,Rain
7/6/2018,51,32,Sunny
```

Listing C.11: weather_data.py

```python
import pandas as pd

df = pd.read_csv("weather_data.csv")

print(df)
print(df.shape)   # rows, columns
```

(Continued)

```
print(df.head())  # df.head(3)
print(df.tail())
print(df[1:3])
print(df.columns)
print(type(df['day']))
print(df[['day','temperature']])
print(df['temperature'].max())
```

Listing C.11 invokes the Pandas read_csv() function to read the contents of the CSV file weather_data.csv, followed by a set of Python print() statements that display various portions of the CSV file.

The output from Listing C.11 is here:

```
        day   temperature   windspeed   event
0   7/1/2018          42          16    Rain
1   7/2/2018          45           3    Sunny
2   7/3/2018          78          12    Snow
3   7/4/2018          74           9    Snow
4   7/5/2018          42          24    Rain
5   7/6/2018          51          32    Sunny
(6, 4)
        day   temperature   windspeed   event
0   7/1/2018          42          16    Rain
1   7/2/2018          45           3    Sunny
2   7/3/2018          78          12    Snow
3   7/4/2018          74           9    Snow
4   7/5/2018          42          24    Rain

        day   temperature   windspeed   event
1   7/2/2018          45           3    Sunny
2   7/3/2018          78          12    Snow
3   7/4/2018          74           9    Snow
4   7/5/2018          42          24    Rain
5   7/6/2018          51          32    Sunny

        day   temperature   windspeed   event
1   7/2/2018          45           3    Sunny
2   7/3/2018          78          12    Snow
```

```
Index(['day', 'temperature', 'windspeed', 'event'],
    dtype='object')
<class 'pandas.core.series.Series'>
        day     temperature
0   7/1/2018        42
1   7/2/2018        45
2   7/3/2018        78
3   7/4/2018        74
4   7/5/2018        42
5   7/6/2018        51
78
```

In some situations you might need to apply Boolean conditional logic to filter out some rows of data, based on a conditional condition that's applied to a column value.

Listing C.12 displays the contents of the CSV file `people.csv` and Listing C.13 displays the contents of `people_pandas.py` that illustrates how to define a `Pandas DataFrame` that reads the CSV file and manipulates the data.

Listing C.12: people.csv

```
fname,lname,age,gender,country
john,smith,30,m,usa
jane,smith,31,f,france
jack,jones,32,f,france
dave,stone,33,f,france
sara,stein,34,f,france
eddy,bower,35,f,france
```

Listing C.13: people_pandas.py

```
import pandas as pd

df = pd.read_csv('people.csv')
df.info()
print('fname:')
print(df['fname'])
print('------------')
print('age over 33:')
```

(Continued)

```
print(df['age'] > 33)
print('------------')
print('age over 33:')
myfilter = df['age'] >  33
print(df[myfilter])
```

Listing C.13 populate the Pandas dataframe df with the contents of the CSV file people.csv. The next portion of Listing C.13 displays the structure of df, followed by the first names of all the people. The next portion of Listing C.13 displays a tabular list of six rows containing either True or False depending on whether a person is over 33 or at most 33, respectively. The final portion of Listing C.13 displays a tabular list of two rows containing all the details of the people who are over 33. The output from Listing C.13 is here:

```
myfilter = df['age'] >  33
<class 'pandas.core.frame.DataFrame'>
RangeIndex: 6 entries, 0 to 5
Data columns (total 5 columns):
fname       6 non-null object
lname       6 non-null object
age         6 non-null int64
gender      6 non-null object
country     6 non-null object
dtypes: int64(1), object(4)
memory usage: 320.0+ bytes
fname:
0    john
1    jane
2    jack
3    dave
4    sara
5    eddy
Name: fname, dtype: object
------------
age over 33:
0    False
1    False
```

```
2       False
3       False
4        True
5        True
Name: age, dtype: bool
------------
age over 33:
  fname  lname  age gender country
4  sara  stein   34      f  france
5  eddy  bower   35      m  france
```

Pandas `DataFrames` and Excel Spreadsheets (1)

Listing C.14 displays the contents of `people_xlsx.py` that illustrates how to read data from an Excel spreadsheet and create a `Pandas DataFrame` with that data.

Listing C.14: people_xlsx.py

```
import pandas as pd

df = pd.read_excel("people.xlsx")
print("Contents of Excel spreadsheet:")
print(df)
```

Listing C.14 is straightforward: the `Pandas` dataframe `df` is initialized with the contents of the spreadsheet `people.xlsx` (whose contents are the same as `people.csv` displayed in Listing C.12) via the `Pandas` function `read_excel()`. The output from Listing C.14 is here:

```
  fname  lname  age gender country
0  john  smith   30      m     usa
1  jane  smith   31      f  france
2  jack  jones   32      f  france
3  dave  stone   33      f  france
4  sara  stein   34      f  france
5  eddy  bower   35      f  france
```

Pandas DataFrames and Excel Spreadsheets (2)

Listing C.15 displays the contents of employees_xlsx.py that illustrates how to read data from an Excel spreadsheet and create a Pandas DataFrame with that data.

Listing C.15: employees_xlsx.py

```
import pandas as pd

df = pd.read_excel("employees.xlsx")
print("Contents of Excel spreadsheet:")
print(df)

print("Q1 sum, mean, min, max:")
print(df["q1"].sum(), df["q1"].mean(),df["q1"].
    min(),df["q1"].max())

print("Q2 sum, mean, min, max:")
print(df["q2"].sum(), df["q2"].mean(),df["q2"].
    min(),df["q2"].max())

print("Q3 sum, mean, min, max:")
print(df["q3"].sum(), df["q3"].mean(),df["q3"].
    min(),df["q3"].max())

print("Q4 sum, mean, min, max:")
print(df["q4"].sum(), df["q4"].mean(),df["q4"].
    min(),df["q4"].max())

sum_col=df[["q1","q2","q3","q4"]].sum()
print("Quarter totals:")
print(sum_col)
df = pd.read_excel("people.xlsx")
print("Contents of Excel spreadsheet:")
print(df)
```

Listing C.15 starts by reading the contents of the spreadsheet people.xlsx (whose contents are the same as people.csv displayed in Listing C.12) into the Pandas dataframe df, just as you saw in Listing C.14. The rest of Listing C.15 displays various statistical values, such as the sum, mean,

min, and max values of quarter 1, quarter 2, quarter 3, and quarter 4. The
output from Listing C.15 is here:

```
Contents of Excel spreadsheet:

         id    fname   lname   gender    title      q1

  0     1000   john    smith     m     marketing  20000

  1     2000   jane    smith     f     developer  30000

  2     3000   jack    jones     m       sales    10000

  3     4000   dave    stone     m      support   15000

  4     5000   sara    stein     f      analyst   25000

  5     6000   eddy    bower     m     developer  14000

          q2      q3      q4      country

  0      12000   18000   25000     usa

  1      15000   11000   35000    france

  2      19000   12000   15000     usa

  3      17000   14000   18000    france

  4      22000   18000   28000    italy

  5      32000   28000   10000    france

Q1 sum, mean, min, max:
114000 19000.0 10000 30000
Q2 sum, mean, min, max:
117000 19500.0 12000 32000
Q3 sum, mean, min, max:
101000 16833.333333333332 11000 28000
Q4 sum, mean, min, max:
131000 21833.333333333332 10000 35000
Quarter totals:
q1    114000
q2    117000
q3    101000
q4    131000
dtype: int64
```

```
Contents of Excel spreadsheet:
    fname  lname   age  gender      country
0   john   smith   30   m           usa
1   jane   smith   31   f           france
2   jack   jones   32   f           france
3   dave   stone   33   f           france
4   sara   stein   34   f           france
```

Reading Data Files with Different Delimiters

This section contains an example of reading a text file that contains different delimiters: some rows use a space as a delimiter, whereas other rows start with a space and use a colon ":" as well as a space as a separator.

Listing C.16 displays the contents of multiple_delims.dat that contains data rows with different delimiters, followed by Listing C.17 that displays the contents of multiple_delims.py that read the contents of multiple_delims.dat into a Pandas DataFrame.

Listing C.16: multiple_delims.dat

```
c stuff
c more header
c begin data
 1 1:.5
 1 2:6.5
 1 3:5.3
```

Listing C.17: multiple_delims.py

```
import pandas as pd

df = pd.read_csv('multidelim.dat', skiprows=3,
                names=['a', 'b', 'c'],
                sep=' |:', engine='python')

print("dataframe:")
print(df)
print(data.head())
```

Listing C.17 invokes the Pandas read_csv() function to read the contents of multidelim.dat into the Pandas dataframe df. Compare the output shown below with the contents of Listing C.16 to understand the code in Listing C.17:

```
dataframe:
   a  b    c
0  1  1  0.5
1  1  2  6.5
2  1  3  5.3
```

Transforming Data with the sed Command (Optional)

The preceding section contains an example of a data file with different delimiters, but there is a limitation: the first set of rows must have the same type and the second set of rows must also be of the same type.

However, you might have a more heterogeneous dataset with a set of rows in random order, where each row contains multiple delimiters. The solution in this section involves three files: an initial randomized dataset `multiple_delims2.dat`, a shell script `multiple_delims2.sh` for creating a clean dataset called `multiple_delims2b.dat`, and a Python script `multiple_delims2.py` that reads the data in `multiple_delims2b.dat` into a `Pandas DataFrame`.

Listing C.18 displays the contents of `multiple_delims2.dat` that contains a mixture of delimiters in multiple rows (in random order).

Listing C.18: multiple_delims2.dat

```
1000|Jane:Edwards^Sales
2000:Tom:Smith^Development
3000|Dave:Del Ray^Marketing
4000^Steven^Andrews:Marketing
```

Listing C.19 displays the contents of the shell script `multiple_delims.sh` that transforms `multiple_delims2.dat` into the dataset `multiple_delims2b.dat`, where the latter dataset has only a comma "," as a delimiter between columns in every row.

Listing C.19: multiple_delims2.sh

```
inputfile="multiple_delims2.dat"
cat $inputfile | sed -e 's/:/,/' -e 's/|/,/' -e
  's/\^/,/g'
```

Listing C.19 specifies the name of a text file whose contents are piped to the Unix `sed` command that replaces all occurrences of the characters ",", "|", and "^" with a comma ",". The trailing `g` in the `sed` command ensures that the replacement is performed globally. The resulting output will contain only a "," as a delimiter (shown in Listing C.18).

Open a command shell and navigate to the directory that contains the shell script in Listing C.19 and execute the following pair of commands:

```
chmod +x multiple_delims2.sh
./multiple_delims2.sh > multiple_delims2b.dat
```

Listing C.20 displays the contents of `multiple_delims2b.dat` that you created in the preceding step.

Listing C.20: multiple_delims2b.dat

```
1000,Jane,Edwards,Sales
2000,Tom,Smith,Development
3000,Dave,Del Ray,Marketing
4000,Steven,Andrews,Marketing
```

Listing C.21 displays the contents of `multiple_delims2b.py` that reads the contents of `multiple_delims2b.dat` into a `Pandas DataFrame`.

Listing C.21: multiple_delims2b.py

```
import pandas as pd

df = pd.read_csv('multiple_delims2b.dat',
                 names=['a', 'b', 'c', 'd'],
                 sep=',', engine='python')
print("dataframe:")
print(df)
```

Listing C.21 imports `pandas` and then initializes the variable `df` with the contents of the text file `multiple_delims2b.dat`. The output from launching the code in Listing C.21 is here:

```
dataframe:
      a      b        c            d
0  1000   Jane  Edwards        Sales
1  2000    Tom    Smith  Development
```

```
2    3000    Dave      Del Ray     Marketing
3    4000    Steven    Andrews     Marketing
```

Once again, the heavy lifting is performed by the cryptic-looking `sed` command in the shell script `multiple_delims2.sh`, which is in appendix 4 of the book *Data Cleaning Pocket Primer* (ISBN: 978-1683922179). This book contains a detailed explanation of the `sed` command that will enable you to understand the contents of `multiple_delims2.sh`, as well as chapters that discuss the `grep` and `awk` commands and numerous examples of how to use them for various data cleaning tasks.

Select, Add, and Delete Columns in `DataFrames`

This section contains short code blocks that illustrate how to perform operations on a `DataFrame` that resemble the operations on a Python dictionary. For example, getting, setting, and deleting columns works with the same syntax as the analogous Python `dict` operations, as shown here:

```
df = pd.DataFrame.from_dict(dict([('A',[1,2,3]),
    ('B',[4,5,6])]),
                orient='index', columns=['one',
    'two', 'three'])

print(df)
```

The output from the preceding code snippet is here:

```
    one  two  three
A    1    2     3
B    4    5     6
```

Now look at the following sequence of operations on the contents of the dataframe df:

```
df['three'] = df['one'] * df['two']
df['flag'] = df['one'] > 2
print(df)
```

The output from the preceding code block is here:

```
    one  two  three  flag
a   1.0  1.0    1.0  False
b   2.0  2.0    4.0  False
```

```
c  3.0  3.0    9.0  True
d  NaN  4.0    NaN  False
```

Columns can be deleted or popped like with a Python `dict`, as shown in following code snippet:

```
del df['two']
three = df.pop('three')
print(df)
```

The output from the preceding code block is here:

```
   one  flag
a  1.0  False
b  2.0  False
c  3.0  True
d  NaN  False
```

When inserting a scalar value, it will naturally be propagated to fill the column:

```
df['foo'] = 'bar'
print(df)
```

The output from the preceding code snippet is here:

```
   one   flag  foo
a  1.0  False  bar
b  2.0  False  bar
c  3.0   True  bar
d  NaN  False  bar
```

When inserting a Series that does not have the same index as the `DataFrame`, it will be conformed to the index of the `DataFrame`:

```
df['one_trunc'] = df['one'][:2]
print(df)
```

The output from the preceding code snippet is here:

```
   one   flag  foo    one_trunc
a  1.0  False  bar    1.0
b  2.0  False  bar    2.0
c  3.0   True  bar    NaN
d  NaN  False  bar    NaN
```

You can insert raw `ndarrays` but their length must match the length of the index of the `DataFrame`.

Pandas `DataFrames` and Scatterplots

Listing C.22 displays the contents of `pandas_scatter_df.py` that illustrates how to generate a scatterplot from a `Pandas DataFrame`.

Listing C.22: pandas_scatter_df.py

```
import numpy as np
import pandas as pd
import matplotlib.pyplot as plt
from pandas import read_csv
from pandas.plotting import scatter_matrix

myarray = np.array([[10,30,20],
    [50,40,60],[1000,2000,3000]])

rownames = ['apples', 'oranges', 'beer']
colnames = ['January', 'February', 'March']

mydf = pd.DataFrame(myarray, index=rownames,
    columns=colnames)

print(mydf)
print(mydf.describe())

scatter_matrix(mydf)
plt.show()
```

Listing C.22 starts with various `import` statements, followed by the definition of the `NumPy` array `myarray`. Next, the variables `myarray` and `colnames` are initialized with values for the rows and columns, respectively. The next portion of Listing C.22 initializes the `Pandas DataFrame mydf` so that the rows and columns are labeled in the output, as shown here:

```
        January  February    March
apples       10        30       20
oranges      50        40       60
beer       1000      2000     3000
```

	January	February	March
count	3.000000	3.000000	3.000000
mean	353.333333	690.000000	1026.666667
std	560.386771	1134.504297	1709.073823
min	10.000000	30.000000	20.000000
25%	30.000000	35.000000	40.000000
50%	50.000000	40.000000	60.000000
75%	525.000000	1020.000000	1530.000000
max	1000.000000	2000.000000	3000.0000000

Pandas DataFrames and Histograms

Listing C.23 displays the contents of pandas_histograms.py that illustrates how to generate histograms from a Pandas DataFrame.

Listing C.23: pandas_histograms.py

```
import pandas as pd

df = pd.read_csv("housing.csv")

print(df.head())
print(df.info())
print(df.describe())

import matplotlib.pyplot as plt
df.hist(bins=50, figsize=(20,15))
#save_fig("housing_histograms")
plt.show()
```

Listing C.23 initializes the Pandas DataFrame df with the contents of the CSV file housing.csv. Next, various portions of df are displayed, such as the first five rows and information about the structure of df.

The next portion of Listing C.23 imports the plt class so that we can display a scatterplot of the data in df: this is done by invoking the hist()

method of the `df` variable, followed by the `plt.show()` command that actually displays the scatter plot. The output from Listing C.23 is here:

Unnamed:

	0	price	lot size	bed rooms	bath rms	stories	drive way	rec room\
0	1	42000.0	5850	3	1	2	yes	no
1	2	38500.0	4000	2	1	1	yes	no
2	3	49500.0	3060	3	1	1	yes	no
3	4	60500.0	6650	3	1	2	yes	yes
4	5	61000.0	6360	2	1	1	yes	no

	fullbase	gashw	airco	garagepl	prefarea
0	yes	no	no	1	no
1	no	no	no	0	no
2	no	no	no	0	no
3	no	no	no	0	no
4	no	no	no	0	no

```
<class 'pandas.core.frame.DataFrame'>
RangeIndex: 546 entries, 0 to 545
Data columns (total 13 columns):
Unnamed: 0     546 non-null int64
price          546 non-null float64
lotsize        546 non-null int64
bedrooms       546 non-null int64
bathrms        546 non-null int64
stories        546 non-null int64
driveway       546 non-null object
recroom        546 non-null object
fullbase       546 non-null object
gashw          546 non-null object
airco          546 non-null object
garagepl       546 non-null int64
prefarea       546 non-null object
dtypes: float64(1), int64(6), object(6)
memory usage: 55.5+ KB
```

None
Unnamed:

	0	price	lot size	bed rooms
count	546.000000	546.000000	546.000000	546.000000
mean	273.500000	68121.597070	5150.265568	2.965201
std	157.760895	26702.670926	2168.158725	0.737388
min	1.000000	25000.000000	1650.000000	1.000000
25%	137.250000	49125.000000	3600.000000	2.000000
50%	273.500000	62000.000000	4600.000000	3.000000
75%	409.750000	82000.000000	6360.000000	3.000000
max	546.000000	190000.000000	16200.000000	6.000000

	bathrms	stories	garagepl
count	546.000000	546.000000	546.000000
mean	1.285714	1.807692	0.692308
std	0.502158	0.868203	0.861307
min	1.000000	1.000000	0.000000
25%	1.000000	1.000000	0.000000
50%	1.000000	2.000000	0.000000
75%	2.000000	2.000000	1.000000
max	4.000000	4.000000	3.000000

Figure C.1 displays the histograms that are generated by launching the code in Listing C.23.

Pandas DataFrames and Simple Statistics

Listing C.24 displays the contents of housing_stats.py that illustrates how to gather basic statistics from data in a Pandas DataFrame.

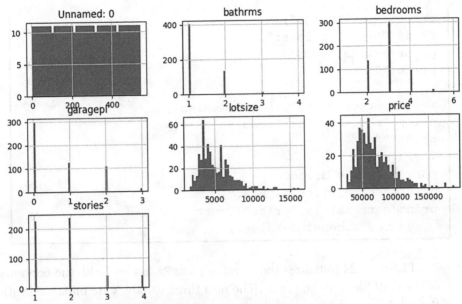

FIGURE C.1 Histograms for the housing.csv Dataset.

Listing C.24: housing_stats.py

```
import pandas as pd

df = pd.read_csv("housing.csv")

minimum_bdrms = df["bedrooms"].min()
median_bdrms  = df["bedrooms"].median()
maximum_bdrms = df["bedrooms"].max()

print("minimum # of bedrooms:",minimum_bdrms)
print("median  # of bedrooms:",median_bdrms)
print("maximum # of bedrooms:",maximum_bdrms)
print("")

print("median values:",df.median().values)
print("")
```

(Continued)

```
prices = df["price"]
print("first 5 prices:")
print(prices.head())
print("")

median_price = df["price"].median()
print("median price:",median_price)
print("")

corr_matrix = df.corr()
print("correlation matrix:")
print(corr_matrix["price"].sort_
    values(ascending=False))
```

Listing C.24 initializes the Pandas DataFrame df with the contents of the CSV file housing.csv. The next three variables are initialized with the minimum, median, and maximum number of bedrooms, respectively, and then these values are displayed.

The next portion of Listing C.24 initializes the variable prices with the contents of the Prices column of the Pandas DataFrame df. Next, the first five rows are printed via the prices.head() statement, followed by the median value of the prices.

The final portion of Listing C.24 initializes the variable corr_matrix with the contents of the correlation matrix for the Pandas DataFrame df, and then displays its contents. The output from Listing C.24 is here:

```
Apples
10
```

Standardizing Pandas DataFrames

Listing C.25 displays the contents of pandas_standardize_df.py that illustrates how to standardize data in a Pandas DataFrame.

Listing C.25: pandas_standardize_df.py

```python
# Standardize data (0 mean, 1 stdev)
from sklearn.preprocessing import StandardScaler
from pandas import read_csv
import numpy

url = 'https://goo.gl/bDdBiA'
names = ['preg','plas','pres','skin','test','mass',
    'pedi','age','class']
dataframe = read_csv(url, names=names)
array = dataframe.values

# separate array into input and output components
X = array[:,0:8]
Y = array[:,8]
scaler = StandardScaler().fit(X)
rescaledX = scaler.transform(X)

# summarize transformed data
numpy.set_printoptions(precision=3)
print(rescaledX[0:5,:])
```

Listing C.25 imports the StandardScaler class from the Sklearn package in order to rescale data values so that they have a mean of 0 and a standard deviation of 1.

Next, the variable url is initialized with the location of a website that returns CSV-based data. The names variable contains an array of column names that are used to label the columns of the CSV-based data. Next, the variable dataframe is initialized with the contents of the CSV-based data (retrieved from the location specified by the url variable).

The next portion of Listing C.25 initializes the variable array with the values in the variable dataframe. Next, the variable X is initialized with the leftmost eight columns of every row in the variable array, and the variable y is initialized with the data in the ninth column of the variable array. The next portion of Listing C.25 invokes the fit method of the Standard-Scaler class in order to fit the data contained in X, and the result is used to initialize the variable `scaler`. The next statement invokes the `trans-form()` method on the contents of X and the results are used to initialize the variable `rescaledX`, which concludes the required data transformations (finally!)

The final portion of Listing C.25 displays all the columns of the first five rows of the variable `scaler`. The output from Listing C.25 is here:

```
minimum # of bedrooms: 1
median  # of bedrooms: 3.0
maximum # of bedrooms: 6

median values: [2.735e+02 6.200e+04 4.600e+03
   3.000e+00 1.000e+00 2.000e+00 0.000e+00]

first 5 prices:
0    42000.0
1    38500.0
2    49500.0
3    60500.0
4    61000.0
Name: price, dtype: float64

median price: 62000.0

correlation matrix:
price       1.000000
lotsize     0.535796
bathrms     0.516719
stories     0.421190
garagepl    0.383302
Unnamed: 0  0.376007
bedrooms    0.366447
```

Pandas `DataFrames`, `NumPy` Functions, and Large Datasets

Pandas `DataFrames` containing numeric data can be used in conjunction with `NumPy` functions such as `log`, `exp`, and `sqrt` (and various other `NumPy` functions). Example of such functions are shown here:

```
df.exp(df)
np.asarray(df)
```

```
matrix multiplication:
df.T.dot(df)
```

the dot method on Series implements dot product:

```
s1 = pd.Series(np.arange(5,10))
s1.dot(s1)
```

However, a `Pandas DataFrame` is not intended to be a direct replacement for `ndarray` as some of its indexing semantics are quite different from a matrix.

Another challenge that you might face: what do you do with large datasets that exceed the memory of your machine? The solution involves a chunking technique for reading portions of data into memory. Chunking enables you to stream data from a file into a `Pandas DataFrame`, and you can specify the number of rows in a chunk of data. An example of chunking is shown here:

```
import pandas as pd
mydata = pd.DataFrame()

#Modify chunksize based on your requirements
for chunk in pd.read_csv('myfile.csv',
    iterator=True, chunksize=5000):
  mydata = pd.concat([mydata, chunk], ignore_
    index=True)
```

Working with `Pandas Series`

A `Pandas Series` is a one-dimensional labeled array that can be populated with any data type: integers, strings, floating point numbers, Python objects, and so forth. The axis labels are collectively referred to as the index.

Create a `Pandas Series` as shown here in the Python REPL:

```
>>> s = pd.Series(data, index=index)
```

The variable `data` in the preceding code snippet can be a scalar value, a Python `dict`, an `ndarray`, and so forth. The variable `index` is a list of axis labels, which consists of different possible values, as discussed in the following subsections.

From `ndarray`

If the variable `data` in the code snippet below is an `ndarray`, then index must be the same length as the variable `data`:

```
>>> s = pd.Series(data, index=index)
```

However, if no index is passed, an index will be automatically created with the values `[0, ..., len(data) - 1]`. Here is another example:

```
>>> s = pd.Series(np.random.randn(5), index=['a', 'b', 'c', 'd', 'e'])
>>> s
```

The output of the preceding code snippet in the Python REPL is here:

```
a    0.4691
b   -0.2829
c   -1.5091
d   -1.1356
e    1.2121
dtype: float64
>> s.index
```

The output of the preceding code snippet in the Python REPL is here:

```
Index(['a', 'b', 'c', 'd', 'e'], dtype='object')
>>> pd.Series(np.random.randn(5))
```

The output of the preceding code snippet in the Python REPL is here:

```
0   -0.1732
1    0.1192
2   -1.0442
3   -0.8618
4   -2.1046
dtype: float64
```

Note that `Pandas` supports nonunique index values. However, if you invoke an operation that does *not* support duplicate index values, then an exception will be raised if you specify data that has duplicate index values.

Here is an example of a Python `Series` that is instantiated from a Python `dict`:

```
>>> d = {'b' : 1, 'a' : 0, 'c' : 2}
>>> pd.Series(d)
```

The output in the Python REPL is here:

```
b    1
a    0
c    2
dtype: int64
```

Pandas DataFrame **from** Series

Listing C.26 displays the contents of pandas_df.py that illustrates how to create a Pandas DataFrame with data from a Pandas Series.

Listing C.26: pandas_df.py

```
import pandas as pd

names = pd.Series(['SF', 'San Jose', 'Sacramento'])
sizes = pd.Series([852469, 1015785, 485199])

df = pd.DataFrame({ 'Cities': names, 'Size': sizes })
df = pd.DataFrame({ 'City name': names,'sizes': sizes })

print('df:',df)
```

Listing C.26 is straightforward: the first portion initializes the Pandas Series names and sizes with cities, and zip codes, respectively. The next portion of Listing C.26 creates the Pandas DataFrame df with the contents of the series names and sizes. The output from Listing C.26 is here:

```
('df:',
     City name    Sizes
0           SF   852469
1     San Jose  1015785
2   Sacramento   485199)
```

Useful One-line Commands in Pandas

This section contains an eclectic mix of one-line commands in Pandas (some of which you have already seen in this appendix) that are useful to know:

Save a data frame to a csv file (comma separated and without indices):

```
df.to_csv("data.csv", sep=",", index=False)
```

List the column names of a `DataFrame`:

```
df.columns
```

Drop missing data from a `DataFrame`:

```
df.dropna(axis=0, how='any')
```

Replace missing data in a `DataFrame`:

```
df.replace(to_replace=None, value=None)
```

Check for NANs in a `DataFrame`:

```
pd.isnull(object)
```

Drop a feature in a `DataFrame`:

```
df.drop('feature_variable_name', axis=1)
```

Convert object type to float in a `DataFrame`:

```
pd.to_numeric(df["feature_name"], errors='coerce')
```

Convert data in a `DataFrame` to `NumPy` array:

```
df.as_matrix()
```

Display the first n rows of a dataframe:

```
df.head(n)
```

Get data by feature name in a `DataFrame`:

```
df.loc[feature_name]
```

Apply a function to a `DataFrame`: multiply all values in the "height" column of the data frame by 3:

```
df["height"].apply(lambda height: 3 * height)
```

OR:

```
def multiply(x):
    return x * 3
df["height"].apply(multiply)
```

Rename the fourth column of the data frame as "height":

```
df.rename(columns = {df.columns[3]:'height'},
          inplace=True)
```

Get the unique entries of the column "first" in a `DataFrame`:

```
df[""first"].unique()
```

Create a dataframe with columns "first" and "last" from an existing `DataFrame`:

```
new_df = df[["name", "size"]]
```

Sort the data in a `DataFrame`:

```
df.sort_values(ascending = False)
```

Filter the data column named "size" to display only values equal to 7:

```
df[df["size"] == 7]
```

Select the first row of the "height" column in a `DataFrame`:

```
df.loc([0], ['height'])
```

This concludes the `Pandas`-related portion of the Appendix. The next section contains a brief introduction to `Jupyter`, which is a Flask-based Python application that enables you to execute Python code in a browser. Instead of Python scripts, you will use `Jupyter` notebooks, which support various interactive features for executing Python code. In addition, your knowledge of `Jupyter` will be very useful when you decide to use Google Colaboratory (discussed later) that also supports `Jupyter` notebooks in a browser.

What Is Jupyter?

The `Jupyter` Notebook is an open-source web application for creating and sharing documents. Moreover, such documents can contain a combination of code, equations, visualizations, and text. The `Jupyter` home page is here:

http://jupyter.org/

`Jupyter` is popular among data scientists, Python developers, and even physicists because it simplifies the sharing of code. Moreover, Google Colaboratory (later in this appendix) supports `Jupyter` notebooks, along with some extra functionality.

First let's take a look at some `Jupyter` features that are discussed in the next section.

Jupyter Features

Jupyter has gained significant traction among various communities because of its ease of use and useful functionality. Some of the features of Jupyter include:

- support for multiple programming languages
- support for Python2 and Python3
- sharing notebooks
- importing notebooks
- download notebooks
- produce different types of output
- big data integration
- multiuser version
- user management and authentication

In particular, the Jupyter Notebook supports more than forty programming languages, including Python, R, Julia, and Scala. Notebooks can be easily shared via email, Dropbox, GitHub and the Jupyter Notebook Viewer. Jupyter notebooks support interactive output that contains a combination of HTML, images, videos, LaTeX, and custom MIME types.

In addition, Jupyter notebooks support big data integration, such as Apache Spark, where the data has been generated from Python, R and Scala. A multiuser version of the Jupyter notebook is also available, and it's designed for companies, classrooms, and research labs. You can also manage multiple users and authentication with OAuth and easily deploy the Jupyter Notebook to all the users in your organization.

Launching Jupyter from the Command Line

Launching Jupyter from the command line is straightforward. First open a command shell, then navigate to the directory that contains the Jupyter notebook basic-stuff.ipynb, and then launch Jupyter with this command:

```
jupyter notebook
```

After a few moments a new browser session is automatically opened and you will see a list of the files in the current directory.

JupyterLab

JupyterLab is an interactive development environment for notebooks containing code and data, that also fully supports `Jupyter` notebooks. `JupyterLab` also enables you to use text editors, terminals, data file viewers, and other custom components side by side with notebooks in a tabbed work area.

`JupyterLab` provides a high level of integration between notebooks, documents, and activities, so that you can:

- drag-and-drop to reorder notebook cells and copy them between notebooks.

- run code blocks interactively from text files (.py, .R, .md, .tex, etc.).

- link a code console to a notebook kernel to explore code interactively without cluttering up the notebook with temporary scratch work.

- edit popular file formats with live preview, such as Markdown, JSON, CSV, Vega, VegaLite (and others)

Develop JupyterLab Extensions

While many `JupyterLab` users will install additional `JupyterLab` extensions, some of you will want to develop your own. The extension development API is evolving during the beta release series and will stabilize in `JupyterLab` 1.0. To start developing a `JupyterLab` extension, see the `JupyterLab` Extension Developer Guide and the TypeScript or JavaScript extension templates.

`JupyterLab` itself is codeveloped on top of PhosphorJS, a new Javascript library for building extensible, high-performance, desktop-style web applications. In fact, `JupyterLab` supports modern JavaScript technologies such as TypeScript, React, Lerna, Yarn, and webpack. In addition, the combination of unit tests, documentation, consistent coding standards, and user experience research helps them maintain a high-quality application.

Summary

This appendix introduced you to Pandas for creating labeled Dataframes and displaying metadata of Pandas Dataframes. Then you learned how to create Pandas Dataframes from various sources of data, such as random numbers and hard-coded data values.

You also learned how to read Excel spreadsheets and perform numeric calculations on that data, such as the min, mean, and max values in numeric columns. Then you saw how to create Pandas Dataframes from data stored in CSV files. Then you learned how to invoke a Web Service to retrieve data and populate a Pandas Dataframe with that data. In addition, you learned how to generate a scatterplot from data in a Pandas Dataframe. Finally, you saw how to use Jupyter, which is a Python-based application for displaying and executing Python code in a browser.

INDEX

A

Accuracy, 79, 93, 211
  complexity and, 65
  of decision tree model, 75
  of neural network, 105
  vs. precision *vs.* recall, 37
Activation functions, 80–82, 129
  common, 82–83
  exponential linear unit, 84–85
  Keras, 84
  LeakyReLU, 157
  multilayer perceptron, 111–112
  nonlinear, 110, 111
  Perceptron, 104
  preferred, 84
  Python. *See* Python activation functions
  in Python, 83
  rectified linear unit, 84–85
  ReLU, 102, 115–117, 157
  sigmoid, 83, 86–87, 111
  softmax, 86, 112, 117
  softplus, 86
  tanh, 83, 86, 111, 112
  work, 81
Activation hyperparameter, 107
Adam optimizer, 110
Adversarial attacks, 152–153
Adversarial images, 152
Adversarial training, 152
Agents, 19, 173, 183
Algorithmic bias, data bias *vs.*, 21
Algorithms, 24, 102
  classification, 64
  clustering, 25, 27–28

deep RL, 185
epsilon-greedy, 159, 180–181
genetic. *See* Genetic algorithm
types, 64
AlphaZero, success of, 11
ALVINN, 13
AM system. *See* Artificial Mathematician
  system
AND function, 110
Android Neural Networks API, 223
Animal intelligence, 3
ANN. *See* Artificial neural networks
Anomaly detection, 26
API
  Android Neural Networks, 223
  tf.rank(), 229
  tf.shape(), 230–231
  tf.tan(), 245
Arithmetic operations, 224
  in TensorFlow 2, 240–241
  caveats for, 241–242
Array variable, 49, 50, 54
Artificial intelligence (AI), 1
  bioinformatics, 17–18
  code samples, 21–22
  definition, 2–4
  evolutionary computation, 14
  expert systems, 7, 9, 12–13
  and games, 10–11
  genetic algorithm, 8
  heuristics, 6–8
  interrogator test, 5, 6
  knowledge representation, 8–9
  major parts of, 18–21
    deep learning, 19